MONOGRAPHS OF THE
SOCIETY FOR RESEARCH IN
CHILD DEVELOPMENT

SERIAL NO. 211, VOL. 50, NOS. 4–5

S0-CPR-824

HISTORY AND RESEARCH IN
CHILD DEVELOPMENT

EDITED BY

ALICE BOARDMAN SMUTS
UNIVERSITY OF MICHIGAN

JOHN W. HAGEN
UNIVERSITY OF MICHIGAN

IN CELEBRATION OF THE FIFTIETH ANNIVERSARY
OF THE SOCIETY

MONOGRAPHS OF THE SOCIETY FOR RESEARCH IN CHILD
DEVELOPMENT, SERIAL NO. 211, VOL. 50, NOS. 4–5

CONTENTS

PART 3: HISTORY OF THE SOCIETY FOR RESEARCH
IN CHILD DEVELOPMENT

ABSTRACT

SMUTS, ALICE BOARDMAN, and HAGEN, JOHN W. History and Research in
Child Development. *Monographs of the Society for Research in Child Development*, 1985, **50**(4–5, Serial No. 211).

The Society for Research in Child Development chose a historical
theme for its fiftieth anniversary meeting in 1983. This *Monograph* consists
of 8 chapters, by both historians and developmentalists, based on papers
delivered as part of the historical program.

Part 1 of the *Monograph*, "History of the Family and of Childhood,"
contains 2 chapters by eminent historians of the family that are addressed
especially to developmentalists. One reviews major findings and
methodological approaches in this relatively new field of history and also
includes original research by the author. The other describes attitudes toward and ways of treating children under 7 years in colonial and early
nineteenth-century America.

Part 2, "Historical Approaches to Child Development," contains 4 chapters, 3 of which discuss scientific developments in the field of child development within their social context. The first explores early research on handedness in the context of the nature-nurture controversy. The second
discusses the founding of *Parents' Magazine*, focusing on the unsuccessful
effort of Rockefeller Foundation officials responsible for child development
programs to control its contents. The third analyzes research on Afro-
American children published in *Child Development* from 1936 to 1980. The
fourth considers the history of anorexia nervosa.

Part 3 is devoted to 2 histories of the Society for Research in Child
Development, both based on archival sources. The first describes the events
from 1925 to 1933 that culminated in the founding of the society. The
second reviews the progress and contributions of the society during its first
25 years. A 6-year project sponsored by the society to preserve historical
materials in the field of child development is described in the Appendix.

INTRODUCTION

This *Monograph* is a pioneer venture, the first publication in which both professional historians and child developmentalists focus on the history of child development and in which historians gear their work to an audience of developmentalists.

The *Monograph* is one result of the decision of the Society for Research in Child Development (SRCD) to make the history of the society, of child development research, of the family, and of childhood the theme of its fiftieth anniversary meeting, held in Detroit, April 21–24, 1983. The program was conceived not as a single event to celebrate an anniversary but as a spur to a continuing agenda that would encourage a historical perspective among developmentalists, interest historians in the rich opportunities for research in the field of child development, and foster an exchange of ideas and information between developmentalists and historians.

As one developmentalist expressed it, the program was an attempt to discover "where we have been and how we got to where we are." In this respect the *Monograph* is an archival volume, a record of some of the characteristics of the society and the field during the society's first half century. It also provides a sample of various approaches to the history of child development and to family history.

The two editors shared the chief responsibility for the historical program: developmentalist Hagen as chair of the 1983 Program Committee and historian Smuts as chair of the subcommittee charged with its planning.

The chapters in this *Monograph* represent a selection of papers from the meeting and reflect the goals of the meeting. They are, however, only the tip of the iceberg. Necessarily excluded are the sights and sounds of the meeting: the early films, the voices on tape of founders of the field (some no longer alive), the photography exhibit, and informal exchanges between developmentalists and historians. Lending a special flavor and excitement to the occasion was the attendance, as honored guests, of some of SRCD's founding members and other developmentalists who contributed to the birth and early growth of the field. Many of these pioneers led conversation hours and commented on films they had participated in making.

The *Monograph* contains about one-quarter of the historical papers from the meeting. Selected personal perspectives from child development pioneers and material drawn from discussion sessions are presented separately in a special supplement to the *Society for Research in Child Development Newsletter* ("Historical Selections from the Fiftieth Anniversary Meeting," in press). We know of several research papers and three complete symposia that have been or will be published elsewhere (Bremner, 1983; Bronfenbrenner, Kessel, Kessen, & White, in press; Reese, 1984; Siegel, 1983; Slaughter & McWorter, 1985; Wohlwill, 1985). Some papers representing work in progress were not completed in time to be included in the *Monograph*. Because this *Monograph* represents only a portion of the program, it could not reflect the interdisciplinary goal of the society nearly as well as the historical program did.

When we suggested the historical theme for the anniversary meeting, we had no inkling of how the society or historians would respond. It is a pleasure to report that support for the program overwhelmed us and was, in large part, responsible for its success. Members of the Subcommittee on History, the Program Committee, the Committee on Interdisciplinary Affairs, and the Committee on the Preservation of Historical Materials supported and participated actively in the formulation and carrying out of the program. So did Joy Osofsky, editor of the *Newsletter;* Robert Emde, editor of the *Monographs of the Society for Research in Child Development;* and Dorothy Eichorn, executive officer of the society. Robert Emde provided early encouragement by suggesting that this *Monograph* might be one outcome of the program.

Individual members submitted 25 papers and eight symposia to the new review panel on history; many wrote or telephoned suggestions for the program. Especially welcome was the response from long-term members. They sent precious photographs from their personal collections, participated in planning the program, and attended the meeting in unexpected numbers.

Historians also responded enthusiastically. Reviewers for the new panel on history included 10 developmentalists and 10 historians. Historians helped with the planning and were well represented on the program. Some historians who were not on the program attended the meeting at their own expense or sent students; others wrote or telephoned their approval and expressed willingness to support a continuing program. Those present singled out the reminiscences of pioneers as particularly interesting and rewarding. To both developmentalists and historians, we express our deeply felt gratitude.

We thank Manfred Waserman, especially, for his participation in the program, for his assistance to the authors of the SRCD histories in obtaining source material, and for his generous help and advice to SRCD and many of its members. Over the years, he gave far more than was required by his official duties as curator of modern manuscripts in the History of Medicine Division of the National Library of Medicine.

Lest we paint too rosy a picture, we should add that, of 25 historical papers submitted by developmentalists, only eight were accepted for the program and one for this *Monograph*. This high rejection rate suggests that many developmentalists who are interested in history need help in doing history. Helping members of each field to understand the perspective and methodology of the other was even more difficult than we had anticipated. Historian and developmentalist reviewers for both the program and the *Monograph* often disagreed widely on ratings. Historians sometimes found papers interesting and worthy but declared them "not history" and suggested placing them elsewhere on the program. Some developmentalists confessed that they felt uncomfortable writing a historical paper; others found that their efforts to place the internal history of scientific theory and methodology within a social context required three or four drafts.

In the course of preparing the program and this *Monograph* we, too, have had to struggle to help each other and our contributors to understand the approaches of each field. But the stimulation we gained from sharing our knowledge and different approaches far outweighed the difficulties. We hope that the program and the publications that have come out of it will encourage continuing, growing, and fruitful interaction between our two fields.

On behalf of SRCD, we gratefully acknowledge financial support for the historical program provided by Ford Motor Company Fund, the Harris Foundation, and Ross Laboratories.

A. B. S.
J. W. H.

PART 1
HISTORY OF THE FAMILY
AND OF CHILDHOOD

HISTORY OF THE FAMILY AND OF CHILDHOOD:
INTRODUCTION TO PART 1

The chapters in Part 1 by Hareven and by Moran and Vinovskis are examples of the nature and content of the relatively new field of family history. When offered at the 1983 meeting, they drew large audiences and were enthusiastically received. Given the importance and relevance of family history to developmentalists, it is appropriate that they introduce the *Monograph*. The authors, in addition to presenting their own research, synthesize the findings in their respective areas, present comprehensive bibliographies, and suggest some of the implications of this expanding, innovative field for developmentalists.

The membership of the Society for Research in Child Development (SRCD) has long been drawn from such diverse fields as psychology, psychiatry, sociology, anthropology, education, nursing, pediatrics, anatomy, nutrition, home economics, and social work—but not history. The society gained its first historian member in 1976 and its second in 1983.

Until recent decades developmentalists have shown little interest in temporal perspectives. Until then, they had few examples from historians of the effect that past environments had on children's lives to stimulate their interest. In contrast, they have long seen the value of cross-cultural perspectives, perhaps because anthropologists such as Margaret Mead (1928, 1930) and sociologists such as Robert and Helen Lynd (1929) were publishing their own pioneering studies on children and family life during the very period in which the field of child development was being established. Anthropologists and sociologists have been active in SRCD from the beginning.

Family sociologists lost interest in the child after World War II, however, and regained it only in the mid-1970s, when new studies "examined the relationship of individual development and family organization across the life span and under varied historical circumstances" (Furstenberg, 1985, p. 283). The reawakened interest was stimulated, in part, by the new historical research. Developmentalists have shown interest in the new sociological as well as the new historical research on the family; the April 1985 issue of

3

Child Development devoted a special section to family development and the child. As Furstenberg pointed out in his introduction to the section, this indicates a welcome departure from "prevailing practice, which often portrays the child as a discrete entity, analytically distinct from the external social environment" (Furstenberg, 1985, p. 281).

The new studies in the history of the family are one offshoot of the new social history, which is interested more in the lives of ordinary people than in elites, more in private experience than in public events. It uses explanatory frameworks from many disciplines, particularly from the social and behavioral sciences. Many family historians are well trained in demography and quantitative techniques, but they also draw on qualitative sources such as letters, diaries, child-rearing manuals, toys, and so on little used by more traditional historians. Good descriptions and examples of family history are available in many anthologies (e.g., Demos & Boocock, 1978; Gordon, 1983; Hareven, 1977a; Rabb & Rotberg, 1971; Rosenberg, 1975).

If the chapters in this part stimulate historian and developmentalist readers to the extent they did the editors, they will persuade professionals from each field of the benefits to be obtained from becoming better acquainted with the perspectives and knowledge of the other.

Hareven, for example, describes a series of recent changes in approaches to family history that find a parallel in child development: from cross-sectional to longitudinal studies, from a narrow focus on internal family life to a consideration of the family in the context of wider kinship groups and of the larger community, from a focus on the effect of social forces on the family to a recognition that the family is an active agent of social change. Also of special interest to developmentalists should be Hareven's discussion of the way in which trends in science and society interact to define and institutionalize life stages and of the effects of household composition on children's development.

Like the early child developmentalists, Moran and Vinovskis focus on the child under 7 and for the same reason—the nearly total neglect of this age group by previous scholars. Like contemporary developmentalists they pay attention to the role of the father as well as of the mother. Their discussion of the conviction of other family historians that there was a link between evangelical religious fervor and authoritarian child-rearing practices provokes one to hope for studies that will examine the interaction of new "scientific" theories and cultural trends for explanations of the shift from authoritarianism to "permissiveness" during the decades preceding and following World War II. The broad view of the Puritan family and of the socialization of Puritan children by church, school, and other institutions includes, in addition to a synthesis of research in this field, the revisionist views of the authors.

HISTORY AND SOCIAL POLICY FOR CHILDREN

Although many have perceived the relevance of the new social and family history to child development research, few have called attention to its potential usefulness to the formulation and execution of social policy for children. From its inception SRCD has aimed at promoting the successful application of research findings as well as encouraging more and better research.

Detailed case histories of successful and unsuccessful attempts to apply social science research in general, and child development research in particular, could be useful. Because the approaches of historians and developmentalists are different and complementary, such studies would be even more pertinent if conducted cooperatively by scholars in both fields. Developmentalists tend to focus on knowledge of children drawn from child development research: how valid it is and how well documented; why, how, and if it can be applied to improve the lives of children and families. They are also concerned with how and to what extent scientific methods can evaluate the effects of application, including human effects that cannot be measured easily.

Historians are trained to take a long-term view of social problems, to look at their knowledge of the past for similarities and continuities as well as for differences and discontinuities. They can help developmentalists to recognize that some problems families and children face today are not unique or, when they are, how and for what reasons.

By their training, historians are also sensitive to trends in public moods and values that sometimes encourage, other times discourage, the acceptance and utilization of research findings. They are familiar with the tension between the American emphasis on the "sanctity of the family" and American zeal for reform. This tension was particularly evident during the late nineteenth and early twentieth centuries, when industrialization, urbanization, immigration, and other changes affected families and children in ways that made former arrangements for their protection appear inadequate.

The passion to protect the family from outside interference aroused the opposition of parents to the weighing and measuring of schoolchildren during the period when G. Stanley Hall was campaigning for the improvement of school health. It delayed the first organized effort to prevent child abuse and must be taken into account in connection with current efforts to deal with child abuse. It also was partly responsible for the delay in founding the Children's Bureau (Bremner, Barnard, Hareven, & Mennel, 1971, pp. 761–774), whose initial function was limited to research. In this instance, reformers' arguments concerning the need for the federal government to gather new and objective information about children carried the day.

THE RELEVANCE OF CHILD DEVELOPMENT TO HISTORY

Since the purpose of the 1983 meeting was to interest historians in child development as well as developmentalists in history, it seems appropriate, at this point, to suggest to historians that the field of child development contains a rich lode, largely untapped, of subjects, primary source materials, and information about children and their families that historians could exploit in their own research.

Lawrence Stone (1974) criticized historians' almost exclusive use of the Freudian model of human development and their narrow application of the model to biography. Citing ego psychology as one example, Stone suggested that other psychological models were available that took into account the effects on human development of the social and cultural environment as well as of internal family dynamics and that were therefore applicable within a broad historical framework. John Demos (1971) has discussed developmental perspectives on the history of childhood and applied them to his own research. Hareven has pointed out the relevance of developmental perspectives and knowledge in her chapter in this *Monograph* and elsewhere.

If historians have been slow to use the fruits of scientific research on children, they have done even less to document the social consequences of the widespread dissemination and application of research findings. The transition from a moral and religious to a more secular and scientific view of childhood is one of the great revolutions of this century, but it remains largely unperceived and little studied. The birth and growth of scientific study of children wrought profound changes in American attitudes and institutions. It altered dramatically the ways in which parents, teachers, physicians, social workers, and many others thought about and treated children. It led to significant changes in the policies and practices of schools, hospitals, orphanages, social welfare agencies, and other institutions that serve children. Through its influence on federal and state legislation, it has had significant effects on all children and families. Whether new historical research deals broadly with the social consequences of child study—for example, with the assessment of fundamental changes in attitudes toward the nature of the child and toward child rearing—or focuses on the effects on specific institutions, it will help to fill a serious void in our current knowledge of twentieth-century American social history and appeal to a broad and diverse audience.

In addition to new subjects, child development offers historians new data. Few historians have taken advantage of the data collected by developmentalists, in some cases continually for more than 50 years. Glen Elder's research in the longitudinal records of the Institute of Human Development at Berkeley, the basis for his book *Children of the Great Depression* (1974), is an outstanding example of the creative use of such data, in this instance, however, by a sociologist rather than by a historian. An inventory of longitudinal research on children has been compiled (Verdonik & Sherrod, 1984). Huge collections of data, unfortunately, still remain in storage in warehouses and basements, where they are likely to stay unless historians show an interest in them.

A. B. S.
J. W. H.

I. HISTORICAL CHANGES IN THE FAMILY AND THE LIFE COURSE: IMPLICATIONS FOR CHILD DEVELOPMENT

TAMARA HAREVEN

Clark University and Harvard University

INTRODUCTION

A relatively new field, the history of the family has provided a time perspective on contemporary issues as well as an understanding of behavior in the past. The questions asked by family historians have much in common with those of psychologists, anthropologists, sociologists, and economists (Elder, 1978b; Hareven, 1971, 1974, 1976; Stone, 1981; Tilly & Cohen, 1982). The uniqueness of historical research on the family is not only in providing a perspective on change over time but also in examining family behavior within specific social and cultural contexts. Historians have thus contributed not just examinations of diachronic changes but investigations of synchronic patterns within discrete time periods as well. The overall effect of studies in the history of the family has been to revise a simplistic view of social change and family behavior over time. These revisions have also generated a host of new questions, which have yet to be answered (Elder, 1981; Hareven, 1977b).

Over the past decade, research in the history of the family has moved from a narrow study of the family as a household unit at one point in time to a consideration of it as a process over the entire lives of its members; from a study of discrete domestic family or household structures to one of the nuclear family's interaction with the wider kinship group; and from a study of the family as a separate domestic unit to an examination of its interaction

Part of the research reported in this chapter was carried out while I was under a research career development grant from the National Institute on Aging. I am grateful for their support.

with the worlds of work, education, correctional and welfare institutions, and such processes as migration.

More recently, efforts to explore internal decision-making processes within the family have led to an investigation of strategies and choices that individual family members and family groups make (Elder, 1978b, 1981; Modell, 1978). In trying to understand the role of the family and its internal dynamics, historical research has gradually moved from a concentration on the family as an isolated unit to an exploration of its interaction with other social processes and institutions, with considerable emphasis on the role of the family in the processes of industrialization and urbanization (Anderson, 1971; Hareven, 1975, 1977a, 1978b, 1982; Smelser, 1959).

The life-course approach has greatly influenced historical research on the family in recent years and has added an important developmental dimension to the history of the family by focusing on age and cohort comparisons in ways that link individual and family development to historical events (Elder, 1978a, 1978b; Hareven, 1978c; Vinovskis, 1977). As will be discussed below, an application of the life-course approach to historical research will also provide a better understanding of child development in a historical context.

A major initial impetus for the historical study of the family came from Phillipe Ariès's book *Centuries of Childhood* (1962), which opened up a new direction by focusing attention both on the concept of childhood and on the changing experience of children in preindustrial French and British society. Ariès argued that childhood as a distinct experience and stage of life was discovered only in the eighteenth century and that its discovery was closely linked to the emergence of the "modern family" (Demos, 1970; Shorter, 1976; Stone, 1977). In linking child development to family structure, social class, and economic and demographic changes, particularly in focusing on sentiment, Ariès provided a model for subsequent historical studies of the origins of the "modern" family, most notably those by John Demos, Edward Shorter, and Lawrence Stone.

In recent years historians have challenged Ariès's thesis that the family as an emotional entity resting on sentimental ties between husband and wife and between parents and children did not exist prior to the eighteenth century and that Western Europe had earlier been characterized by indifference to children. Ariès himself has recently conceded that, had he examined medieval sources, his own conclusions might have been different. But his major contribution, the recognition that childhood, adolescence, and other stages of life were not historical monoliths but rather subject to change of historical time, has survived.

This essay examines the major findings in the history of the family, with special attention to their relations to childhood and child development. The focus is on three areas in which most of the historical research has been

9

accomplished to date: family and household structure and the wider kin group, the life course, and the relation between the family and social change.

FAMILY AND HOUSEHOLD STRUCTURE AND ORGANIZATION OF KINSHIP

One of the major findings in the early stages of research in the history of the family was the continuity of a nuclear household structure in Western Europe and the United States since the preindustrial period. The prevailing assumption had been that the predominant household form in preindustrial society was the extended family, in many cases involving the harmonious coresidence of three generations, and that industrialization destroyed this family structure and led to the emergence of the isolated nuclear family.

Research in the 1960s has demolished some of these myths. Laslett and his group firmly established the predominance of a nuclear family structure in preindustrial Western Europe and its persistence over at least the past three centuries (Laslett & Wall, 1972). These findings for Western Europe, combined with similar findings for colonial American communities, have shown the three-generational household in preindustrial society to be a myth (Demos, 1970; Goode, 1963; Greven, 1970). In most early American communities the typical form of household structure was nuclear. Members of the nuclear family were enmeshed, however, in close ties with extended kin and, as Greven found in Andover, Massachusetts, aging parents did not reside in the same household with their adult son but lived in the vicinity, on the same land, in what would be labeled a "modified extended" family structure (Demos, 1970; Greven, 1970; D. S. Smith, 1973).

Similarly, in American urban communities in the nineteenth century, the dominant household structure was nuclear. Only about 9%–12% of these households were extended, and only about 1%–3% contained solitary residents. The remaining households were nuclear (Blumin, 1977; Hareven, 1977a; Sennett, 1971). Nuclear households, however, were not always restricted to family members, for they often included nonrelatives. Nor was the nuclear residential family unit always isolated; even when kin were not present in the household, the family could be extended through kinship ties outside the household (Anderson, 1971; Greven, 1970; Hareven, 1978a, 1982; Yans-McLaughlin, 1977).

Since the family functioned as a workshop and a vocational training and welfare institution in the preindustrial period, it included nonrelatives who were engaged in various degrees of economic and social relationships with the members of the nuclear family. These nonrelatives were usually apprentices or servants, other people's children who were placed in the household for discipline and socialization, and homeless or dependent individuals who were placed with families by town authorities. For youths in their teens, leaving home and living with another family was a common pattern of transition to adult roles. In the nineteenth century, following the decline of apprenticeship and particularly of the practice of live-in apprentices, non-relatives residing in the household were predominantly servants, boarders, and lodgers (Demos, 1970; Modell & Hareven, 1973).

In nineteenth-century American communities, only 12%–15% of urban households contained relatives other than members of the nuclear family, while 20%–30% of all households included boarders and lodgers. Boarding and lodging was a life-course phenomenon and was therefore part of the regular process of individual and family development; but it was also part of a migration process (Modell & Hareven, 1973).

For young men and women in the transitional stage between departure from their parents' households and marriage, boarding offered housing they could afford in a family setting. It provided some surrogate family arrangements without the accompanying obligations and parental controls. For migrants and immigrants, boarding represented an opportune use of other people's households as a means for access to jobs and social supports, through the connections of the head of the household with whom they were boarding. It was no coincidence, therefore, that migrant boarders clustered in the households of members of the same ethnic group, often former townsmen (Modell & Hareven, 1973).

For heads of households, taking in boarders augmented the family budget and provided surrogate children after their own sons and daughters had left home. In addition to its economic functions, boarding thus provided a surrogate family arrangement and an important form of exchange between younger people and those in the later years of life. In working-class families during the late nineteenth century, the contribution of boarders and lodgers to family income was most significant as a substitute for (or, depending on family need, as a supplement to) the work of women and children. Taking in boarders thus enabled wives to stay out of the labor force and old people to continue to live in their own household after their children had left home (Hareven, 1982; Modell & Hareven, 1973).

With several exceptions for the colonial period, the majority of studies in the earlier stage of research in family history were limited in their concentration on family and household at one point in time or, at best, at several points in time, thus conveying the impression that family and household structures were constant over the entire lives of their members. A profile of the household limited to one point in time obscured the constant movement of family members in and out of different forms of household organization over their lives. Households were like a revolving stage on which individual members entered and exited, under their own momentum or through the influence of external conditions (Berkner, 1972; Hareven, 1974).

Wherever individuals had kin available nearby, they turned to them for assistance rather than to nonrelatives (Anderson, 1971; Hareven, 1978a, 1982). Especially in a regime of economic insecurity with hardly any other available institutional supports, the very autonomy of the nuclear family depended on reciprocity with extended kin.

Extended kin fulfilled a central role in mediating between the nuclear family and other institutions. They were crucial in organizing migration, in facilitating settlement, labor recruitment, and finding employment, and in cushioning the shock of adaptation to new conditions. Even the migration of individuals to urban areas followed a pattern of chain migration; it was directed, organized, and supported by kin. Migrants from rural areas to industrial centers carried over their kinship ties and modified them to meet new conditions (Hareven, 1982).

Kinship networks effectively interacted with the modern, industrial system in the late nineteenth and early twentieth centuries and cushioned the adaptation of immigrant workers to new settings (Hareven, 1978b, 1982). Relatives often acted as major brokers between the workers and the industrial corporations. Relatives initiated the young and the new immigrants into the work process, technology, and industrial discipline and provided protection on the job (Hareven, 1975, 1978a, 1982). At the same time, they socialized newly arrived immigrant workers to collective working-class behavior while cushioning the adaptation of young workers and of newly arrived immigrants without excessively restricting their mobility. Kinship networks were instrumental in serving the industrial employer as well as advancing relatives' interests and trying to protect them (Hareven, 1982).

These important roles that kin fulfilled in their interaction with the workplace in modern corporations exemplify both the continuity in the functions of kin as mediators between the nuclear family and public institutions and their taking on new functions in response to the requirements of the industrial system.

The salient role of kin extended beyond the immediate community to encompass long-distance functions as well. To be sure, kinship ties were most effective in interaction with local institutions and in meeting immediate crises. Yet networks typically stretched over a region and were most useful when conditions failed in the local community or during migration. The strength of locally based kinship networks lay in stability; the strength of extended networks lay in their fluidity and continuous reorganization (Hareven, 1978a, 1982).

Underlying family relations both in the nuclear family and in the wider kinship group during the nineteenth century and the first two decades of the twentieth was a corporate view of family relationships and a collective family economy that required an unwavering commitment of individual effort to collective family needs. Work careers of individual members were integrated in a collective family economy. The timing of life transitions, migration, and occupational choices was determined to a large extent by family needs rather than individual preferences (Chudacoff & Hareven, 1978, 1979; Hareven, 1978a; Modell, Furstenberg, & Herschberg, 1976; Modell & Hareven, 1978). This commitment to collective family goals was also a major determinant for the participation of children, teenagers, and married women in the labor force. It was a carryover from rural society into urban areas and was reinforced by the traditions of various immigrant groups.

Historical study of the household and the extended kinship group has thus delineated several patterns that are significant for the socialization and development of children growing up within the family. In the preindustrial period and throughout the nineteenth century and the early part of the twentieth, the majority of children were growing up in households that did not include grandparents or other extended kin.

The absence of grandparents from households does not mean, however, that children grew up without contact with grandparents and other extended kin. The fact that the nuclear family was engaged in interaction with extended kin outside the household would suggest some degree of involvement in child rearing and child care on the part of grandparents and other kin. The extent of this involvement and its meaning for the socialization of children have not been examined historically, however. In addition to their own parents and siblings, within the household children were likely to be exposed to nonrelatives, such as apprentices, servants, boarders, and lodgers, who may have provided additional role models, ones usually absent in contemporary society.

The effect of household composition on children needs more study. Did children growing up in extended households or in households including nonrelatives experience a different kind of socialization and personality development from children growing up in nuclear households containing no unrelated individuals? While Talcott Parsons argued that a tight, intimate nuclear family situation was more conducive to preparing its members for coping with a complex external world, Phillipe Ariès has claimed that exposure to a diversity of role models within the household may have been more conducive to equipping children for functioning later as adults in a complex and diversified society.

On the basis of the historical evidence, it would appear that the difference between Parsons's and Ariès's conclusions on the relation between the composition of the household and personality development also hinges on the internal dynamics of the household and its functions. The type of preindustrial households described by Ariès was actively engaged in interaction with the larger community and fulfilled public functions within the domestic sphere, while the isolated nuclear household described by Parsons had withdrawn from the outside world and had become more domestic and private. It is thus possible that not simply household membership itself but also the diversity of functions ascribed to the household and the family, especially their public function, may have had a significant influence on the development of children.

FAMILY DEVELOPMENT OVER THE LIFE COURSE

The Life Course

The influence of the life-course approach on family history has been most powerful in understanding three areas of family behavior: the synchronization of individual life transitions with collective family changes, the interaction of individual and collective family transitions with historical conditions, and the effect of earlier life transitions on later ones. "Timing" takes into account the historical context defining the social circumstances and cultural conditions that affect the scheduling of life events, on both an individual and a familial level (Baltes, 1979; Elder, 1978b; Hareven, 1978c; Neugarten & Hagestad, 1976; Riley, 1978; Riley, Johnson, & Foner, 1972).

Life transitions are determined by changes in family status and in accompanying roles as well as by age. Timing involves life transitions on both the nonfamilial and the familial levels in areas such as entering and leaving school, joining or leaving the labor force, migration, leaving or returning home, marriage and setting up an independent household, and, in the later years of life, movement out of active parenting into the "empty nest" and retirement.

Historical Changes in the Timing of Life Transitions

Central to the understanding of any life pattern is the effect of historical processes on the timing of individual or family transitions. Such timing is influenced by the interaction of demographic, social, and economic factors as well as by familial preferences shaped by the family members' cultural background.

Especially during periods when most educational, economic, and welfare functions were concentrated within the family, decisions on timing of transitions that would be considered "individual" today were family based and regulated according to family priorities, within the constraints of external economic and institutional conditions. Institutional and legislative changes, such as compulsory school attendance, child labor laws, and mandatory retirement, have affected the transitions of different age groups into and out of the labor force. At the same time, however, the ways in which the various individuals or groups responded to these opportunities or constraints were also influenced by their cultural traditions.

From his examination of life-course patterns of white American women from 1879 to 1939, Peter Uhlenberg concluded that the sequence of marriage, family formation, the rearing and launching of children, and survival until age 50 with the first marriage still intact unless broken by divorce, although always modal, was by no means prevalent for most of the population before the twentieth century (Uhlenberg, 1974, 1978).

Over the past century, the decline in mortality has tended to effect greater uniformity in the life course of American families and has made it considerably more likely that the family unit will survive intact for many years. The decline in mortality has also enabled an increasing proportion of the population to enter prescribed family roles and, except in cases of divorce, to live out their lives in family units (Uhlenberg, 1974). The decline in mortality, especially in the earlier years, means that the chances of children's surviving into adulthood and growing up with their siblings and both parents alive increased considerably. Similarly, the chances of women's surviving to marry, raise children jointly with a husband, and live with a husband through the launching stage increased steadily from the late nineteenth through the early twentieth century (Uhlenberg, 1974).

For women, these changes, combined with earlier marriages and earlier completion of child rearing, have meant a more extended period of life without children in their middle years. At the same time, women's tendency to live longer than men has resulted in a protracted period of widowhood in later life. Men, on the other hand, because of lower life expectancy and a greater tendency to remarry in old age, normally remain married until death (Glick, 1947, 1955, 1977; Glick & Parke, 1965).

The most marked discontinuity in the life course that has emerged since the nineteenth century has occurred in the middle and later years of life, namely, the emergence of the empty nest in a couple's middle age as a result of earlier marriage, fewer children, child bearing occurring in the early stages of the family cycle, and children's leaving home at an earlier point in their parents' lives (Glick, 1977).

In the nineteenth century, later marriage, higher fertility, and shorter life expectancy led to different family configurations from those characterizing contemporary society. Children were spread over a broader age range within the family; frequently, the youngest child was starting school when the oldest was preparing for marriage. For large families, the parental stage with children remaining in the household extended over a longer period of time, sometimes over the parents' entire lives. Since children were spread in families along a broad age spectrum, younger children could observe their older siblings and near relatives moving through adolescence and into adulthood. Older siblings in turn trained for adult roles by acting as surrogate parents for younger siblings (Hareven, 1977b). The combination of a later age at marriage and earlier mortality meant that the "empty nest" was a rare phenomenon. Fathers surviving the child-rearing years rarely lived beyond the marriage of their second child.

Demographic factors account only in part for the occurrence or nonoccurrence of the empty nest. Children did not remain in their aging parents' household simply because they were too young to move out. Even where sons and daughters were in their late teens and early twenties and therefore old enough to leave home, at least one child remained at home to care for aging parents if no other assistance was available (Chudacoff & Hareven, 1979; Hareven, 1982). Nineteenth-century families did not go through clearly marked stages. Leaving home did not so uniformly precede marriage, and the launching of children did not necessarily leave the nest empty. Frequently, a married child would return to the parental home, or the parents would take in boarders or lodgers. Familial obligations, dictated by the insecurity of the times and by cultural norms of familial assistance, took precedence over strict age norms (Chudacoff & Hareven, 1979; Hareven, 1982). Recent developments in the 1970s have begun to revive some of the "historical" patterns, thus blurring the contrast between past and present. Most notable among these are late marriages and the late commencement of child bearing among professionals, the return of young adults to the parental home, or their delayed leaving.

The important historical change in the timing of life transitions since the beginning of this century has been the emergence of a greater uniformity in the pace at which a cohort accomplished a given transition. This is particularly evident in the transitions to adulthood (leaving home, marriage, and establishment of a separate household). As Modell et al. (1976) have shown, over the past century transitions have become more regularly sequenced, more rapidly timed, and more compressed.

In contrast to our times, in the late nineteenth century transitions from the parental home to marriage and to household headship were more gradual and less rigid in their timing. The time range necessary for a cohort to accomplish such transitions was wider, and the sequence in which transitions followed one another was flexible. In recent decades transitions to adulthood have become more uniform for the age group undergoing them, more orderly in sequence, and more rigidly defined. The consciousness of embarking on a new stage of life and the implications of movement from one stage to the next have become more firmly established.

The timing of life transitions has become more regulated according to specific age norms rather than in relation to the family's collective needs (Modell et al., 1976). The increasing rapidity in the timing of transitions and the introduction of publicly regulated and institutionalized transitions have converged to isolate and segregate age groups and at the same time have generated new pressures on timing within the family as well as outside its confines.

STAGES OF LIFE

Changes in the timing of life transitions discussed above are related to the segmentation of the life course into specific developmental stages. This process has involved the gradual societal recognition of new stages of life, their acceptance in the culture, and their public recognition. This has been accomplished through the passing of legislation and the establishment of institutions and agencies for the realization of the potentials of specific stages of life and their protection within those stages. To the extent that it is possible to reconstruct a historic model, it appears that the "discovery" of a new stage of life is itself a complex process. First, individuals become aware of new characteristics in their private experience. The articulation of such a stage and of the conditions unique to it is then formulated by the professionals and eventually recognized in the popular culture. Finally, if the conditions seem to be associated with a major social problem, it attracts the attention of public agencies, and its needs and problems are dealt with in legislation and in the establishment of institutions. Those public activities in turn affect the experience of individuals going through such a stage and clearly influence the timing of transitions in and out of it.

In American society childhood was "discovered" first in the private lives of middle-class urban families in the early part of the nineteenth century. The discovery itself was related to the emergence of the domestic family, the segregation of the workplace from the home, the redefinition of the mother's role as the major custodian of the domestic sphere, and the emergence of sentiment as the basis of familial relationships. The new child-centeredness of urban domestic families in the early nineteenth century was also a response to two major demographic changes: a decline in infant and child mortality and an increase in the conscious practice of family limitation. After it emerged in the lives of middle-class families, childhood as a distinct stage of development became the subject of the voluminous body of child-rearing and family advice literature commencing in the first half of the nineteenth century. The movement for the regulation of child labor and the legislation of compulsory school attendance were the first steps of the public recognition of a new stage of life and its institutionalization.

The "discovery" of adolescence followed a similar pattern. While puberty in itself is a universal, biological process, the psychosocial phenomena of adolescence were only gradually defined, most notably by G. Stanley Hall

17

(1904). The experience of adolescence itself, particularly some of the problems and tensions associated with it, was apparent in the private lives of people reaching puberty during the second half of the nineteenth century (Demos & Demos, 1969). The congregation of young people in peer groups and the symptoms of what might be characterized as a "culture of adolescence" were also observed by educators and urban reformers from the middle of the nineteenth century on. Anxiety over such behavior increased particularly where it was connected with new immigrants. Adolescence was also widely discussed in popular literature. The extension of school age through high school, in the second part of the nineteenth century, the further extension of the age limits for child labor, and the establishment of both juvenile reformatories and vocational schools were all part of the public recognition of the needs and problems of adolescents (Kett, 1977).

The boundaries between childhood and adolescence, on the one hand, and between adolescence and adulthood, on the other, became more clearly demarcated during the twentieth century. As Keniston (1971) has suggested, the extension of a moratorium from adult responsibilities beyond adolescence has resulted in the emergence of another stage, youth. However, despite the growing awareness of these preadult stages, no clear boundaries on adulthood in America emerged until "old age" became prominent as a new stage of life, and with it the need to differentiate the social and psychological problems of "middle" from those of "old" age. The overall boundaries of adulthood are not yet sharply defined, and the transitions into middle age are still fuzzy. "Old age," however, is now recognized as a specific period of adulthood. On the public level it has a formal beginning, age 65 (at least where an individual's working life is concerned), and it is institutionalized by a rite of passage, retirement and eligibility for social security (Fischer, 1977; Hareven, 1976).

Whether childhood, adolescence, youth, and middle or old age were first experienced on the private, individual level or acknowledged on the public, collective level, their very appearance and increasing societal recognition have affected the timing of family transitions in the past. Thus not only has the very experience of these stages of life changed over time, but also the timing of people's entry into and exit from such stages and the accompanying roles involved in such timing have changed as well.

The existential as well as the institutional changes that have buttressed the extension of a moratorium from adult responsibilities have also affected the timing of individual and familial transitions. Thus the postponement of the assumption of adult responsibilities would have meant that children resided longer in the household without contributing to the family's economic effort and that an increase in the state of "dependency" or "semi-dependency" as a typical experience of adolescence resulted.

HISTORY OF THE FAMILY AND SOCIAL CHANGE

Recent work in the history of the family has had a profound effect on our understanding of the family's response to changing social and economic conditions. Since the family has acted as a mediator between individuals and larger social processes, the history of the family also helps us understand how change takes place.

The most important consensus in recent historical study of the family has occurred around the question of the effect of industrialization on the family. Historians now agree that industrialization did not bring about the characteristics of demographic behavior and family and household patterns previously attributed to it. One of the patterns associated with "modern" family behavior—family limitation, the spacing of children, a later age of marriage, and a nuclear household structure—had actually preceded industrialization.

Historians also agree that industrial capitalism in itself did not cause a breakdown of traditional family patterns, that the family most "fit" to interact with the modern industrial system is not the isolated nuclear type but rather a nuclear family embedded in an extended kinship network, and that industrialization and migration to urban areas did not destroy traditional kinship patterns.

While rejecting the assumption that industrialization generated a new type of family structure, historians agree that industrialization has affected family functions, family values, and the timing of family transitions. Many of these changes were not necessarily linked directly to industrialization but emerged as consequences of the restructuring of the economy and of increased urbanization following industrialization. The most crucial change wrought by industrialization was the transfer of functions previously held by the family to other social institutions. As has often been pointed out, the preindustrial family served as a workshop, church, reformatory, school, and asylum (Demos, 1970). Over the past century and a half, these functions have become in large part the responsibility of other institutions. The household has been transformed from a place of production to a place of consumption, and the family's major purpose has become the nurturing of children. The family has withdrawn from the world of work, and the workplace has generally become nonfamilial and bureaucratic.

The home is viewed as a retreat from the outside world. The family has turned inward, assuming domesticity, intimacy, and privacy as its major characteristics as well as ideals. The privacy of the home and its separation from the workplace have been guarded jealously as an essential feature of family life (Cott, 1977; Degler, 1980; Welter, 1966). The commitment to the domesticity of the family is itself the outcome of a long historical process that

19

commenced in the early modern period in Western Europe, a process characterized by Phillipe Ariès as follows: "The modern family . . . cuts itself off from the world and opposes to society the isolated groups of parents and children. All the energy of the group is expended in helping the children to rise in the world, individually and without any collective ambition, the children rather than the family" (1962, p. 404).

By contrast, writes Ariès, the premodern family "was distinguished . . . by the enormous mass of sociability which it retained" (1962, p. 404). Both family and the household were the foundation of the community. Reacting to economic growth and industrialization, the family became a specialized unit, its tasks limited primarily to consumption, procreation, and child rearing.

The question is still open, however, as to what effect the loss of many of the family's former functions, combined with shrinking household membership, has had on the internal dynamics and the quality of family relationships. According to Ariès, the contracting of family functions and the resulting privatization of family life marked the emergence of the modern family; the family has become nuclear, intensive, inward turning, and child-centered—at the expense of sociability and greater integration with the community. Ariès concluded that these developments weakened the family's adaptability and deprived children of the opportunity to grow up in a flexible environment with a variety of role models to follow. To date, however, historians have done little to document and to explore closely the effect of these changes on internal relations within the family (Ariès, 1962).

Since the family changes more slowly than other social institutions do, and since, as has been shown, the family does not passively respond to change but also generates it, it has been difficult for historians to develop a typology of change in the family over time. Historians attempting to date the emergence of the "modern family" in the West place it somewhere between 1680 and 1850. Ariès and Lawrence Stone have singled out the late seventeenth and early eighteenth centuries, while Edward Shorter dates its emergence in the late eighteenth and early nineteenth centuries. Stone holds that the "closed domestic nuclear family" emerged sometime between 1640 and 1800. American historians generally date its emergence in the late eighteenth or early nineteenth century (Ariès, 1962; Degler, 1980; Shorter, 1976; Stone, 1977).

Stone, Ariès, and Shorter have focused on the rise of affective individualism as the major criterion of the modern family. They generally agree that the modern family is privatized, nuclear, domestic, and child-centered and that its crucial base is the sentimental bond between husband and wife and between parents and children. They have all pointed to the weakening influence of extended kin, friends, and neighbors on family ties and to an isolation of the family from interaction with the community as a consequence of privacy and child-centeredness. Marriages are based on "emotional bonding" between husband and wife and are a result of personal and sexual attraction rather than of alliances between sets of parents or lineages. Stone, as to some extent does Degler, sees the weakening of bonds with kin as an inevitable consequence of this type of family.

While there has been general agreement on these characteristics of modern family life, there is some disagreement and, at times, lack of clarity as to which class first initiated these changes. The scholars discussed above follow basically a "trickle down" theory. Ariès, Stone, and, more implicitly, Degler view the bourgeoisie and the gentry as the vanguard, while Shorter has assigned a crucial role to peasants and workers. For American society, Degler places the origins of the modern family in the middle class, although he generalizes from the experience of the middle class to the entire society. The most important aspect still absent from historical studies of long-term changes in the family over time are more systematic distinctions between social classes and a more detailed understanding of the historical process by which modes of family behavior were adopted by other classes, if indeed that was the case, and, conversely, of what class differences have survived (Ariès, 1962; Degler, 1980; Shorter, 1976; Stone, 1977). These studies of broad change over time also hold in common their acceptance of ideological and cultural factors as the major explanations of change in family behavior rather than social and economic ones. Shorter is the only one among them to cite "market capitalism" as the major cause for the emergence of family sentiment, but, as his critics have pointed out, he does not provide an explicit connection between these economic forces and the transformations of family relations (Tilly & Cohen, 1982).

Stone offers a "multicausal" explanation rather than one single factor, but he tends to favor the predominance of cultural and ideological explanations over social and economic ones, as does Degler (Degler, 1980; Stone, 1981). This is precisely where the most fundamental disagreements about social change and the family are likely to emerge among historians. Not only is there a lack of consensus over the relative importance of ideological or socioeconomic causes in long-term changes in the family, but there is also a greater need to know how the changes took place and what the nature of interaction among these different factors was. The "grand" explanations of change are vulnerable particularly in some of these studies' claims for linear change over time.

The characterization of what was typical behavior for the middle-class modern family does not necessarily hold true for other classes. In the United States, for example, there has not been sufficient research over time to identify specific differences between middle-class, working-class, black, and immigrant families. There is, however, sufficient evidence to suggest that privatism, child-centeredness, affective individualism, and isolation from extended kin, which emerged as characteristic traits of urban middle-class families—carriers of the modern family type—were not necessarily typical of other classes and ethnic and racial groups. Among working-class and ethnic families, some preindustrial family characteristics have persisted, although in modified form (Hareven, 1982; Scott & Tilly, 1975).

The overall pattern of historical change has moved in the direction of an adoption by other classes and ethnic groups of middle-class family patterns. As Modell (1978) shows, even consumption patterns and tastes of immigrant families began to conform to those of the native born. But the adoption of native-born, middle-class family styles by other classes and ethnic groups was by no means linear and uniform (Hareven & Modell, 1980). How this process took place and at what pace is still a major subject for future research. It is clear from several studies that the adoption of "modal" patterns of behavior by different ethnic groups and various classes was selective and unevenly paced.

The realization that historical changes in the family have not taken place uniformly throughout society has led historians to react against a simplistic, linear interpretation of change and to focus instead on research that is carried out on a synchronic level, examining family interaction with societal processes and institutions within specific community contexts. While such work has already helped to revise earlier generalizations, it must still be integrated into a more systematic pattern ranging over a longer historical period.

At the moment, the contribution of historical knowledge to the overall understanding of social change and the family lies in emphasizing, first, that, in the process of changes, families are *active* agents in their contacts with social, economic, and cultural forces; second, that changes in family behavior (as well as in many other aspects of society) do not follow any simple linear trend (as postulated in modernization theory); and, third, that stages of individual development and the timing of life transitions were subject to interaction with the family as a collective unit in the context of changing historical and social conditions.

The historical study of the family has contributed to the study of child development by providing a basic understanding of the rough patterns of historical change in the family and in the status of children. Perhaps the most vital message coming from historical research is a revision of simplistic notions of linear change and an understanding of the social, economic, and cultural factors affecting human development. Most significantly, a historical approach suggests that stages of human development, rather than being universal, were subject to changing social and cultural definitions and that individual development was strongly linked to the collective development of the family unit.

Further research is needed, however, both in the history of the family and in child development in order to achieve an adequate understanding of patterns of development in a changing historical context. Since most of the work in the history of the family has focused on functions and structures, more attention to internal dynamics and relationships is required before the interaction between family and kinship patterns and personality development can be fully understood.

II. THE GREAT CARE OF GODLY PARENTS: EARLY CHILDHOOD IN PURITAN NEW ENGLAND

GERALD F. MORAN

University of Michigan—Dearborn

MARIS A. VINOVSKIS

University of Michigan

The history of early childhood in premodern America remains to be written. While interest in early American childhood has remained high since the 1960s, most of it has been focused on older children—particularly adolescents. The lack of historical attention paid to young children is unfortunate because efforts on behalf of the young child by their families, churches, and schools can provide us with useful insights not only about the child but also about the dynamics of these institutions in the socialization of the young.

This chapter will focus on three aspects of the young Puritan child in the seventeenth and eighteenth centuries.[1] First, we will analyze Puritan ideology and how it may have influenced attitudes toward children—especially how views of infant damnation and of the child's will may have affected the responses of adults. Second, we will investigate whether Puritans really saw young children as distinct and different from others or

We would like to thank John Hagen, John King, Kenneth Lockridge, Alice Smuts, and R. M. Smuts for very useful comments on an earlier version of this chapter.

[1] Although the phrase "young children" was a fairly vague chronological category for Puritans, we will use it to refer to children generally below the ages of 6 or 7. In addition, while we will try, whenever possible, to consider the behavior or views of young children themselves, we are concerned primarily with adult perceptions and treatment of young children. Furthermore, while we refer throughout to Puritanism as a factor that shaped parental attitudes toward children, we do not attempt to distinguish between it and New England or Protestant culture, which overlapped in many areas of child rearing.

whether they regarded them merely as miniature adults. Finally, we will analyze early childhood education in New England, considering the roles of the family, the church, and the schools in the socialization of the young child and speculating on the relative importance of the mother and the father in this process. While this chapter should be regarded only as a tentative foray into the analysis of the care of young children in the past, it will offer a synthesis of previous investigations and will serve as a guide for further research.

I. PURITAN IDEOLOGY AND THE CHILD

No aspect of New England theology has been more damaging to the historical reputation of Puritan treatment of childhood than the doctrine of infant damnation. Historians have asked, How could the Puritans have loved their children and at the same time have consigned deceased infants to eternal damnation? In theory, all infants and children who died unconverted suffered the eternal torments of hell. Since few infants were thought to experience conversion, this meant that the great majority of deceased infants were considered damned (Stannard, 1977, p. 49). The awful fate awaiting children at their demise was magnified in the minds of Puritans by their depiction of hell as a place of unremitting and unmitigated torment and horror.

The theory of infant damnation remained generally unchallenged among orthodox New Englanders well into the eighteenth century. But in actual practice the Puritans avoided the implications of the doctrine. New England ministers were reluctant to dwell on the subject and avoided discussing it in detail (Slater, 1977), while Puritan parents often refused to apply the doctrine to their own deceased children. It was a great temptation to consider a dead infant among the few God had selected for salvation. In such cases, the character of the deceased child was idealized and the meaning of his death rationalized. His demise was considered a welcome departure from the cares and sorrows of the world, while he was invested "with superior characteristics, often in invidious contrast to still living siblings" (Slater, 1977, p. 39). Some parents also sought to sustain relationships with dead children, as the gravestone iconography of the period suggests.

In time, Puritans also began to accept the possibility of infant regeneration. Such was the increasing emphasis placed on the proneness of elect babes to achieve salvation at death that, by the time of the Great Awakening in the early 1740s, the New Lights, who subscribed in theory to the doctrines of original sin and infant damnation, had difficulty in practice consigning unregenerate infants to hell. Even Jonathan Edwards (quoted in Fiering, 1981, p. 210), one of the most ardent defenders of infant damnation, con-

25

cluded that "'tis generally supposed to be a common thing that the infants of the godly die in infancy are saved." As a result, the concept of infant damnation was jettisoned by the religious liberals of the eighteenth century and increasingly ignored by Old Light Calvinists.

Another aspect of New England theology that has damaged the historical reputation of Puritan treatment of children is original sin. According to most historians, the doctrine of original sin and human depravity was responsible for Puritan repression of children (Axtell, 1974; Demos, 1970). Puritan parents sought to counteract original sin in children by breaking and beating down their wills. Once established, this mode "of parental discipline was probably maintained for quite a number of years" (Demos, 1970, p. 139).

Central to the argument of Demos and others is the child-rearing theory of John Robinson, an early seventeenth-century English minister and the Pilgrim's first pastor. In a treatise published in 1625 entitled "Of Children and Their Education," Robinson (quoted in Ashton, 1851, p. 246) writes, "And surely there is in all children, though not alike, a stubborness, and stoutness of mind arising from natural pride, which must, in the first place, be broken and beaten down."

Robinson's is perhaps the most frequently cited passage in the secondary literature on Puritan childhood. But how representative of English and American Puritans were Robinson's attitudes toward children? Some historians (Axtell, 1974, p. 147) argue that they were typical of the seventeenth century, while a few others (Sommerville, 1982, pp. 124–125) contend that they were not.

Despite the popularity of Robinson's views among historians of the child, we suspect that he was not as representative of seventeenth-century Puritans as has been suggested. Robinson was a radical separatist—a sect with only a very small following in England, very few of whom migrated to New England. In addition, a recent study (Greven, 1977) suggests that the repressive mode of child rearing was not typical of all Puritans but was common only among those of an evangelical temperament. But how prevalent was evangelicalism in the seventeenth century?

Greven emphasizes continuity over change, arguing that evangelicals and their authoritarian mode of child rearing persisted over the course of 3 centuries—from the seventeenth through most of the nineteenth. While he is reluctant to indicate the extent of repressive child-rearing methods in early New England, he does suggest a crucial connection between evangelicalism and religious revivalism (Greven, 1977, pp. 10, 142), one that allows us to add a temporal dimension to his analysis. Revivals were not common to all periods of New England history but ebbed and flowed across the eighteenth and nineteenth centuries. If one can establish a connection between the periodic eruption of religious revivals and the popularity of authoritarian child-rearing practices among the participants, then the static picture of child care suggested by Greven should be modified.

A recent history of the English family suggests such a link between religious revivals and authoritarian modes of child rearing. Stone argues that "in England an era of reinforced patriarchy and discipline lasted from about 1530 to about 1670, with the high point in the 1650s. This in turn gave way to an era of growing individualism and permissiveness which was dominant in the upper middle and upper classes from about 1670 to 1790. The next stage in the evolution of the family was marked by a strong revival of moral reform, paternal authority and sexual repression, which was gathering strength among the middle classes from about 1770." "The driving force behind this movement," he goes on to say, "was the spread of Evangelical piety. God was again seen as directly controlling day-to-day events within the household, in which capacity he was a severe and pitiless masculine figure" (1977, p. 666). "With this reassertion of patriarchal authority in the early nineteenth century, the status of women inevitably declined" (1977, p. 667). Moreover, there was a "renewed stress on the preeminence of the father, and the subordination of the children. The family became increasingly 'a stifling fortress of emotional bonding', while relations between parents and children grew more intrusive. Supervision was more intense and oppressive since it was now motivated by an intense religious zeal. The seventeenth century Puritan theory of the innate sinfulness of the child was revived" (1977, p. 669).

Stone's analysis parallels that of other historians. In a recent work, Sommerville (1982, pp. 124–125) observes that "the phrase 'breaking the will,' which was not very current in the seventeenth century, seems to have increased in popularity" in eighteenth-century England and America. The classic statement of this view comes from the pen of John Wesley, the noted English evangelist, whose preaching helped to bring about the revivals in mid-eighteenth-century England. Wesley's counterpart in America, Jonathan Edwards, the premier theologian of the Great Awakening, used similar language in his discussions of children and favored the same repressive mode of child rearing. In fact, the Wesley and Edwards family papers have given historians the richest store of evidence on that method of child rearing.

As for the attitudes of the many other families who participated in the same revivals and shared the same temperament, much less is known. But the language of authoritarian parenthood reappeared throughout the remainder of the eighteenth century and into the nineteenth. It surfaced during the early nineteenth century among the descendants of the New England revivalists in Utica, New York (Ryan, 1981, pp. 70–71); it persisted among evangelical families of the antebellum South (Mathews, 1977, pp. 98–101); and it was to be found in the writings of the nineteenth-century Baptist minister Francis Wayland (Greven, 1977, p. 39).

A few individuals like Robinson who advocated the breaking of the wills of young children could be found in the seventeenth century, but they were not predominant. Moreover, considerable evidence exists to suggest that the early Puritans were not the snake in the child's paradise, as the traditional historiography would have it. As Edmund Morgan (1966, pp. 185–186) argued as early as 1944, Puritan parents loved their children as much or even more than modern parents, sometimes even to the extent of allowing them to usurp a higher place than God in their affections. The Reverend Samuel Willard (1726, p. 601), a typical New England minister, expressed in vivid language the positive assessment of children that was characteristically Puritan: "The Love of Parents of their Children is such as admits not of suitable words to express it, it being so intense and influential, so that God himself is pleased to resemble His Love to His Children by this, there being no Comparison that better resembleth it."

The Puritans expressed fondness for their offspring in other ways as well. The literature of the Great Migration contains numerous references to parental solicitude for children as a compelling motive for the exodus. In the privacy of their diaries, many parents contemplated how removal to America might protect their progeny from Old World corruption and profanity and might ensure their physical and especially spiritual well-being. In addition, the 1660s in New England offer an unusual spectacle of a whole society caught up in a dramatic dialogue over the religious fate of children. The eventual outcome of this debate was the halfway covenant, which extended baptism to the children of the unregenerate sons and daughters of the elect. Moreover, as one historian (Morgan, 1966, p. 77) has argued, New England parents put their children out to other families lest they spoil them with lavish displays of affection. Simply put, they did not trust themselves with their own children.

This is not to say that seventeenth-century Puritans were always positive in their assessment or treatment of children, nor does it mean to imply that they were child-centered, as were many nineteenth-century Americans (Hoffer & Hull, 1981). They were far removed from the cult of the child, but they were equally far removed from the indifferent, neglectful attitudes toward children held by many of their contemporaries and forebears. In this respect they were born "half modern," as a historian (Slater, 1977, p. 19) has recently noted. Furthermore, they shared with evangelicals an ambivalent attitude toward children, believing that the infant soul was tainted with original sin. In the words of the Reverend Samuel Willard, children were "innocent vipers," prone to commit evil at an early age but not to be held responsible for their acts until they had achieved the age of reason. The Puritans held a complex view of human nature, one that is more in accord with modern attitudes than with the romantic version of the nineteenth century.

Whereas evangelicals stressed fear over love in their approach to infants, most early Puritans were more inclined in the opposite direction. They sought a middle way of child rearing, one that balanced discipline with indulgence, severity with permissiveness. They used the rod only as an instrument of last resort. With evangelicals, Puritans shared an intense concern for the spiritual destiny of their children, but they were less anxious about their ability to achieve it. They desired to bend, shape, and mold the will, not to break it. They exercised an authoritative, not an authoritarian, mode of child rearing.

Puritan child-rearing efforts were directed less at the will than at the affections and reason. The affections were to be cultivated early in life, so that children would come instinctively to love God and his word. In their attention to affections, the Puritans, especially the women, anticipated the romanticists of the nineteenth century (Ulrich, 1982).

Reason was also to be nurtured in children at an early age, so that they could understand the right doctrine and be able to discern the Lord's body at the time of their admission into the church. The child's mind was considered an empty receptacle, one that had to be infused with the knowledge gained from careful instruction and education. While evil had to be restrained in the child, his mind had to be enlightened. All good had to come from the outside. In their belief that the infant's mind was a blank receptacle with a great capacity to reason, the Puritans anticipated the child-rearing theories of John Locke and other eighteenth-century Enlightenment thinkers.

II. CHILDREN AS MINIATURE ADULTS

According to some of the earliest historians of the Puritan child in New England (Earle, 1899; Fleming, 1933), the notion of a separate and distinct childhood did not exist. The idea that children in the past were regarded and treated as miniature adults received reinforcement from the work of Philippe Ariès (1962), who traced the nature of childhood in Western Europe from the Middle Ages to the seventeenth century. The work of Ariès was particularly significant because American colonial historians (Demos, 1970, 1974; Wells, 1982; Zuckerman, 1970) in the 1960s and early 1970s relied heavily on his interpretation of the role of the child in the past and assumed that children in early America were also treated as miniature adults.

Yet Puritans did see children as different and separate from adults. Children below age 6 or 7 were treated very differently than were older ones, and even older children were distinguished from adults (Axtell, 1974; Kaestle & Vinovskis, 1978, 1980; Stannard, 1975, 1977). Indeed, it is important to note that, much like contemporary parents, Puritans believed that different children possessed different abilities and temperaments and that child rearing had to be molded to fit the particular "temper" of each child. Every infant was considered an individual, an attitude reflected in the personalized naming patterns of the Puritans (Sommerville, 1982, p. 109). As Anne Bradstreet observed, "Diverse children have their different natures; some are flesh which nothing but salt will keep from putrefaction; some again like tender fruits are best preserved with sugar: those parents are wise that can fit their nurture according to their nature" (quoted in Ellis, 1867, p. 50). Perhaps particular deference was accorded the eldest son, whose responsibility it would be to carry on the traditions of the family after the death of the parents. In any case, Puritan parents had to know their children well and had to raise them accordingly.

Similar distinctions were made with respect to the capacities of consecutive age groups of children, as Puritan catechisms, which offer a rich but unexamined source of information on New England views of the intellectual and moral development of children, indicate. Of the many catechisms that were published during the seventeenth century, a good number were written especially for children of different ages. Some were written so that even the youngest children could begin learning the rudiments of Christian doctrine. In some instances ministers assembled graduated catechisms in one volume, as was the case with the Westminster Assembly (Grant, 1968, p. 198). Special catechisms were also developed for mothers for the "catechising of children in the Knowledge of God, Themselves, and the Holy Scriptures" (Grant, 1968, p. 121). It was also the parents' responsibility to know the individual abilities of their children and to adjust their instruction of them accordingly.

While Puritans did distinguish between adults and children and even among children, their conception of the intellectual capabilities of young children was quite different from contemporary views of young children today. Puritans believed that children developed intellectually more rapidly than we usually expect young children to develop today. To observe these differences, it is useful to consider the ages at which Puritans expected children to learn to read as an index of their view of the intellectual capabilities of the child.

Since most early Americans simply assumed that everyone agreed on the proper age for training young children, they did not devote much time or energy to this topic. On the basis of our reading of colonial documents as well as earlier work in this field, it appears that Puritans expected children to learn to read as soon as possible in order to prepare themselves in this world for salvation in the next. As Cotton Mather put it, "The Children should LEARN TO READ the Holy Scriptures; and this, as Early as may be" (quoted in Smith, 1973, p. 27).

There appears to have been considerable variation in the ages at which children learned to read in colonial America since there was little effort to synchronize reading with a certain chronological age. Yet the thrust of Puritan religious and educational ideas was to encourage reading as soon as possible. In seventeenth-century England, children were expected to learn to read at early ages, entering school at about 4 or 5 in urban areas and 6 or 7 in rural ones (Cressy, 1980). English spiritual autobiographers reveal that most of them began their schooling at age 6, although some began as early as 4 (Spufford, 1979). John Locke (1964, p. 186), one of the most widely read educators in England and New England, assumed that children should be taught to read as soon as possible but cautioned parents against injuring them or discouraging their natural curiosity.

While both Locke and the New England Puritans agreed on the desirability and possibility of early reading, they differed considerably on the precise age for achieving this objective. Whereas Locke saw early reading as desirable, he was unwilling to coerce the young child into reading. Many New England Puritans, on the other hand, saw the reading of the Bible as indispensable to the child's salvation, especially in a world still characterized by high infant mortality, and therefore encouraged or even forced their offspring into learning to read at very early ages. Thus the sense of urgency and importance attached to early reading by the Puritans may have been tied to the changes in their own religious beliefs and enthusiasm.

The importance and practice of early reading received a major boost in the early nineteenth century when the infant school movement swept the country (Kaestle & Vinovskis, 1978, 1980; May & Vinovskis, 1977). Although initially intended to help poor children ages 2–4 receive an early education, which would help them to overcome their disadvantaged backgrounds, infant schools were soon opened to the children of middle-class families as well. By the 1830s and 1840s in Massachusetts, for example, as many as 40%–50% of 3-year-olds may have been enrolled in a public or private school.

Not all infant school instructors were eager to teach such young children the alphabet as well as the rudiments of reading. But parents, reflecting their view of the intellectual capabilities of the young as well as their desire to have their offspring keep up with the training received by other children, insisted that the infant schools provide their pupils with instruction in the alphabet and reading. Thus as late as the 1820s and 1830s almost all parents in America agreed that very young children could be taught to read, although some of them did not believe that early intellectual development was essential—especially since the belief in infant damnation had been abandoned by almost everyone since the seventeenth and eighteenth centuries (Slater, 1977).

The belief that young children could and should be taught to read at an early age persisted virtually uncontested during the first 2 centuries of American development. But in the 1830s, partly as a reaction to the growing popularity of the infant school movement, this idea was forcefully and successfully challenged by Amariah Brigham (1833), a physician, who saw early education leading to the insanity of the child.

The warnings of Brigham were soon picked up and echoed by educators and popularized through the mass media (Kaestle & Vinovskis, 1978). From about 1830 to 1920 the term "precocity" was applied not to extraordinarily gifted children but to normal ones experiencing pressures for accelerated intellectual or social development, which was increasingly seen as being harmful to their health and development (Kett, 1978). Advocates of early childhood education now reversed themselves and discouraged intellectual precocity among young children (Sigourney, 1838). Furthermore, writers of popular advice books admitted their previous mistake in advocating early intellectual activity (Humphrey, 1840, pp. 11–12).

The effort to convince parents that they should not attempt to teach their young children reading at an early age was not immediately successful, as many of them continued to send their children to the infant schools. But most of the infant schools, which had been heavily dependent on the financial contributions from middle-class female reformers, were soon forced to close as this better-educated and more widely read group abandoned the idea of early childhood education (May & Vinovskis, 1977). By 1860 the transition was complete; almost no 3- or 4-year-olds attended schools in Massachusetts. Indeed, the start of the kindergarten movement at this time revealed the changes—it was directed at children older than those who had gone to the infant schools, and it did not try to teach them how to read (Kaestle & Vinovskis, 1978, 1980).

This reexamination of the societal views of the young child in the past suggests that, while early Americans did not view their children as miniature adults, they did see them as capable of intellectual development at a very young age. This idea persisted unchallenged for 200 years and was reinforced in the early nineteenth century by the infant school movement. But starting in the 1830s the belief that early intellectual activity among children ages 3 and 4 was possible and desirable underwent a major change that resulted in an entirely different view of young children by the eve of the Civil War.

III. EARLY CHILDHOOD EDUCATION IN NEW ENGLAND

The centerpiece of Puritan efforts to educate children was the family. Though household religion was part of the general Protestant tradition in England, the Puritans emphasized it more than other groups. They assumed that the family would play a key role in educating their own children and servants and that the state would intervene only when the family failed in its educational mission.

The family was expected to instruct its members not only in the art of reading and writing but also in religion. Children were expected to be catechized by their parents at home as a normal part of their initial religious training. In fact, the stress on reading rather than writing was to insure the ability of everyone to comprehend the Bible. For example, when Watertown officials admonished parents for not educating their children, they focused only on the ability to read the English language (Bremner et al., 1970, p. 41).

Though the Puritans relied on the family for the early education of their children, they also developed a comprehensive system of schooling. Most of their initial efforts in formal education were directed toward the creation of grammar schools to prepare those children going on to a university. A few towns such as Salem did maintain petty or dame schools, but most towns simply assumed that the parents would teach their children enough reading and writing for their religious needs or their entrance into grammar school.

While it is difficult to assess the success rate of Puritans in educating their children, an estimate of the literacy of Puritans will at least provide some idea of their achievements in this area. Information on the literacy levels of Puritan parents will also give us some sense of the potential for educating their children at home if they had wanted to do so.

Most analysts assume that New England Puritans were better educated than their counterparts in England or in the other colonies were since they stressed the importance of education in their religion more than most other groups. Yet there is a growing debate about the actual extent of literacy in New England as well as about the role of Puritan religion in fostering it.

The most comprehensive study of literacy in colonial New England is Kenneth Lockridge's (1974) analysis of signatures on wills, which he uses as a crude index of literacy. Lockridge concludes that there were significant differences between the literacy of men and women in colonial New England. Among the early settlers, about 60% of the men and only about 30% of the women could sign their own wills. By the end of the colonial period the literacy of both men and women increased, so that 90% of males could sign their names and 50% of females signed their wills. In rural New England, however, female literacy continued to be below that of urban women and even declined slightly in the first half of the eighteenth century.

To explain the relatively high rate of literacy among New England males, Lockridge (1974, p. 83) rejects the argument that it was the fear of the wilderness that motivated Puritans to invest so heavily in the education of their children. The mechanism for this increase was not the transmission of literacy by the families but the growing availability and efficacy of schools

(Lockridge, 1974, pp. 65–69). Whereas in the second half of the seventeenth century the Puritan school laws were ignored by many towns because their population was so widely dispersed throughout the settlement, in the eighteenth century most towns complied with these laws since the greater concentration of population now made the establishment of public schools feasible.

Thus Auwers (1980), Daniels (1979), Lockridge (1974), and Soltow and Stevens (1981) stress the increasing density of settlement and the resultant growth of primary schools in New England as the major factor in the rise of male and female literacy. Indeed, Lockridge (1974, p. 58) explicitly dismisses home education as a possible source of increased literacy.

While we agree with these scholars about the importance of schools in fostering literacy in colonial New England, we also suspect that some of the rudiments of that literacy may have been acquired in the home. That females continued to use mark signatures more than males did does not exclude the home or neighborhood as a possible source of literacy. If women were much less likely to be taught to write than their brothers were, then it is not at all surprising that they were less able to sign their names, even though both males and females were taught the alphabet and reading, if not writing, within their own homes or those of neighbors. Furthermore, although Auwers (1980) correctly points to the higher rates of female literacy in those areas of Windsor that were closest to the schools, her data on the three settlements furthest removed from the center of the town (Pine Meadow, Poquonnoc, and Wintonbury) suggest a sharp increase in female literacy well before they acquired easy access to local schools.

Another issue in the socialization of the young in colonial America is the relative role of the mother and the father in teaching children. Many scholars (Cressy, 1980; Lockridge, 1974) assume that it was unlikely that fathers played a major role in teaching their children. Yet very little effort has been made to ascertain the role of the father in early childhood education. Although much has been written about the mother's role in childhood education in the nineteenth century (Kuhn, 1947), relatively little has been said about the maternal care and education of young children in early America.

It appears that fathers played a much larger role in the education of their children in colonial New England than in the nineteenth century. Fathers were expected to play the leading role in the catechizing of their children and servants. For example, according to a 1648 law, the masters of the household (usually the fathers) were expected to catechize the children and servants (Bremner et al., 1970, p. 40). Whether the father was also expected to teach the children the rudiments of reading and writing is not clear. But since males were usually better educated than females in colonial America, perhaps there was little choice in many households as to which parent would instruct the child. Indeed, Auwers (1980) found that female literacy in seventeenth-century Windsor was associated with the literacy of the father but not of the mother. As literacy was often considered a prerequisite for spiritual preparedness, the teaching of reading and the catechizing of children probably occurred simultaneously under the direction of the father and often with the assistance of the mother (Morgan, 1966; Todd, 1980). Perhaps, in some households, there was even a differentiation of instructional tasks, as some Puritan diaries suggest (Mather, 1961, p. 278).

In the first generation most fathers were probably able to carry out their household religious and educational duties since at least 60% of them could sign their names (and many of the others could probably at least read the Bible) and most belonged to the church. The problems came in the mid-seventeenth century, when males increasingly stopped joining the church (Moran, 1979), and the church's membership became feminized (Moran, 1980, p. 49). Surely some of the anxieties over educational decline in mid-seventeenth-century New England stemmed from the fact that many fathers were either no longer thought fit to prepare their children spiritually or unwilling to shoulder the responsibility (Stone, 1977, p. 241).

The solution to this dilemma was to reassign the responsibility for catechizing and educating young children to the wives since they continued to join the church even as their spouses declined to do so. Yet these women were handicapped in carrying out this assignment since they were less literate than their husbands. Furthermore, though Puritans were willing to teach women to read and to allow them to help in the education of their children, they may have been reluctant in the 1640s and 1650s to entrust them entirely with the responsibility of directing and catechizing the children and servants in the wake of the radical religious activities of Anne Hutchinson and her followers during the Antinomian crisis of the late 1630s (Hall, 1968).

Perhaps the dilemma posed by the inability or the unwillingness of many males to catechize their households and the reluctance of the Puritan leadership to entrust women to replace them in this function helps to explain the growing willingness of the churches to catechize the children themselves. At first the churches merely reminded their brethren of the importance of catechizing their children and servants at home, but gradually they began to offer public catechizing (Axtell, 1974).

At the same time, colonial officials sought to establish more local schools. In Connecticut the General Court shifted responsibility for schooling from the town as a whole to the individual parishes, thereby ensuring greater participation in local educational affairs on the part of the church and the ministers. While the effects of this change have not been studied, Auwers's (1980) analysis of Windsor suggests that the increased role of the church in local school affairs, at a time when church membership was becoming heavily feminized, led to increasing educational opportunities for women.

Though the Puritan ministers appear to have been reluctant at first to place the full responsibility for catechizing and educating children on the women's shoulders, they gradually changed their minds. As women became increasingly literate, at least in regard to reading the Bible, and as they continued to join the church in larger numbers than males, ministers began to emphasize their role in the religious education of their children. From the late seventeenth century on, they showed an increasing willingness to praise women for piety and literacy skills. For the period 1668–1735 Evans's bibliography (1941) lists 55 eulogies, memorials, and funeral sermons for women in addition to other works of practical piety devoted wholly or in part to females, with the great bulk of these tracts appearing in print during the 1710s, 1720s, and early 1730s. From these treatises a composite picture of the Puritans' image of the virtuous woman emerges. Not only did the ideal Puritan woman express her inordinate piety through early seeking of God, fasting, and prayer, but she also conversed well, read Bibles and devotional literature, and wrote (Malmsheimer, 1973; Ulrich, 1976).

New England ministers were also increasingly inclined to advise women on their educational responsibilities. John Cotton (quoted in Morgan, 1966, p. 42) told women to "Keep at home, educating of her children, Keeping and improving what is got by the industry of the man." In a sermon published in 1692, Cotton Mather (1741, p. 107) devoted whole passages to the religious responsibilities of mothers. The devoted mother, he said, introduces to her "little Vessels" such works as "Histories and Sentences fetch'd from the Oracles of God, and Institutions how to pray in secret unto their heavenly Father. She then proceeds to make 'em expert in some orthodox catechisms, and will have 'em learn to read and write, as fast as ever they can make it; and so she passes to the other Parts of an ingeneuous Education with them." As Benjamin Wadsworth (1719, p. 60) counseled mothers, "While you lay them in your bosomes, and dandle them on your knees, try by little and little to infuse good things, holy truths into them." Letters, diaries, and other records provide numerous examples of women teaching children, reading to children, and exerting a general influence over their religious development (Axtell, 1974, p. 175; Ferris, 1855, pp. 16–17; Jedrey, 1979, p. 15; Morgan, 1966, p. 96; Slater, 1977, p. 100).

One dilemma that might be associated with this redefinition of the role of women and men in the household is that it may have appeared to undercut the traditional authority and responsibility of the father as the head of the household. The solution to this problem was to declare women's particular sensibilities in religious activities and their special skills in raising young children. Thus the shift in the religious socialization of young children from the fathers to the mothers may have contributed to the development of the idea of special spheres of responsibility for women in the household—eventually leading to the "cult of domesticity" in the nineteenth century.

While the family had been assigned the major responsibility for educating and catechizing its children in the early seventeenth century, by the end of the eighteenth century it was clear that public schools and churches in New England had assumed some of those tasks. Yet even at that late date, the family was entrusted with the task of teaching its children the rudiments of literacy and religion since many public schools and churches expected to deal only with children who already knew the elements of the alphabet and simple reading. It was not until the late eighteenth and early nineteenth centuries that the responsibility of the family for early childhood education changed, as primary schools throughout New England began to take over the tasks of teaching students how to read and write. Furthermore, this transfer of functions from the family to the public schools was not one that was imposed on reluctant families by an aggressive school system—rather it was a responsibility hesitatingly accepted by most schools and teachers, who would have preferred to leave the care of very young children to their parents (Kaestle & Vinovskis, 1980). Indeed, by the twentieth century the role of the state in the provision of education for young children is virtually unchallenged.

PART 2
HISTORICAL APPROACHES TO
CHILD DEVELOPMENT

HISTORICAL APPROACHES TO CHILD DEVELOPMENT:
INTRODUCTION TO PART 2

From its beginnings, the field of child development has been buffeted by the culture, sent first in one direction, then another, by changing political, economic, social, and intellectual trends. Early leaders struggled to create a scientific discipline out of research that was intimately tied to practical concerns about child rearing and the conditions under which children lived. (See the histories of the Society for Research in Child Development in Pt. 3 below.) Since people will always use new information about children for personal and political ends, child development will always be vulnerable to powerful and pervasive social pressures.

Several developmentalists have pointed out that professionals in the field are not sufficiently aware of the extent to which society affects their scientific work. In his commentary on the Milton J. E. Senn Oral History Collection in Child Development, William Kessen observed that Senn's respondents "may have been looking in the wrong places for the sources of change in the field" and that they "tended to see themselves and their institutions or research findings or theoretical ideas at the center, as the causes and sources of our variegated history. A more skeptical reader," Kessen continues, "might see the students of children not as movers or shakers but as moved and shaken" (Senn, 1975, p. 101). The discussion session on the history of developmental psychology (F. Kessel, Chair) at the 1983 meeting of the society focused on implicit, underlying assumptions in the field that are based more on ethical values than on science (Bronfenbrenner, Kessel, Kessen, & White, in press).

An examination of the programs of regional and national meetings of the Society for Research in Child Development and the American Psychological Association over the last 5 years or so and of the latest developmental handbooks reveals an unprecedented interest in the philosophy of science and in the history of science and medicine in general and of child development in particular. This interest may have been stimulated by pathbreaking books on the philosophy of science and the history of science and medicine that have appeared within the last 2 decades.

These developments, however, have not yet produced much in the way of new histories of child development. Historians and developmentalists, together, have published less than a dozen articles on the history of the field and no full-length history. The content of the historical program revealed the paucity of published studies and the narrow focus of most historical research. In preparing the program, however, we discovered a variety of innovative historical studies in progress by both developmentalists and historians. The chapters in this section are in the vanguard. Two by developmentalists, two by historians, they offer a sample of new approaches to the history of science applied to the field of child development.

The chapter by Harris demonstrates that research on the work of earlier scientists need not be an antiquarian exercise but instead may recover both theory and research findings of direct relevance to contemporary researchers. Harris reviews the early theoretical and research literature on handedness and places it within the larger context of the nature-nurture controversy. In 1921, John Watson concluded that handedness is learned, contradicting James Mark Baldwin's earlier research indicating that it is instinctual (Watson & Watson, 1921). The psychological literature of the 1920s, a decade of rampant environmentalism, accepted Watson's conclusion, although we now know that Baldwin was closer to being right. This episode is a striking example of how scientific conclusions can be influenced by the dominant assumptions of the times and by chance events, in this case, Baldwin's expulsion from academe.

Schlossman is one of the few historians who has published articles on the early parent education movement and its relation to the founding of the Laura Spelman Rockefeller Memorial institutes of child development. His chapter illustrates the assumption, widespread during the 1920s, that parent education in the new scientific child-rearing methods could save the world. The contempt for traditional child-rearing techniques and the preference for reliance on the "expert" is reflected in Ernest Groves's comment (1932, p. 216) that "parents who rely on tradition socially menace their children." Schlossman tells the previously untold story of the founding of *Parents' Magazine* and of the unsuccessful effort of the two chief Laura Spelman Rockefeller Memorial Fund program officers to maintain some control over its content.

McLoyd and Randolph analyze the research on Afro-American children that appeared in *Child Development* between 1936 and 1980. They found dramatic changes in the frequency and type of research on this population and identified some of the changing social issues and perspectives that are reflected in the research. A major role in the study of black children has been played recently by the Conferences on Empirical Research in Black

Psychology, funded by the Russell Sage Foundation in 1974 and convened by A. Wade Boykin and J. Frank Yates. By 1983, eight conferences had been held that addressed some of the issues raised by McLoyd and Randolph and others. Six other historical papers by developmentalists on research on black children were presented at the meeting, but there were no papers on the history of research on children of other minority groups. We deeply regret that a paper by Marie Peters on 50 years of research on black children that was provisionally accepted by the first review panel could not be included because of her death.

Brumberg's chapter is the only representative in the *Monograph* of the history of medicine. Her reflections on the history of anorexia nervosa provide a new perspective on a disorder of great current interest and suggest that the psychodynamics of the disorder have not always been what they appear to be today. This conclusion is also supported by the fact, not discussed by Brumberg, that anorexia nervosa among very young children was of great concern to pediatricians during the 1920s and early 1930s (Brennemann, 1932; Powers, 1935) and was one of the subjects considered at the National Research Council Third Conference on Child Development in 1929 (Roberts, 1929NP, pp. 85–86, 99–100). One may wonder if feeding problems in young children and in adolescent girls represent the same disorder, but it is interesting that, in both instances, those involved usually came from middle- and upper-class families. Brumberg's chapter, which she is expanding into a book, whets the appetite for additional histories of changing interpretations and treatment of disorders of children and adolescents. An important subject, for example, would be autism, the first disorder of childhood diagnosed as a psychosis.

We have suggested that attention to the complicated interaction of science and society is an important aspect of the research on the history of child development. So also is the interaction of the various movements that we lump together under the umbrella term "child development movement": research on children, the clinical study of children, the parent education movement, the movement for early education, the movement by a small group of pediatricians to expand pediatrics to include the study and treatment of behavioral disorders, and, finally, the movement for child welfare reform, to which all the above are related. We do not have a history of the founding of institutionalized research on children, of the child guidance movement, of behavioral pediatrics, or of the Children's Bureau. No comprehensive history of child development can be undertaken until all these histories have been written, but the task has hardly begun.

A. B. S.

J. W. H.

43

III. JAMES MARK BALDWIN ON THE ORIGINS OF RIGHT- AND LEFT-HANDEDNESS: THE STORY OF AN EXPERIMENT THAT MATTERED

LAUREN JULIUS HARRIS

Michigan State University

INTRODUCTION

After many years of neglect, the work of the American philosopher-psychologist James Mark Baldwin (1861–1934) has finally begun to arouse interest among developmental psychologists. To date, however, attention has been focused on Baldwin's theoretical and philosophical contributions, while his empirical work, including studies of infancy and early childhood and laboratory investigations of adult memory and reaction time, has won only passing mention (e.g., Broughton & Freeman-Moir, 1982). This is understandable, since these studies occupied Baldwin only briefly early in his career (1889–1896) and are regarded to have been of negligible value in their own right. As Boring said, "Baldwin's genius did not lie in experimentation. He was a philosopher at heart, a theorist" (1957, p. 532). That verdict continues to stand (e.g., Mueller, 1976). I do not question this judgment, although Baldwin's investigations of infancy and early childhood are worth examination, given their critical role in the formation of his thinking about development (see Wozniak, 1982). At least one of these early investigations, however, proved to be important in its own right—a study of the development of hand preference in the infant (Baldwin, 1890a), which was completed during Baldwin's brief tenure at the University of Toronto (1889–1893).[1]

Research for this paper was supported, in part, by a grant from the Spencer Foundation.

[1] Baldwin first reported his experiment in a brief communication to *Science* (1890a) and then gave more extensive accounts in an article in *Popular Science Monthly* (1894) and in

44

This study is worth recalling for several reasons. It seems to have been the first investigation conceived for the express purpose of testing theories about the origins of handedness; as such, it significantly influenced debate on this question while providing the model for experimental procedures used in subsequent work. It reflects Baldwin's early thinking about evolution, including an example of his application of the recapitulation hypothesis of Ernst Haeckel. It constitutes an exposition and early application of Baldwin's "law of mental dynamogenesis," that is, his proposition that knowledge originates in action on objects. Finally, in his analysis of handedness, Baldwin brilliantly anticipated a host of "modern" issues in developmental and neuropsychological theory that to date have not been associated with his name.

HISTORICAL CONTEXT FOR BALDWIN'S STUDY

Theories of Handedness

To tell the story of this experiment, some of the background events must first be sketched in. The early years of Baldwin's career, between the 1880s and the turn of the century, saw the continuation of a vigorous scientific debate about human handedness: was it a native expression of some physical asymmetry of the brain or body, or was it more fundamentally a consequence of custom, special training, and education?[2]

Nativist theories.—Among the nativists, explanations ranged broadly. One proposal, alluded to by Baldwin (1895), was that of the Scottish physiologist Andrew Buchanan (1862). On the supposition that the body's center of gravity usually lay to the right because of an asymmetry in the weight of the viscera, Buchanan concluded that "dynamic balance" would shift to the left, "leaving the right leg—and right arm—freer for action" (1862, p. 152). The effect, however, would become apparent only when the child could

his book *Mental Development in the Child and the Race* (1895). For the account given here, I have depended primarily on these three sources. Baldwin's initial purpose was to improve the study of color perception over earlier techniques used by Preyer and Binet, among others. Details of Baldwin's apparatus appear in *Mental Development in the Child and the Race* in the chapter "Distance and Colour Perception by Infants."

[2] Baldwin's interest in handedness very likely was sparked by Sir Daniel Wilson, the president of the University of Toronto. Wilson had published a series of papers on handedness in 1885–1886 (subsequently published in a book in 1891), which Baldwin called the "best *résumé* and general discussion of the question" (1890a, p. 247). Baldwin recalled that Wilson was "greatly interested" in his experiments on handedness (1926, p. 43). Wilson described them as having "followed up on my own researches," noting, however, that Baldwin, being "a specialist in the department of psycho-physics, . . . carried his inductive research beyond the range embraced in the present treatise" (1891, p. 128).

walk because only then would he be strong enough to put forth sufficient effort to realize the mechanical advantage of the right side.

In the new light of Broca's (1861, 1865) studies of aphasia, the critical organ shifted from the viscera to the brain. Now handedness was seen as linked with speech to one side of the brain—the left hemisphere in the typical right-handed case. Comparisons thus began to be made of the weight, density, complexity, and blood supply of the two hemispheres on the assumption that the left hemisphere would prove to be physically superior (Harris, 1980a). Broca himself contemplated all such possibilities (e.g., 1865, 1877). He also (1865) suggested that the critical factor was maturational: his colleague, the comparative anatomist Pierre Gratiolet (Leurat & Gratiolet, 1857, pp. 241–242), had observed that in fetal human brains the frontal convolutions form earlier on the left side than on the right. Broca (1865, p. 393) thus proposed that it was just this earlier development of the left anterior cortex that predisposed its usual leading role in the control of speech as well as of handedness.

Nurture theories.—"Nurture" theorists also had a range of ideas. One was that handedness was caused by how the infant was cradled. As G. Stanley Hall noted, "Nurses carry children on their own right arm, leaving the child's right arm a freer field of motion" (Hall & Hartwell, 1884, p. 101). (See also Comte, 1828; Harris, 1983b, pp. 189 ff.) But many more (e.g., Féré, 1889; Marion, 1890; Wilson, 1891, p. 127), including Baldwin himself, observed that right-handers usually hold the child on the *left* arm. As Baldwin said, "This would leave the child's left arm free, and so a right-handed mother would be found with a left-handed child" (1895, p. 59), which was manifestly not the case.

Another proposal cited by Baldwin was "that infants get to be right-handed by being placed on one side too much for sleep" (1895, p. 59). He did not say which side but perhaps meant the right, meaning that the right hand, if extended, would be brought into closer proximity to the infant's line of sight, thus affording a better vantage point for visual-motor practice. Baldwin did not consider the possibility that newborn infants spontaneously assume the head-right position, something the educator Edouard Seguin had pointed out in 1875 (see Seguin, 1976).

Finally, right-handedness was said to be inculcated in young children through deliberate training, encouraged by a broad cultural bias against the use of the left hand. Indeed, in surveying the European scene, the French sociologist Robert Hertz declared, wryly, "One of the signs that distinguish a 'well-brought-up child' [*bien élevé*] is that his left hand has become incapable of any independent action" (1909, p. 556).

Certain nurture theorists saw dangers in all such practices, for in the dominance of one hand (and, so it was supposed, one half of the brain) they saw man using only half his mental endowments. In England, in 1904, a schoolteacher from Belfast by the name of John Jackson even formed the Ambidextral Culture Society for the promotion of equal training of the hands. Numerous benefits were promised, including (as a result of left-hand training) the creation of supplementary speech centers in the right cerebral hemisphere, thereby mitigating the effects of left-hemisphere injury (Harris, 1985).

Infant Handedness and Evolution

The time of Baldwin's early career was the age of Broca but still more the age of Darwin. The question of the existence of functional and anatomical asymmetries in human infants thus was seen as relevant not only to extant theories of handedness in man but to fundamental ideas about human evolution as well. Nativists argued that handedness not only was innate but also signified a more advanced state in the evolution of the species. Note was taken of reports that the right-arm bones of prehistoric man were heavier and more massive (e.g., Lehmann-Nitschke, 1895), suggesting, as D. J. Cunningham, a leading British anatomist, said, that "right-handedness assumed form as a characteristic of man at a very early period in his evolution" (1902, p. 279). Nurture theorists spurned any such view. As John Jackson saw it, dextral superiority would imply a corresponding *deterioration* of the other limb. How, he asked, could that possibly benefit, and therefore constitute a more advanced state in, those animals so affected? (1905, p. 91).

The evolutionary argument soon became conflated with the biogenetic theory of Ernst Haeckel, according to which the human child recapitulates in its development the adult stages of phylogeny (Haeckel, 1874/1905). As the physician Sir William Gowers put it, "If 'the child is Father to the man' the child may also exemplify the primitive paternity of the race" (1902, p. 1719). Many embraced this idea, including Baldwin and G. Stanley Hall (see Broughton, 1981; Sewny, 1945). The implications for the analysis of handedness through the study of infants were quickly seen. Cunningham regarded infant study to be of "very especial value," since it could identify "the period in the evolution of man at which right-handedness became a fixed and permanent human characteristic" (1902, p. 280).

Early Studies of Infant Hand Preference

The human infant thus appeared to be the perfect means for testing competing theories of the origins of handedness. If handedness developed in the absence of social training, that would favor the "nature" explanation. Otherwise, "nurture" must be held responsible. Each side cited evidence for its own position. For example, to support his dynamic balance theory, ac-

47

cording to which hand preference would appear only after the first year, Buchanan stated that "All observant persons" will admit that infants before this time "exhibit no tendency to use the one hand in preference to the other, as they employ indifferently the nearest hand to clutch at any object within their reach" (1862, p. 144). Broca, however, reflecting on Gratiolet's observation that the frontal convolutions form earlier on the left side, said, "One therefore understands why, from the first moments of life, the young child prefers to use the limbs having the more perfected innervation, why, in other words, he becomes right-handed" (1865, p. 383). The French scientist Jobert, although a follower of Broca, claimed that the infant becomes "clearly right- or left-handed" only by the end of the second year (1885, pp. 12–13). A recapitulationist as well, Jobert named this as the period corresponding to the rise of handedness in evolution. Finally, Ambidextral Culturists declared the human infant their shining example of the naturalness of symmetry and evenhandedness—at least until, as one early advocate put it, "some grown fool interferes and mutilates it" (Reade, 1878, p. 175).

Were any of these different assertions based on actual evidence? There is no way to tell. As the German physiologist Karl von Vierordt said, "Reliable data are lacking concerning this question of primary importance—the use of the left and right arms in the first grasping movements of infants" (1881, p. 428).

Baby biographies.—The popular baby biographies of Baldwin's time helped little, for they usually described the child's spontaneous behavior in natural settings rather than in controlled tests. Consequently, although the best diarists, such as the behavioral embryologist Wilhelm Preyer (1888), frequently provided rich descriptions of motor development, they did not present convincing data on the development of hand preference (see Harris, 1983a). Along with these methodological shortcomings, Baldwin saw a more grievous problem: the biographers had put a ban on theory, the "life blood of all science," and had caught science "in the straight-jacket of barren observation" (1895, p. 37). Whence Baldwin issued his famous call: "Give us theories, theories, always theories. Let every man who has a theory pronounce his theory! This is just the difference between the average mother and the good psychologist—she has no theories, he has; he has no interests, she has. She may bring up a family of a dozen and not be able to make a single trustworthy observation; he may be able, from one sound of one yearling, to confirm theories of the neurologist and educator, which are momentous for the future training and welfare of the child" (1895, p. 38). As the quotation suggests, Baldwin's scorn was directed not at Preyer and other scientist/biographers (Preyer's biography, in particular, was rich in theory) but rather at the rank amateurs, usually mothers (and fathers) and women in reading circles and clubs who were publishing anecdotal and often naive and sentimental accounts of their children (see Ross, 1972, p.

124). Consequently, when Baldwin himself addressed the question of the development of handedness, his intent was a wedding of theory and experimental method.

BALDWIN'S EXPERIMENT

Hand Movements, Mental Development, and "Dynamogenesis"

To start, Baldwin saw in the child's hand movements for reaching and grasping a significance transcending the limited question of the origins of handedness; hand movements were no less than a window to mental development.

> The hand reflects the first stimulations, the most stimulations, and, becoming the most mobile and executive organ of volition, attains the most varied and interesting offices of utility. We have spontaneous arm and hand movements, reflex movements, reaching-out movements, grasping movements, imitative movements, manipulating movements, and voluntary efforts—all these, in order, reflecting the development of the mind. . . . It has accordingly seemed to me worth while to find whether a child's reaching movements would reflect with any degree of regularity the modifications of its sensibility, and, if so, how far this could be made a method of experimenting with young children. [Baldwin, 1895, p. 43]

Baldwin further proposed that the intensity of the hand movement would be proportional to the intensity, or "dynamogeny," of a given stimulus, much as—to use Baldwin's own example—the physiologist François Magendie had suggested measuring changes in sensibility by the corresponding changes in blood pressure. By this "dynamogenic" method, Baldwin proposed that a wide range of issues in addition to handedness could be studied, including color perception, color preference, and distance estimation.

Tests of Current Theories of Handedness

With respect to handedness, Baldwin wished to put certain proposals to test, in particular, Buchanan's (1862) dynamic balance theory; the "infant cradling" theory (e.g., Hall & Hartwell, 1884); and the "reclination" theory, according to which the infant's handedness was determined by its position while lying supine.

Subject and method.—For his experimental subject, Baldwin chose his own first child, Helen, born in 1889. To eliminate all the aforementioned sources of influence, "certain precautions" were "carefully enforced": "She was never carried about in arms at all—never walked with when crying or sleepless (a ruinous and needless habit to cultivate in an infant); she was frequently turned over in her sleep; she was not allowed to balance herself on her feet until a later period than that covered by the experiments. Thus the conditions of the rise of the right-handed era were made as simple and uniform as possible" (Baldwin, 1895, p. 60).[3]

For his test, Baldwin designed a special chair that kept Helen's posture constant, leaving her arms free to move. A set of rods attached to the chair displayed objects, one at a time, at different positions and distances. The objects used included pieces of newspaper and squares of blotting paper of different colors.

From the beginning of Helen's fifth month to the end of her tenth, Baldwin administered over 2,000 "experiments" (i.e., trials) at short distances (9 inches, within easy reach) and always at midline. On these trials, Helen showed no trace of hand preference. For a 24-day-long period, during the eighth month, Baldwin added trials at longer distances (12–15 inches). "This resulted in very hard straining on her part, with all the signs of physical effort" (1895, p. 61). Under these conditions, the right hand was preferred by a ratio of almost 15:1. Finally, during the last 10 days of this period, Baldwin presented objects from 1–5 inches to the right or left. The result was further enhancement of the right-hand preference. Baldwin therefore concluded that Helen's dextrality could not have derived from using the closer hand for such acts as reaching, grasping, and holding because her right hand "intruded regularly upon the domain of her left" (1895, p. 63). By her thirteenth month, Helen was "a confirmed right-hander" (1890a, p. 248).

Given his results, Baldwin dismissed the cradling, reclination, and dynamic balance theories and cast his lot squarely with the brain physiologists: "Right handedness in the child is due to differences in the two half-brains, reached at an early stage of life, . . . the promise of it is inherited, and . . . the influences of infancy have little effect upon it" (1895, p. 74).

Why, though, had the right-hand preference appeared only with muscular effort? Baldwin answered that the expression of right-handedness

---

[3] Considering the privations (to child as well as to parents) imposed by this regimen, it is understandable that Baldwin volunteered his own daughter; other parents might not have agreed. Still, we perhaps should not accept Baldwin's description of Helen's treatment at face value. In the account of the experiment that appeared in the 3d ed. (1906) of *Mental Development in the Child and the Race*, the phrase "she was never carried about in arms at all" that was used in the 1st ed. (1895, p. 60) and the 2d ed. (1900, p. 60) as well as in the *Popular Science* article (1894, p. 607) was changed to "she was carried about in arms very little" (1906, p. 58). Had Mrs. Baldwin in the interim confessed to her husband her own transgressions, or had Baldwin conveniently overlooked some of his own?

varies directly with the dynamogenic influence of the stimulus, the far distance drawing this out more than the near. What is more, the finding was consistent with an "efferentist" rather than an "afferentist" theory of movement: "Why did the child prefer the right hand uniformly for effort, if not under the feeling of stronger outward nervous pressure [efferent feeling of innervation] in the case of that hand?" (Baldwin, 1890a, p. 248).

Early Left-Hand Preference and the Recapitulationist Theory

Baldwin's study confirmed an early right-hand preference but did not support Broca's (1865) statement that hand preference would appear "from the first moments of life." Instead Helen's right-hand preference developed later, apparently rather suddenly, and then only on far-distance trials. Furthermore, Baldwin noticed that, during the eighth month, Helen showed a temporary preference for her left hand, using it for short distances at the same time as she used her right for far distances. To explain this apparent anomaly, Baldwin drew on the principle of genetic recapitulationism. For other recapitulationist theorists (e.g., Gowers, 1902; Jobert, 1885), the phylogenetic principle to be recapitulated in ontogeny was the initial absence of handedness followed by the emergence of right-handedness. Because Helen, instead, had shown an earlier and transient period of left-hand preference, Baldwin concluded that any invocation of the recapitulationist principle would mean that "lower animals" should be left-handed rather than evenhanded (1894, p. 607; 1895, pp. 73–74, n. 1). He went on to cite various reports supporting this extrapolation, including an assertion by Vierordt (1881, pp. 427–428) that parrots grasp and hold food with the left claw and that lions strike with the left paw; Vierordt's quotation from the explorer David Livingstone that "all animals are left-handed"; and a personal communication from the neurologist William Ogle about a left-handed chimpanzee, a late denizen of the Zoological Garden in London. (Baldwin also mentioned that Ogle, 1871, had made observations on parrots and monkeys, without saying, however, what Ogle had found.) Baldwin (1895) acknowledged the need for further data and even sent inquiries to zoo officials. In the second (1900) and third (1906) editions of *Mental Development in the Child and the Race*, Baldwin did not report any replies, although in the second edition he did note that he had confirmed Vierordt's report that parrots are left-handed: "My birds [parrots] stand on the right and hold the food with the left claw" (1906, p. 71).

Handedness and Language Development

Before Broca (1865), the development of handedness could be understood only in the limited context of the theories of laterality of the day. With the establishment of the principle of cortical localization of speech and the proposed relation to handedness, a new implication emerged: both the development of handedness and the development of speech could be linked to the hypothesized ascension in functioning of one side of the brain, in other words, to functional changes in a common cortical system. Following Broca, Baldwin thus identified both speech and handedness as functions coordinated in one hemisphere only, "functions which are crippled only if one selected hemisphere is damaged" (Baldwin, 1895, p. 68).

An evolutionary scenario.—The fact of a functional and cortical coordination between handedness and speech provoked Baldwin to consider how the two traits might have been linked in evolution. Baldwin's analysis of this question seems to foreshadow his subsequent (1896) theory of "coinciding variations." By this formulation—what Simpson (1953) called the "Baldwin effect"—Baldwin tried to reconcile the predominant role of natural selection with the Lamarckian theory of heredity of acquired characteristics by postulating that traits individually acquired may eventually, under the influence of selection, be reinforced by similar hereditary characters (see Cairns & Ornstein, 1979; Gottlieb, 1979). Baldwin thus proposed that a functional change in hand use could have mediated a structural (hereditary) variation:

> If . . . heredity be brought to the aid of these "experience" theories [i.e., theories of handedness that Baldwin felt justified in rejecting], it is possible to claim that, as structure is due to function, experience of function must have been first in race history; and only thus could the modification in structure which is now sufficient to produce right-handedness in individual cases have been brought about. On the other hand, if we go lower in the animal scale than man, analogies for the kinds of experience which are urged as reasons for right-handedness are not present; animals do not carry their young, nor pat them to sleep, nor do animals shake hands! It must therefore be shown that animals are right- or left-handed, or that they differ in some marked respect in regard to function, in their nervous make-up, from man. Admitting the need of meeting these requirements; admitting again that we have little evidence that animals are dextral in their functions; admitting also the known results as to the control of the two halves of the muscular system by the opposite brain hemispheres respectively; admitting further that the motor speech function is performed by the hemisphere which controls the stronger side of the body; and is adjacent to the motor arm centre in that hemisphere; and admitting, finally, that the speech function is one in which the animals have little share— all these admissions lead us at once to the view that there is a fundamental connection between the rise of speech and the rise of right-handedness. [1895, pp. 66–67]

Time of first appearance of hand preference and speech.—Having linked the emergence of speech and handedness in evolution, Baldwin turned to the ontogenetic question—whether speech and handedness would be coordinated in individual development. Broca himself seems to have implied a close connection from the outset: the functions of the left hemisphere for guiding fine movements and for speech were both habits carried from earliest childhood ("dès notre première enfance") (1865, pp. 384–385). Baldwin, however, noted that Helen's right-handedness had developed before she had learned to "utter articulate sounds with much distinctness," that is, "while the motor speech centre is not yet functioning" (1890a, p. 247). Nevertheless, "the speech function follows this right-hand preference up pretty closely, beginning to be slightly voluntary in the shape of verbal imitations about the eighth or ninth months." Baldwin therefore concluded that voluntary speech "proceeds upon an earlier predominant dextral function" (1895, p. 424).

Gesture and speech.—The near synchronous development of speech and handedness, along with the proximity of the cortical substrates, provoked a more fundamental question. What psychological functions did speech and dominant-hand movement have in common? Baldwin's answer was that speech is "*par excellence* the function of expression"; all movements "are in a sense expressive"; and "details of expression and its relative fulness are matters of co-ordination," which has attained "its ripest and most complex form, apart from speech, in movements of the hand." Right-handedness thus is a form of "expressive differentiation of movement" (Baldwin, 1895, p. 69). To support this hypothesis, Baldwin cited evidence from philology and customs of various ethnic groups of the direct influence of hand movements on spoken language. He also remarked that "it would be interesting . . . to inquire how far the right hand is predominant in gesture and sign languages, which precede articulate speech," and he cited two reports that addressed this question. One by Cushing (1892), on the use of the hands by the Zuni Indians in counting and summing, indicated that for such functions the left hand is usually a passive instrument manipulated actively by the right. The other report, by Colonel Garrick Mallery (1881) on the sign languages of the North American Indians (see Baldwin, 1895, pp. 67–68, n. 1), revealed that, when either hand was used alone or predominantly, it was the right hand, not the left. Baldwin concluded that this "supports the view that the right hand was pre-eminently the 'expressive' member in prehistoric times." Furthermore, "The *common signs* among different tribes, found also in deaf-mute sign language, show that many of these forms of expression are not late conventions, but rather matter of real aboriginal usage. If, then, they date back to the period before the development of speech, we have much reason for believing that right-handedness is originally a one-sided expressive function" (1895, app. B, p. 492).

INFLUENCE OF BALDWIN'S EXPERIMENT

Baldwin's experiment (1890a) found a wide audience. The editor of *Nature* (1890) called it "interesting" and quoted it extensively. Subsequently, it was cited in leading German and French journals (*Zeitschrift für Psychologie und Physiologie der Sinnesorgane*, 1891; Weber, in *Zentralblatt für Physiologie*, 1904; Mazel, in *Revue Scientifique*, 1891, 1892); listed by the eminent German anatomist Karl von Bardeleben in his influential bibliography of works on laterality (1909); discussed at length by Tracy in his textbook *The Psychology of Childhood* (1893); analyzed by the anatomist D. J. Cunningham in the Huxley Memorial Lecture for 1902 before the Anthropological Institute of Great Britain; mentioned by the leading British physician Sir James Crichton-Browne in an important paper on handedness (1907); cited by Robert Hertz, the French sociologist and heir apparent to Durkheim, in his seminal essay "La Prééminence de la main droite" (1909) (Hertz had read the French ed. of *Mental Development in the Child and the Race*); and mentioned in a variety of books on child psychology and general articles on handedness (e.g., Beeley, 1919; Carrington, 1908; Gould, 1904; Lundie, 1896; Nice, 1918; O'Conner, 1890; Smith, 1917; Stevens, 1908; Sully, 1896). Baldwin's work, along with Wilson's (1891), also figured importantly in Joseph Jastrow's (1901) article on "Dexterity" in Baldwin's own *Dictionary of Philosophy and Psychology*. Finally, the popular press paid notice, including the *Illustrated London News* (1891) and *McClure's Magazine* (Brewster, 1913). The story in *McClure's* called dexterity a "universal and peculiar human quality" and one of the earliest to appear in life (Brewster, 1913, p. 170).

Influence on Extant Theories of Handedness

Why was this one experiment so influential? Certainly it won attention by being the first experimental study of its kind and by its initial publication in *Science*, a leading scientific journal. Moreover, its young author was already a well-known figure.[4] But above all, it was heralded for shedding real light on long-disputed questions about the origins of handedness. For instance, the damage to Buchanan's dynamic balance theory was obvious. As Crichton-Browne said, "unmistakeable right-handedness" declares itself about the eighth month, "before the infant can have profited by experience or has assumed the erect posture" (1907, pp. 639–640). The results proved

[4] The current Baldwin revival notwithstanding, some psychologists today still may not realize the extent of Baldwin's stature in his own time. Even as early as 1890, when his study first appeared, he had already published the first volume of his *Handbook of Psychology* (1889). By 1903, he was ranked the fifth most eminent contributor to psychological research, behind James, Cattell, Münsterberg, and Hall, but ahead of such luminaries as Dewey and Titchener (Cattell, 1929).

that right handedness "is unquestionably congenital and innate, and not acquired in any way" (pp. 639–640). The critical factor thus must be the brain itself, and an American physician (O'Connor, 1890), recalling one of the several physiological theories, credited Baldwin's results to the superior blood supply of the left hemisphere. Baldwin himself seems to have been partial to this explanation (1895, p. 74), although, as Jastrow (1901) correctly said, there was no clear evidence.

The experiment also was seen in larger theoretical perspective. For instance, Cunningham called Baldwin's findings "most suggestive" in connection with the evolutionary question (1902, p. 280). The American physician George Gould was more specific: Baldwin's findings meant that "the period in phylogenous savage life to which this of the infant corresponds must, therefore, be that of the earliest phase of humanization" (1904, p.

Cunningham also regarded Baldwin's results to be corroborated by neuroanatomical evidence on the timing of the myelination of the motor paths in the brain and spinal cord. Such evidence would predict what, indeed, Baldwin had found—that right-handedness would appear only when "the paths which connect the higher and lower motor centers are fully established and have been systematically practiced" (Cunningham, 1902, p. 281). Cunningham went on to note that the portion of cortex devoted to speech is fully developed only by the end of the first postnatal year. Thus on purely anatomical grounds Cunningham presumably would have predicted what Baldwin had found—hand preference first, then speech.

Influence on the Scientific Debate on Ambidextral Training

Baldwin's experiment also figured in a scientific dispute about John Jackson's Ambidextral Culture Society. By the early 1900s, the society had attracted much attention—support from a devoted coterie, including some distinguished scientists, and criticism from others, who objected to its scientific claims and were dismayed by what had become its cultist trappings (Harris, 1985). At least two critics—Crichton-Browne (1907) in England and George Gould (1904) in America—saw the polemical value of Baldwin's experiment. Ambidextral culturists had called ambidexterity the natural state of being, but here was young Helen declaring right-handedness to be her natural state, quite in the absence of any outside pressure. Gould (1904) took obvious satisfaction in using Helen to scuttle Jackson.

Influence on Methodology

Finally, the experiment contributed to methodology. Sir Daniel Wilson stated that identifying the "initial proclivities" toward hand preference could be accomplished only with Baldwin's procedure—prolonged observations "made at the first stage of life, and based on the voluntary and unprompted actions of the child" (1891, p. 209). The American psychologist T. L. Bolton called Baldwin "a master of the method he advocates" (1895, p. 143). And the anatomist Cunningham spoke of "this ready means of investigation" (1902, p. 280). (All these writers were referring to Baldwin's longitudinal method and testing procedure. If they also admired the Baldwins' treatment of their daughter, they did not say.)

Despite the acclaim, a dozen years passed without a comparable study. Cunningham said it was "a matter of regret . . . that Baldwin's method has not been more fully taken advantage of" (1902, p. 280). But in another dozen years at least six new studies had appeared, either fashioned after Baldwin's or at least mindful of his approach (Marsden, 1903; McDougall, 1908; Myers, 1908; Valentine, 1914; Voelckel, 1913; Woolley, 1910). The first three used reaching primarily to study color perception. Nevertheless, hand preference was reported, and the results as well as those of the other studies supported Baldwin or at least offered little comfort to the nurturist position. The support, in some cases, was impressive. For instance, both Marsden (1903) and Woolley (1910) found that their infant subjects, like Baldwin's daughter, began using their right hands preferentially at about 7 months and also showed the same relationship between target distance and lateralized responding. Woolley called her results "one more proof" of the already accepted view that "right-handedness must be a normal part of physiological development, not a phenomenon explicable by training" (1910, pp. 40–41). Similarly, Voelckel, who tested 52 infants ranging in age from 3.5 to 17 months, found no hand preference (for reaching) under 7 months and increasing right-hand usage after that point. He therefore sided with Baldwin and "modern opinion"—right-handedness develops about midway through the first year of life and reflects the inherent superiority of the left cerebral hemisphere.

Like Baldwin, some of the new investigators (Marsden, 1903; Valentine, 1914; Woolley, 1910) also found signs of an early transient period of left-hand use. Unlike Baldwin, however, no one invoked recapitulationism. Instead, they either ignored the finding, called it anomalous, or linked it to adventitious and temporarily effective training. Valentine made the interesting suggestion that, in the right-handed child, the left hand "may tend to specialize in actions which are very simple, thus setting free the right hand for more serious work" (1914, p. 384).

A few of the new investigators also raised the question of the temporal coordination of hand preference and speech development. For example, Woolley's subject (her daughter) first showed a preponderating use of the right hand at just the time (7 months) when she "began to babble syllables." At 10 months, she showed decided right-handedness and also said her first word. Woolley nevertheless concluded on the same note as had Baldwin: her daughter's early development of right-handedness was not accompanied by an early acquisition of speech, since at 18 months she had but 15 or 20 words, "many of them very indistinctly pronounced" (1910, p. 41).

Critics

Although praise for Baldwin's experiment was strong, a few brickbats were thrown along with the bouquets. One was from William James, which Baldwin himself invited through what can only be called a deliberate provocation. I said earlier that Baldwin saw Helen's preferential use of her right hand in an effortful task to be consistent with an efferent rather than an afferent theory of movement, that is, "under the feeling of stronger outward nervous pressure [efference] in the case of that hand." Baldwin then remarked: "Professor James, no doubt, can explain [the findings] with his 'kinaesthetic memories,'—that sword with which he decapitates so many points of evidence in his 'Principles of Psychology,'—but he does not succeed in convincing many of us. . . . If memories of former movements with effort give 'the cue,' then how do you know that there are no memories of 'innervation' among them? . . . Perhaps Professor James or some other 'afferentist' will explain this case" (1890a, p. 248).

James immediately obliged, in print (1890) and in a private letter (cited in Baldwin, 1895, p. 79). His answer was that Helen might have been guided by her sense of greater success or ease, in the case of earlier right-hand movements—all of which would involve peripheral, not central, elements. In a rejoinder, Baldwin (1890b) rejected this possibility but later confessed that he was not "strenuous" for his original interpretation and that James's interpretation now seemed to him to be "more natural and simple" (1895, p. 79). Nevertheless, Baldwin saw certain remaining problems with an afferentist account such as Helen's use of her right hand even when circumstances would seem to discourage it, for example, to grasp objects lying to her left side. Baldwin (1895, p. 79) also noted that the functionalist psychologist George Trumbull Ladd had endorsed an efferentist interpretation in his own theory of the origins of movement (Ladd, 1894, p. 222).

Baldwin's execution of his experiment also drew criticism. Whereas Bolton (1895) had called him "a master of the method he advocates," the American psychologist Margaret Schallenberger pointed out various shortcomings, including inconsistencies (in Baldwin's 1895 account) between text and numerical tables in the designation of any particular distance as within or beyond the child's reach.[5] "Professor Baldwin's new dynamogenic

---

[5] Schallenberger's criticisms, in fact, were aimed at Baldwin's color and distance-perception studies, but they apply as well to the handedness study, since it had made use of the same logic and the same reaching method.

method, then, ingenious as it is in its conception, and attractive as it is in its simplicity, has, nevertheless, been so carelessly carried out by its author that no reliance can be placed in the results obtained. True, the idea still remains; and it is left, possibly, for some less brilliant but more accurate experimenter to demonstrate its worth" (Schallenberger, 1897a, p. 576).

In 1893 Baldwin had left Toronto to occupy the Stuart Chair in psychology at his alma mater, Princeton. From there, Baldwin defended himself only briefly, suggesting, with perhaps a tinge of condescension, that his critic did not understand the problems in conducting this new kind of experimental research. "I have before advised experimental purists to 'first catch' a live, warm baby, and attempt to work it; my present critic shows that she does not know the difficulties of the task at first hand. While thanking her, therefore, for her minute examination of the chapter and promising to reconsider the points if I get the chance of a future edition, I yet fear that another revision would leave the matter still very unsatisfactory from a hypercritical point of view" (1897, p. 62). Schallenberger replied in kind: "As to Professor Baldwin's concluding remarks, I really cannot see that the investigation of any baby, of whatever sort its 'vital differences' and whatever grade its temperature, is furthered by inaccuracy of observation and record on the part of the investigating parent" (1897b, p. 62).

Whatever their misgivings, neither critic had challenged Baldwin's major conclusion about the innateness of handedness. There were some who did. One was Sir Daniel Wilson, who, while acknowledging that right-handedness is traceable to specific organic structure, called the bias "slight" and said that, with the great majority, "right-handedness is largely the result of education," beginning in infancy. As an example, Wilson noted how nurses and mothers commonly encourage the infant to use the right hand to hold a spoon (1891, pp. 127–128).

Bolton (1895) likewise objected to Baldwin's conclusion that "the influences of infancy have little effect on handedness" as well as to his reduction of right-handedness to "a spontaneous variation in the equality of the two hemispheres" (1895, p. 143).

Baldwin's fiercest critic was John Jackson, the president of the Ambidextral Culture Society. Stung by Gould's (1904) use of Baldwin's report against his society, Jackson asserted that "no reliable or general deduction, such as Professor Baldwin offers, can logically be drawn from the phenomena of a single case" (1905, p. 82). Jackson developed this point in an unsigned review ("Ambidexterity," 1904)[6] of Gould's (1904) own paper. Citing an 1871 report by Ogle (ironically, the same report mentioned by Baldwin in

---

[6] Although the review was unsigned, I have little doubt that its author was Jackson himself, judging from the content and rhetorical style.

connection with his speculations on animal laterality), Jackson acknowledged that when Ogle

> gave us certain deductions . . . based on his examination of *two thousand
> consecutive patients,* as to their one-handedness, we felt that those deduc-
> tions commanded our respect and necessitated the greatest caution on
> the part of any one who attempted to challenge or criticise them.
>   But what about this so-called "experimental demonstration" by
> Professor Baldwin?
>   Did he examine two thousand infants? Did he test one thousand
> babies in their incipient outbuddings of intelligent prehension and ma-
> nipulation? Did he carry out his experiments on one hundred atoms of
> humanity to ascertain the mode of hand development? Or did Profes-
> sor J. Mark Baldwin go through just *one course* of tests with *just one child;*
> and is the "experimental demonstration" decided by one set of supple-
> mental tests [the effortful trials] extending over exactly fifteen days?
>   . . . and it is from this short series that Dr. Gould's experimental
> demonstration of a fundamental and determining universal law of
> physical and dextral development has been derived!
>   Is it thus that science is to be taught, truth to be demonstrated, and
> belief to be shaped and determined? ["Ambidexterity," 1904, pp. 656–
> 657]

Still, how to explain this "single case"? Jackson answered this question in
his book. Baldwin's child was nothing other than a "freak of nature," "just as
mysterious and unexplainable as are other abnormalities that are occurring
all round us in precisely similar or approximate degrees of frequencies, and
in exactly the same quasi-hereditary, irregular, or sporadic manner" (1905,
p. 97).

If Baldwin knew of Jackson's animadversions on himself as well as
Helen, there is no sign that he replied. In any case, on the matter of sample
size, Baldwin had anticipated any such objection: "I have cited only points
which have their own value,—points on which observations on one child are
as valuable as on many,—determinations concerning the order of development of the mental functions with the physical, not determinations merely
of the time of development, which may vary. Observations on single children may also be valuable as showing that an event may happen, as opposed
to theories according to which such an event may not happen, under given
circumstances" (1890a, p. 248).[7]

---

[7] Jackson was not alone in his views about sample size. The issue also was raised by
Bolton (1895), which may account for his general skepticism about Baldwin's conclusions,
as cited earlier. Bolton's statement on this point (as expressed in his review of *Mental
Development in the Child and the Race*) also typifies the reaction of the experimentalists to
Baldwin's by then well-established penchant for grand theorizing: "After the first three or

BALDWIN'S DECLINE

Despite his early eminence, Baldwin slipped into near oblivion. In 1974, Mueller (cited by Broughton & Freeman-Moir, 1982, pp. 3–4) found not a single mention of his name in a review of 12 introductory psychology textbooks and only three citations in a review of four major psychology and sociology journals in the 1960s. Baldwin's study of handedness and his provocative speculations on the subject suffered a similar fate.[8]

As Mueller (1976) has pointed out regarding the body of Baldwin's work, this "amnesia" can be laid to a combination of factors. In mid-career, Baldwin bucked the positivist stand by shifting his attention to the advance of theory, a characteristic already abundantly evident in his 1895 work, as Bolton (1895) had noted (see n. 7 above). Baldwin wanted to strengthen relations between psychology and philosophy just when G. S. Hall and others were working to free psychology from metaphysics and epistemology. Along with diminished interest in laboratory research, Baldwin failed to develop a cadre of students who would promote and expand his ideas. Finally, in 1908, at the height of his fame, he was personally embarrassed by a sexual scandal and was forced to leave Johns Hopkins and American academic life.[9]

---

four chapters very few observations and experiments made upon his own or other children are given, and the book is devoted almost entirely to theorizing and speculation. It is true that in many of the fields traversed by the author, no facts are yet established. But, then, why not have waited for them, or given time to gathering them, instead of elaborating theory in their absence?" (Bolton, 1895, p. 143). Joseph Jastrow, in his article on dextrality for Baldwin's *Dictionary*, took a more moderate position on the adequacy of the data: "Experiments on children as to original right- or left-handed tendencies are not sufficient to show positive results, but in some cases reveal a decided congenital right-handedness at a well-marked period" (Jastrow, 1901, p. 277)—a statement with which Baldwin, as editor, presumably concurred.

[8] Except for my own historical reviews and empirical reports (Carlson & Harris, 1985; Cornwell et al., 1985a, 1985b; Harris, 1980a, 1983b), I have not found a single reference to Baldwin's experiment and writings on handedness in any papers or books published in the last 20 years. In the 1930s and 1940s, there are frequent citations (e.g., Dennis, 1935; Giesecke, 1936; Heinlein, 1930; Hildreth, 1949; Jones, 1931; Lederer, 1939), but they are perfunctory references to the experimental findings without any discussion of Baldwin's ideas. The study by Dennis (1935), however, at least took very seriously Baldwin's methodology—his controlled upbringing of the infant subject. Dennis did not go to quite the same lengths with his subjects, the twin boys Del and Ray, as Baldwin had with Helen, but the result was the same: from the seventh month on, dextrality was evident in the absence of social transmission.

[9] According to Mueller (1974; cited in Broughton & Freeman-Moir, 1982, p. 4), the scandal erupted when Baldwin was discovered with black prostitutes in a Baltimore brothel. Although Baldwin convincingly protested that his visit had been the result of a practical joke, the incident left a stain on Baldwin's reputation that was never erased in American academic circles. Baldwin spent his last years in Mexico and then in France.

Nowhere is the amnesia more startling than in the treatment of Baldwin's handedness experiment by John B. Watson—Watson, to whom Baldwin himself, in 1908, had offered the chair of psychology at Johns Hopkins. When, a few years later, Watson and his student Rosalie Raynor began their famous infant tests for the purpose of determining which behaviors were instinctive and which learned, Watson ignored Baldwin's and others' earlier work, named handedness as one of the behaviors that needed to be assessed, and dismissed all discussion of this question to date as being "of the 'armchair' variety" (Watson & Watson, 1921, p. 500).

Since his own infant tests failed to show evidence of reliable hand preference, Watson (1924) concluded that handedness must be strictly a matter of conditioning and social training. Watson, however, had not brought forth any direct evidence for his conditioning explanation. Nor is it clear that his results had failed utterly to support the genetic model (Harris, 1983a). What is clear is that Watson not only ignored all previous work but also failed to consider the question of the relationship between handedness and cerebral lateralization, as Baldwin and the others had. In other words, Watson treated the subject of human handedness totally outside the major theoretical context in which it had been considered since Broca's (1865) time.[10] Baldwin, by then an expatriate in France, was in no position, either geographically or in other respects, to challenge Watson's analysis of handedness, much less, as Kessen (1965, p. 229) has said, to control Watson's other excesses. William James, the only other man who, in Kessen's estimation, might have acted as a brake on Watson, had died in 1910.

WAS BALDWIN RIGHT? A CONTEMPORARY APPRAISAL

How should we appraise Baldwin's experiment and theoretical analysis today? On the question whether human handedness, as Watson put it, is "instinctive" or "learned," the consensus today is squarely with Baldwin: human handedness is recognized as a fundamentally biological characteristic, such that in right-handers the skills of the dominant hand reflect the intrinsic specialization of the contralateral (left) cerebral hemisphere. In left-handers, as Baldwin did not foresee, the story is more complicated (see

---

Mueller adds that, compared to the Americans, the French apparently took a more light-hearted view of the incident.

[10] Why Watson acted as he did is a story in itself. At least three factors probably played a role: the apparent absence of hand preference as a species characteristic in monkeys and apes (e.g., Lashley & Watson, 1913); a demonstration by Lashley (1917) that hand preference in a monkey could be established through training; and vigorous criticism by S. I. Franz (1912) of certain extreme cortical localization models being proposed at the time (Harris, 1983a).

the papers in Herron, 1980). Nor did Baldwin or Broca foresee that the "nondominant" hand would prove to be skilled in its own right (e.g., Brizzolara, de Nobili, & Ferretti, 1982; Harris, 1980b). The reasons for left-hemisphere specialization remain unclear; among recent proposals, one of the more provocative is a maturational growth gradient hypothesis (Corballis & Morgan, 1978) reminiscent of what Broca himself had suggested (1865; see Harris, 1984).

As for the timing of first appearance of hand preference, about the middle of the first year seems close to the mark for a visually directed reaching task like Baldwin's, with right-hand preference becoming increasingly strong through 20 months (Cornwell, Harris, & Fitzgerald, 1985a). Many individual infants, however, also show wide fluctuations in hand use over this period (Carlson & Harris, 1985; Liederman, 1983).

Where Baldwin probably went too far, although his own experiment gave him cause, was in declaring that the "influences of infancy" have "little effect" on handedness. If, for early infancy, the question is still open (see reports in Young, Segalowitz, Corter, & Trehub, 1983), it is clear that, when the child begins to learn to use eating utensils and drawing and writing instruments, social training can significantly affect hand preference and skill (e.g., Komai & Fukuoka, 1934; Teng, Yang, & Chang, 1976).[11]

In addition to methodology and the question of the first appearance of hand preference, several other aspects of Baldwin's results have relevance today. For example, it has been suggested that, at about 6 or 7 months of age, the infant will not reach across the midline (Bruner, 1969, p. 231). Recent work has disconfirmed this idea (Carlson & Harris, 1985; Provine & Westerman, 1979), but Baldwin was there first. As he said, Helen's right hand "intruded regularly upon the domain of the left" (1895, p. 63).

Baldwin also anticipated current research on the matter of early left-hand use in infants who eventually show a stable right-hand preference. Some such indications have been reported (e.g., Anderson & McDonnell, 1979; Carlson & Harris, 1985), although the phenomenon is of uncertain reliability (see Young, Segalowitz, Misek, Alp, & Boulet, 1983). No one today, in any case, speaks of recapitulationism, as Baldwin did, but other explanations have been proposed. For example, one possibility is that certain movements of the infant's left hand actually serve a spatial localizing, rather than motor-manipulative, function, thereby reflecting early expres-

[11] It is noteworthy that, among the "training" explanations that Baldwin tested and rejected, two—reclination and infant cradling position—lately have become the subject of considerable interest in their own right. In the supine posture, young infants do turn more often to the right (e.g., Harris & Fitzgerald, 1983) not because they are placed that way but probably as an expression of an endogenous motor bias (Turkewitz & Creighton, 1974). As for cradling, left-side, not right-side, cradling is the more common practice, as Baldwin observed (e.g., Saling & Tyson, 1981), although the reason remains obscure.

sion of right-hemisphere specialization for spatial localization (see Bresson, Maury, Pieraut–le Bonniec, & de Schonen, 1977). The question is provocative but remains unresolved.

Equally provocative is Baldwin's conclusion that dominant-hand preference arises only under effortful or highly motivated conditions. Although Marsden (1903) and Woolley (1910) confirmed this effect for single infants, Carlson and Harris (1985) did not in a sample of 32 infants. Still, the question of the relationship between motivation and hand use—Baldwin's principle of dynamogenesis—has scarcely been raised in contemporary research. The time seems ripe.

Where Baldwin as theoretician may have been most insightful and most prescient is in his analysis of what he called "the fundamental connection between the rise of speech and the rise of right-handedness." With respect to the phylogenetic question, there is intense interest once again, so that the issue of animal laterality has reemerged as a major focus (see Glick, 1985; Harnad, Steklis, & Lancaster, 1976). The particular combination of right-handedness and left cerebral dominance for speech would seem to be uniquely human, as Baldwin (1895) foresaw. What is unclear is whether other primate species show some approximate tendency, such as hand preference as a species characteristic. Many investigators have concluded that they do not (e.g., Warren, 1980), but there is some strongly suggestive evidence to the contrary, and here the evidence goes against Baldwin, since it indicates that, for both monkeys (e.g., Beck & Barton, 1972) and the great apes (e.g., Fischer, Meunier, & White, 1982), hand preference for object manipulation is for the right hand, not the left. Aside from primates, evidence for species "handedness" thus far is absent, with one remarkable exception: in the third edition of *Mental Development in the Child and the Race* (1906), Baldwin, following Vierordt (1881), appears to have been correct in his observation that parrots—or at least the limited number of species studied to date—hold food in the left foot while perching on the right (see Friedman & Davis, 1938; Rogers, 1980).[12]

As for the ontogenetic question, Baldwin's analysis of the linkage be-

---

[12] In Ogle's (1871) report of his observations of parrots and monkeys, which, as I noted earlier, Baldwin (1895) had cited but not described, Ogle actually reported evidence consistent with some of the current reports. Of 23 monkeys, 20 in the great majority of cases preferred to use the right hand for extending and grasping an object outside the cage, while only three preferred the left. Ogle therefore concluded that monkeys, "like men, are as a general rule right-handed" (p. 287). As for parrots, Ogle, like Baldwin as well as more recent investigators, had observed that parrots perch on the right foot and use the left for holding food, but Ogle suggested that the bias might be considered dextral, not sinistral, since the original selection is of the foot that is to serve as support, not the foot to be used for feeding. Inasmuch as Baldwin had cited Ogle's report in the context of his (Baldwin's) speculations on the left-sidedness of lower animals, it would seem that Baldwin either had forgotten the contents of the report or disagreed with Ogle's interpretation.

tween the development of hand preference and speech closely anticipates contemporary analysis (Cornwell, Harris, & Fitzgerald, 1985b; Ramsay, 1980). The same can be said for Baldwin's characterization of handedness as "expressive differentiation of movement" and his speculations about hand differences for gesture during speech and for deaf communication. Current research confirms Baldwin's surmise that the right hand predominates in gesture and sign language (e.g., Bellugi, Poizner, & Klima, 1983; Kimura, 1976, 1979; Vaid, Bellugi, & Poizner, 1984). Where today we would depart from Baldwin and his contemporaries is in the inference he drew from Cushing's (1892) and Mallery's (1881) studies of hand use in sign languages by North American Indians—that is, that because the right hand was favored whenever either hand was used alone or predominantly, the right hand would have been "pre-eminently the 'expressive' member in pre-historic times" (Baldwin, 1895, app. B, p. 492). Baldwin thus appears to have assumed that aboriginal peoples are living fossils. We know today that they are *not*, although, as Shipman (1985) has observed, the old, mistaken view has been hard to dislodge.

We also can say that, in demonstrating the development of hand preference in the absence of social transmission, Baldwin provided perhaps the first empirical evidence of lateral cerebral specialization in infancy. In contrast, a radical and highly influential theory of the 1960s based on studies of brain-injured children and adults was that in infancy the cerebral hemispheres are unspecialized and equipotential and that lateral specialization increases with age (Lenneberg, 1967). This theory has been challenged, partly in light of recent demonstrations of the same sort of asymmetries as Baldwin himself had discovered (see the review in Kinsbourne & Hiscock, 1977). One wonders, then, whether the theory ever would have taken so extreme a form or been so influential had the work of Baldwin and his contemporaries been known.

Finally, in the light of the insights that psychologists today have drawn and are continuing to draw about language, cognition, and neurological development from the analysis of the development of manual specialization, it should be obvious how deeply we have assimilated one of Baldwin's central principles—that the study of hand movements can be a window to the growth of the mind.

Here, then, has been the story of an experiment that mattered in Baldwin's own time and that holds useful lessons for today. History has shown that Watson's verdict on human handedness was wrong, that Baldwin's was right. It seems altogether fitting that Baldwin has been vindicated on this question just as he is beginning to be on so many others.

IV. PERILS OF POPULARIZATION: THE FOUNDING
OF *PARENTS' MAGAZINE*

STEVEN SCHLOSSMAN

Rand Corporation

The modern field of child development, most scholars would readily agree, owes its very existence as a respectable academic enterprise to the generous financial support provided by the Laura Spelman Rockefeller Memorial Fund (LSRM) in the 1920s and 1930s. To the LSRM, especially to its chief program officers Beardsley Ruml and Lawrence K. Frank, child development represented not merely a field of scientific inquiry but the birth of a broader social movement. Starting at rock bottom with child-rearing practices in the home, the movement would, its philanthropic sponsors confidently believed, radiate outward and eventually transform all social institutions. The LSRM agreed to invest so heavily in scientific research on children only because it assumed that the results of research would be immediately practicable and that extensive programs in parent education (also partially funded by the LSRM) would carry the latest findings to mothers for immediate home use. The LSRM, in short, was committed to spreading what I have elsewhere termed the "gospel of child development" in readily accessible form to the lay public (Schlossman, 1981).

Nobody believed more avidly in the gospel of child development as the key to happier children, more enlightened parents, and a more just social order than Lawrence Frank. To some more cautious scholars in the 1920s, Frank's enthusiasm for deriving immediately practicable results from scientific research seemed occasionally naive and boundless. Convinced that mass dissemination of research findings was imprudent until a secure knowledge base had accumulated, they attempted to placate Frank on the

Views expressed in this paper are the author's own and are not necessarily shared by the Rand Corp. or its research sponsors.

issue of parent education so as not to jeopardize funding from the LSRM for purely scientific inquiries. In fact, however, Frank himself was always deeply concerned about the "perils of popularization." He was very much aware that the enormously popular child study movement of the 1890s, pioneered by G. Stanley Hall, Earl Barnes, and numerous educators and middle-class parents, had collapsed in intellectual disarray and disgrace after being pummeled by such leading psychologists as William James, Hugo Münsterberg, and Edward L. Thorndike (Hendricks, 1968; Joncich, 1968; Kessen, 1965; Ross, 1972; Schlossman, 1976). From his first formulations of the LSRM program in child study and parent education in the early 1920s, Frank sought to contain the danger of what he called "boom over-enthusiasm and probable disillusioned deflation," which had earlier befallen Hall's efforts (Frank, 1926NP).

This chapter highlights only one of the LSRM's various strategies for monitoring the direction and growth of popular child study in the post–World War I era: its decision to subsidize a mass circulation periodical, originally called *Children, a Magazine for Parents*, which first appeared in October 1926 and whose name was soon after changed to the more familiar *Parents' Magazine*. During the 1930s and 1940s *Parents' Magazine* was acclaimed as the most popular educational periodical in the world, and it was the only commercial periodical whose circulation and advertising revenues climbed steadily upward during the course of the Great Depression. The magazine's links to the elite of the child development community were clear: Helen Thompson Woolley, director of Teachers College's Institute of Child Welfare Research, and Sidonie Gruenberg, director of the Child Study Association of America, served on its board of editors, while such distinguished scholars and educators as John Anderson of Minnesota, Bird Baldwin of Iowa, Arnold Gesell of Yale, Ernest Groves of Boston University, Patty Smith Hill of Teachers College, Lois Hayden Meek, the educational secretary of the American Association of University Women, and Michael Vincent O'Shea of Wisconsin lent their names as advisory editors.

My analysis of *Parents' Magazine* is limited to the process by which it was created in 1924 and 1925 (Schlossman, 1983). The story has never been told, yet the episode remains one of the most intriguing in the entire history of the child development movement and illuminates the LSRM's concerted effort to contain the "perils of popularization." This chapter represents, I hope, a small beginning toward filling the need Orville Brim, Jr., recognized a quarter century ago for research on "the use of mass media in parent education" (Brim, 1959).

To begin, let us recall some basic chronology regarding the LSRM's investment in research and parent education as of January 1924, when George J. Hecht, a businessman and part-time editor of a social service magazine, first approached Beardsley Ruml with his idea for the periodical

Children. (For background on Hecht, the LSRM, and the larger context of educational popularization in the 1920s, see Cravens, 1979; Lomax, Kagan, & Rosenkrantz, 1978; Schlossman, 1976, 1981, 1983; Senn, 1975; Shea, 1980; Smuts, 1979; Takanishi, 1979; Wollons, 1983.) There is suggestive evidence that Hecht's proposal caught the LSRM very much off guard. Ruml and Frank had as yet barely sketched the outlines of the future child development and parent education movement. None of the institutional apparatus for expanding scientific research on children was in place. Although the LSRM had advanced small sums to support ongoing research on children at Teachers College, Iowa, and Yale, the creation of the first LSRM-funded research institute at Teachers College was still six months off and hardly in the process of early negotiation. Nor was a plan for disseminating the results of scientific research through parent-training programs much more than a glimmer in Lawrence Frank's eye. To date, the LSRM had done little more than subsidize the Child Study Association (then known as the Federation for Child Study) in publishing previously completed self- and group-instructional materials and a small bulletin for limited distribution (Schlossman, 1981). Thus in January 1924 Frank and Ruml were slowly, cautiously, and patiently nurturing their big idea for creating a new science of child study when in walked George Hecht ready to popularize and commercialize whatever knowledge already existed in a mass circulation periodical. One can well imagine that they thought Hecht was putting the cart before the horse and that, unless his venture could somehow be monitored, he posed a considerable threat to the integrity of the larger social and scientific movement they were planning to launch.

A NEGLECTED PIONEER IN CHILD DEVELOPMENT: GEORGE J. HECHT

As the least well-known of the major figures responsible for the growth of the child development movement, Hecht's personal life merits more than passing attention. When he first approached the LSRM with his idea for a magazine on child rearing, Hecht was 28 years old and a businessman in search of a larger cause. He later explained his lifelong business philosophy as follows (*George Joseph Hecht,* 1975, p. 8): "I won't permit going into anything that doesn't render a useful educational service and which doesn't have the prospect of being profitable. Those are the two requirements. They don't have to make much money but they have to have good prospects. But I wouldn't go into any moneymaking project which I cannot be proud of."

Hecht came to both facets of this philosophy quite naturally. Born in New York City on November 1, 1895, to German-Jewish parents and raised in the Victorian brownstone his immigrant grandfather had built (on the site that is now occupied by Radio City), Hecht grew up accustomed to bourgeois comforts and ensured of entry into his family's lucrative hide and skin import business. Hecht's parents possessed the means, the leisure, and the inclination to participate in the various civic reform crusades of the Progressive Era. Hecht's mother was particularly active in welfare concerns and served on the board of directors of such charitable agencies as the East Side Free School and the Hudson Guild, one of the nation's most famous social settlements. Both by their example and by their choice of schools, Hecht's parents sought to convey to their son their sense of moral and social responsibility for those less fortunate than they, especially to the thousands of immigrants who were then arriving daily in New York. They sent George to the Ethical Culture School, which not only upheld high standards of intellectual and moral attainment but also, unlike most private schools, used liberal scholarships to ensure a student body of mixed ethnic, religious, and income backgrounds. Field trips at Ethical Culture included visits to the seamier sites in the city and to its numerous charitable institutions. Hecht, like many other students at the time, claimed especially to have come under the spell of the school's ethics teacher, John Lovejoy Elliott, a nationwide leader in the social settlement movement who taught a secular imperative to "do something useful." Hecht chose quite consciously to attend college at Elliott's alma mater, Cornell, where he majored in economics (*George Joseph Hecht*, 1975; Schlossman, 1979).

While Hecht did well at college, his forte lay in extracurricular activities. He was an active participant in the debating society and in the oldest college magazine, the *Cornell Era*, whose business manager he became by securing for it more advertising than any other student publication in the country. Hecht promoted the magazine's virtues mightily, tripled its circulation within a year, and persuaded a book wholesaler to give national distribution to a collection of the *Era*'s best articles. The collection, *Beyond Cayuga's Waters*, would soon become a Cornell classic; the book distributor, Baker and Taylor, would later be bought by Hecht with profits partially generated by the success of *Parents' Magazine* and transformed into the largest book wholesaler in the country (*George Joseph Hecht*, 1975; Schlossman, 1979).

Hecht graduated a month after the United States entered World War I, and after being denied entry into Officers' Training School because of poor vision, he enlisted and was assigned to the Statistical Division of the General Staff of the Army in Washington, DC. In addition to his regular duties, Hecht developed the concept of using cartoons for wartime propaganda. He founded and supervised (as a second job) the Bureau of Cartoons, which in 1918 became part of George Creel's Committee on Public Information. Hecht initiated the idea of issuing weekly circulars to more than 750 of the nation's cartoonists listing patriotic themes that various government agencies wanted conveyed to build popular support for the war effort. Following the war Hecht gathered and annotated a collection of 100 of the best of the war cartoons. This collection, published as *The War in Cartoons* (Hecht, 1919), appeared on the *New York Times* list of best books of 1919. Hecht obviously had a good nose for what would sell (*George Joseph Hecht*, 1975; Schlossman, 1979).

On return to civilian life in December 1918, Hecht entered the family business. Finding that it offered few outlets for his talents of salesmanship or his quest to do something useful, he soon became involved in the work of the United Neighborhood Houses (UNH), an organization of 40-plus social settlements (Hecht's mentor, John Lovejoy Elliot, had by then become president of the National Federation of Settlements). As chairman of UNH's publicity committee, Hecht decided that the best way to publicize its activities was by means of a monthly newspaper (it later became a weekly). Almost entirely by his own effort and with his customary flair for promotion, Hecht created the diminutive *Better Times*, "the Smallest Newspaper in the World" at 3¾ inches by 5 inches. Hecht hoped to capitalize on the war-induced spirit of sacrifice and empathy for one's fellow Americans. "Through the war everyone, everywhere, has been imbued with the spirit of service," Hecht wrote. "During the period of belligerency no sacrifice was too great for the American people. This devotion to our democracy must not be permitted to diminish. The spirit that won the war must be kept alive." To achieve these aims, *Better Times* would strive to stimulate New Yorkers' interest in "community work" and reinforce their "faith that through neighborhood organization many difficult social reconstruction problems will be solved" (*Better Times*, 1920a, p. 6).

Under Hecht's aggressive leadership (albeit unpaid—his main job remained the family business), the size and length of *Better Times* soon expanded (Hecht now proclaimed it "a Little Paper with a Big Purpose"), and it began to receive advertising. Hecht freely utilized the names of his most prominent subscribers to promote the venture (e.g., Jane Addams, Dwight Morrow, Mrs. Pierpoint Morgan, Mrs. John D. Rockefeller, etc.), and, remarkably for such a minor publication, it quickly accumulated 9,000 subscribers. The leading New York dailies praised *Better Times* and, indeed, often borrowed directly from it to cover social welfare activities they might otherwise have ignored. Yearly dinners celebrating *Better Times*'s achievement became major social occasions among New York's upper crust.

Hecht kept *Better Times* lively and informative. It was, he proudly noted, a "trade paper for charity" that would pioneer new means of communicating the most advanced knowledge to laymen. Social workers had too often "given the results of their work to the public in voluminous, uninteresting reports and unattractive, unillustrated bulletins," Hecht observed. "Consequently many genuinely public-spirited citizens have lost whatever interest they had in welfare work. It has been said that 'he who makes goodness uninteresting sins against virtue.' We are attempting, by giving up-to-date methods of editorship, to make *Better Times* as attractive and readable as possible without making it sensational or inaccurate" (*Better Times,* 1920b, p. 22).

Better Times did not skirt controversial issues. It came out against government efforts to repress postwar radicalism by force (the famous Palmer raids, which had several New York counterparts) and criticized the growing hostility toward immigrants manifested in the campaigns for immigration restriction and efforts to prohibit public use of foreign languages. In supporting Americanization efforts by schools and other government agencies, *Better Times* mediated between those who emphasized the advantages of "cultural pluralism" and "immigrant gifts," on the one hand, and those who railed against immigrants' unwillingness to forsake their mother tongues and qualify for citizenship, on the other. Hecht championed the causes of better housing for all and the government's responsibility to provide sex education in the schools. He also spoke out strongly in favor of sensitive efforts to teach new, distinctively American ideas on child nutrition to immigrant mothers.

I do not want to exaggerate the liberalism of *Better Times* under Hecht's leadership. The periodical sometimes supported a strident form of Americanization, referred to black children as "pickaninnies," and sought more to tap its readership's sense of noblesse oblige than its concern for social justice. Alongside announcements of the latest courses offered by the New School for Social Research were advertisements for the newest models of Rolls-Royce. Nonetheless, *Better Times* remained a unique venture in seeking to popularize the social settlements' mission in New York. Hecht's initiative cultivated a much larger and more knowledgeable lay audience than had previously existed regarding the innovative work that social settlements performed and their unique perspective on contemporary social and political problems (Schlossman, 1979).

I have elaborated Hecht's early educational and publishing experiences prior to his contact with the LSRM primarily in order to make two points regarding the creation of *Parents' Magazine.* First, while scholars affiliated with *Parents' Magazine* often thumbed their noses at Hecht for his crass commercialism, there is no reason to doubt that his passion for helping others was ingrained and genuine. Promotion and advertising may have been his true loves, but from the very beginning of his career he believed that the popularization and dissemination of new knowledge was the key to a more just social order. The particular body of knowledge, the audience, and the scale of *Parents' Magazine* were different from those of *Better Times,* but the basic conviction underlying Hecht's involvement in both enterprises was the same. Second, though still a young man whose primary job was importing hides and skins, Hecht's accomplishments in publishing were already considerable by the time he broached the idea for *Parents' Magazine* to the LSRM. Hecht was imaginative, worked hard, fast, and persistently to bring his ideas to fruition, had excellent instincts for what would sell, enjoyed sufficient independent means to launch new projects without concern for immediate financial gain, and was intent on doing good. He was clearly a man to be taken seriously, for there could be little doubt he would follow through on his ideas.

By 1923 *Better Times* was secure enough for Hecht to turn over most of the operation to others and to seek more ambitious avenues of service and influence for himself. First, he founded and became secretary to the Welfare Council of New York City, an organization he created after synthesizing ideas from a contest *Better Times* had sponsored for the best plan to coordinate the city's 2,000-odd charitable agencies. Hecht turned down the presidency of the organization in favor of the more distinguished philanthropist Robert W. de Forest (president of the Charity Organization Society and the Metropolitan Museum of Art). Then, continuing his pursuit of the useful, Hecht began attempting to drum up support among well-to-do friends and acquaintances for a popular magazine to help parents rear children (*George Joseph Hecht*, 1975; Schlossman, 1979).

Precisely how Hecht originated the idea for *Parents' Magazine* remains unclear; he himself recounted somewhat different versions of how the idea took shape. On some occasions Hecht traced the idea to a specific encounter in the early 1920s when, returning by ship from Europe, he had met a well-to-do woman deeply troubled by the disappointments her children had caused her and her husband (*George Joseph Hecht*, 1975, p. 27). " 'I have failed,' she said, 'where every woman wants to succeed—as a mother. As parents, both of us meant well, but we didn't know how to bring up our children.' " However, Hecht told Milton Senn a different story. From his observations of the social welfare scene while running *Better Times*, Hecht claimed (Senn, 1972aNP, pp. 2–3), he had reached

> the conclusion that the work that was the most productive and the most longlasting was work with children and work with parents in teaching them how to bring up their children. Just about that time my sister was having children of her own and, being a very intelligent girl, she tried to read some of the books on child psychology that were published at that time. They were all great big thick books, unillustrated, and she didn't finish reading, I think, any of them; and I tried to read some of them just as a matter of interest and I had a great deal of difficulty reading that kind of book. I came upon the idea that a popular publication for mothers and fathers on the rearing of children was sorely needed. I was also impressed by the fact that some of the best educated women I knew made a sort of a mess out of bringing up their own children, partly because they didn't know how to go about it.

However the idea originated, by the end of 1923 Hecht had invested $10,000 of his own money to begin the periodical and had secured commitments from his acquaintances for perhaps twice that amount. He soon realized, however, that launching the venture would require much more advance capital than he initially anticipated—at least $100,000. After failing to interest several small magazines to consolidate to serve his ends, Hecht decided to approach Beardsley Ruml to see whether his idea might be integrated into the LSRM's plans for the child study and parent education movement and whether he might secure a $50,000 subsidy. Hecht was already superficially acquainted with both Ruml and Frank as a result of his work at *Better Times* and the Welfare Council. Hence he was in a position to make the overture without appearing out of line or seeking to feather his own nest.

THE VIEW FROM THE LSRM

Hecht's need for capital provided the LSRM with an opportunity to try to transform his basic idea or, at least, to make sure that the proposed periodical did not offer parents advice that was inconsistent with the findings of scientific research. If the LSRM helped fund the periodical, it could presumably exert some control over its editorial policy. Precisely how to do so, however, remained uncertain. Direct subsidy or participation was out of the question; it was impolitic, if not strictly illegal, for a foundation to promote or operate a commercial venture intended for private profit. During the several months following Hecht's initial overture Ruml and Frank appeared to give serious consideration to how they might influence Hecht, while they kept him largely in the dark as to their intentions. That the issue was very much on their minds, though, was clear from an internal document Frank circulated among his LSRM colleagues in the spring of 1924 (Frank, 1924bNP). "The danger . . . of a meretricious or even vicious publication arising is very real," he warned, because of the profitability of the women's magazine market and the new body of consumers for ideas on child rearing that the LSRM's program in parent education was likely to generate. This peril could be averted, Frank suggested, by preempting the field and quickly beginning a magazine under the "supervision and editorial direction" of the LSRM's two principal grantees, the soon-to-be-opened Institute of Child Welfare Research at Teachers College and the Child Study Association. The purpose in doing so, Frank felt, was sufficiently important to warrant subsidy from the LSRM. So monitored, "the promotion of such a magazine . . . could be carried out so as to give a real impetus to the parent training movement in the states."

While Hecht was willing to wait patiently for a formal response from the

LSRM, he was not one to sit idly by while others decided his fate. In addition to continuing to try to raise money among his friends and getting advice from leaders in child welfare circles whose opinion Ruml respected, Hecht prepared a full prospectus and took out a patent on the name *Children, a Magazine for Parents* in June. Whether Hecht's decision to patent the name reflected simple business prudence or distrust as to whether the LSRM or other potential competitors might steal the idea is uncertain. What is clear is that Ruml now began to take more serious action in regard to Hecht's request for subsidy. Ruml sent Hecht's proposal to LSRM president Arthur Woods, informing him that Hecht had already got advice from all the right people and that, while LSRM trustee Raymond Fosdick felt differently, "I thought that if you felt this might be an important thing to do, we might find some way of forwarding it" (Ruml, 1924NP).

Evidently, Woods gave Ruml the go-ahead to continue discussions with Hecht and—sometime toward the end of the summer, without making any specific commitment of LSRM monies—Ruml advised Hecht that the LSRM was genuinely interested in the success of his magazine and would subsidize the planning of several issues with which he could approach a commercial publisher. The key question now, from the LSRM perspective, was how to act on Frank's earlier suggestion and coax its recent grantee, the Teachers College Institute of Child Welfare Research, to participate in the venture and help keep Hecht in line. The LSRM decided (for reasons that remain unclear) to let Hecht take the lead in developing the link with Teachers College, and Hecht, as eager for the prestige of the academic imprimatur as he was for the $50,000 subsidy, agreed to initiate the effort.

THE BATTLE FOR TEACHERS COLLEGE'S PARTICIPATION

In the fall of 1924, prior to the appointment of Helen Thompson Woolley, the acting director of the Institute of Child Welfare Research was Otis W. Caldwell, who also served as director of the progressive Lincoln School (where, incidentally, LSRM president Woods sent his children). After talking informally with Hecht, Caldwell received a lengthy letter from him describing several options for the Institute's participation in *Children* and intimating that the LSRM was fully behind him. Caldwell immediately informed Teachers College president James Earl Russell of Hecht's letter and proposed to speak with Woods to determine, first, the depth of the LSRM's commitment to Hecht and, second, how much pressure the LSRM was ready to exert on the institute to become actively involved in supervising a magazine just as it was struggling to get its research program off the ground.

Caldwell and Woods met, and, as Caldwell ruefully told Russell (Caldwell, 1924aNP), the LSRM was "rather more keen about the matter than we had thought." It was obvious that neither Caldwell nor Russell wanted to pursue the relationship with Hecht, but they were hesitant to say so directly in light of Teachers College's financial ties to the LSRM. Nevertheless, when Caldwell, Hecht, and Lawrence Frank met several days later at a luncheon sponsored by the Child Study Association, Caldwell told Hecht plainly that the Institute "could [not] enter that kind of venture at this time." Later on at the luncheon Frank approached Caldwell in private to assure him that he did not want Teachers College "to have the notion that they [i.e., the LSRM] were in any sense urging the matter." Caldwell was surely too shrewd to accept Frank's assurances at face value; in any event, he told Russell that he truly "hoped that we can let it ride for a bit" (Caldwell, 1924bNP).

George Hecht was not ready to let the matter ride any longer, however. The day following the luncheon he met with Frank at the LSRM offices and took the offensive, saying that he had already followed Ruml's earlier advice and, without benefit of LSRM subsidy, had "worked out a plan" for several issues in order to approach a commercial publishing house. Hecht shared with Frank his frustration in dealing with Caldwell, commenting "that he had been made rather apprehensive of the success of the publication if the conservative and academic attitude manifested by the Columbia people were to dominate the editorial policy." Hecht proposed a meeting soon between himself, Ruml and Frank, Caldwell and Russell, and several other key figures in child welfare to secure their commitment to the periodical. Doubtless Hecht figured that Teachers College would prove more cooperative with both Frank and Ruml on hand to boost his venture. Frank, sensing perhaps that the growing animosity between Hecht and Caldwell might sabotage the enterprise, urged Ruml that it was now time to let Hecht know "as soon as possible" whether the LSRM was ready to back him and persuade Teachers College to cooperate (Frank, 1924aNP).

Ruml appears not to have followed Frank's advice; he did not put immediate pressure on Teachers College to cooperate and left Hecht once again to his own devices to raise money, perhaps secure in the knowledge (as conveyed to him by other publishers) that Hecht had underestimated the start-up costs for the venture and so would be unlikely to begin publication without trying again for an LSRM subsidy. Ruml may also have been hoping that, once the Institute of Child Welfare Research was securely underway and had hired a permanent director, Teachers College would be more willing to participate. The likelihood of cooperation increased when Woolley accepted the institute's directorship in 1925. She had had several prior discussions with Hecht and was enthusiastic about the educational possibilities of his magazine.

In any event, when Hecht submitted a new prospectus for *Children* to the LSRM in the summer of 1925 in the hope of renewing the earlier stalled negotiations, Ruml asked to be kept informed of his progress in raising capital (Hecht still wanted $50,000 from the LSRM; he had already raised $50,000 on his own but now recognized that it would take a total of $150,000 to get underway). Hecht reported 2 months later that he had raised additional monies and was confident he could soon secure a total of $100,000 on his own if the LSRM would guarantee him $50,000. Ruml was now persuaded that it was time for the LSRM to act. He secured a $50,000 commitment to Hecht from LSRM president Woods and then delegated to Lawrence Frank the still delicate task of gaining Teachers College's cooperation.

Initially, the negotiations between Frank and Teachers College went smoothly. On November 16 Frank told Russell that the LSRM wanted to invest $50,000 in a corporation to be formed to publish *Children* "but that we did not wish to take stock in our own name" (Frank, 1925cNP). He asked Russell whether Teachers College would agree to be the funnel through which the LSRM subsidized *Children*, with the understanding that any dividends earned on the corporation stock that Teachers College "purchased" with LSRM money would go to support the Institute of Child Welfare Research. Teachers College would name one member of the board of directors in the proposed corporation, Frank concluded, but would have no voting rights; management would remain in the hands of the businessmen Hecht had convinced to invest in his venture. Russell agreed and, 3 days later, convinced the Teachers College board of trustees to confirm the arrangement. Russell's formal request to the LSRM for $50,000 to invest in *Children*, however, left little doubt that he was participating in good measure out of gratitude for the LSRM's support of the institute. "We are willing to put our resources at [the proposed magazine's] disposal," Russell wrote. "Knowing your interest in the project, we make this request for the common good" (Russell, 1925NP).

While Russell was willing to cooperate with Hecht to please the LSRM, he clearly trusted Hecht or liked the proposed relationship no more than he had a year earlier. Two weeks after agreeing to take stock without voting rights in *Children*, Russell, probably at the urging of his trustees, changed his mind and insisted that Teachers College be given voting rights equal to Hecht's before they would agree to the final arrangement for incorporation. Russell's change of mind clearly distressed Frank, who thought that the final stumbling blocks had already been cleared. He telegraphed Ruml in Cedar Rapids, Iowa, with the bad news (Frank, 1925aNP): "Russell wants voting rights with Hecht stock and Hecht fears academic control may blight popular magazine. . . . I told Russell earlier we did not favor voting rights for his stock but he says his Board believes safeguard necessary. . . . Am arranging conference . . . with both sides. . . . Have you any advice or suggestions. Please wire." Ruml responded firmly, obviously unwilling at this late stage to do anything to jeopardize Teachers College's involvement, which had already taken so long to induce (Ruml, 1925NP): "Suggest Teachers College take voting stock equal to largest other single stockholder."

Frank called both Hecht and Russell into his office to discuss the matter of voting rights for Teachers College. The meeting was evidently spirited (Frank, 1925dNP). "After considerable discussion," Frank reported,

> it developed that Dean Russell was primarily concerned about safeguards against possible exploitation of the Magazine for the personal benefit of Mr. Hecht. While Mr. Hecht, on the other hand, is concerned in protecting his expectancy in the venture because he proposes to work without salary until the Magazine has become successful and then he expects to be given one third of any surplus earnings. Russell, while voicing no objections to this proposed compensation, did think that there was nothing to prevent Mr. Hecht, if he so desired, from voting to himself the entire net proceeds, and he felt that the corporation ought not to tie itself up irrevocably to Mr. Hecht's management, since occasion might arise wherein it would be imperative to separate Mr. Hecht from the Magazine because of possible undesirable conduct on his part which would reflect back on Teachers College. . . .
>
> On the other hand Mr. Hecht thinks quite justly that at some future date Dean Russell's successor or the faculty generally might be inclined to the position that he should not receive the division of profits which he proposes, because they are accustomed to the moderate scale of academic salaries. Furthermore, he believes that Teachers College might later on try to change the Magazine from a popular publication to a scientific educational journal if they were given too large a control.

Bickering between Hecht and Russell continued for several days following this heated meeting, with Frank serving as mediator. The LSRM was now too close to cementing this unique alliance between a foundation, a major university, and a commercial publisher in order to disseminate knowledge on child rearing to a mass audience to risk the improbability of Hecht and Russell resolving their differences on their own. With Frank's insistent mediation over the next several days, Hecht finally capitulated to Russell's request that Teachers College have voting rights in the corporation, but only on condition that Teachers College disperse its voting rights among 10 individuals (several to be approved by Hecht), so that no other individual would hold as large a bloc of votes as did Hecht. In late December 1925 Frank advised Ruml that the delicate negotiations were at last complete and that the LSRM could now issue Teachers College a check with which to purchase stock in the publishing venture. Consistent with the LSRM's desire not to be identified publicly with *Children,* Frank got Russell to agree "to consider the $50,000 as a contribution to child welfare or to the Institute, to be reported as such by him [in his annual report to the Teachers College trustees] and by the Memorial" (Frank, 1925bNP).

Many modern-day scholars in child development know full well that Hecht's magazine often caused Teachers College—and, later, Yale, Iowa, and Minnesota, who, at the LSRM's instigation, joined the corporate board of directors—considerable regret and much annoyance at having agreed to participate in its management. Moreover, the dividends promised to the participating universities for their cooperation did not materialize for over a quarter century and ultimately did little to further the cause of child development research. Though the LSRM and its successor foundations within the Rockefeller philanthropies did what they could to restructure the magazine's corporate management so as to diminish Hecht's control, Hecht outmaneuvered them at nearly every turn and used *Parents' Magazine* as a base on which to amass a personal fortune. *Parents' Magazine* soon acquired a life and rationale of its own that was only marginally related to the growth of scientific knowledge in child development (Schlossman, 1983).

Nonetheless, the details of the founding of *Parents' Magazine* in 1924 and 1925 help us to understand more fully the scope and purpose of the LSRM's original investment in the child development movement. Once Ruml and Frank committed themselves to the field, they were on guard to try to protect it against vulgarization in the mass media, even if that required behind-the-scenes machinations, unorthodox corporate liaisons, and leaning on academic grantees to accept more responsibility for monitoring the popular uses of their research than they might be comfortable with or prefer. However one judges the long-term value of *Parents' Magazine* as an educational medium, its very existence attests to the remarkable faith in the everyday *uses* of scientific research on children in the post–World War I era, without which the child development movement could never have come into being (Cravens, 1979; Joncich, 1968; Kessen, 1965; Lomax, Kagan, & Rosenkrantz, 1978; Schlossman, 1981; Sears, 1975; Shea, 1980; Smuts, 1979; Takanishi, 1979; Wollons, 1983).

V. SECULAR TRENDS IN THE STUDY OF AFRO-AMERICAN CHILDREN: A REVIEW OF *CHILD DEVELOPMENT*, 1936–1980

VONNIE C. MC LOYD

University of Michigan

SUZANNE M. RANDOLPH

Howard University

Almost since its inception, the psychological study of Afro-American children has spawned heated debate. At issue most often have been the appropriateness of comparing the behavior of Afro-American children to that of Euro-American children, labeling as deficits differences found between these two groups, and using tests normed on Euro-American children to assess the development of Afro-American children (Howard & Scott, 1981; McLoyd & Randolph, 1984; Myers, Rana, & Harris, 1979). In the main, critics argue that the study of Afro-American children has been impoverished by the tether of the comparative framework and point to biases in procedures, instruments, and the interpretation of data that, in their view, invalidate a major portion of comparative research (Hall, 1974; Howard & Scott, 1981; Myers et al., 1979; Weems, 1974).

In the present study, we examine secular trends in studies of Afro-

Portions of this chapter were presented in a symposium entitled "The Study of Afro-American Children: A Historical Analysis" at the biennial meeting of the Society for Research in Child Development, Detroit, April 1983. Portions of the research were completed while the first author was a postdoctoral fellow in the Department of Psychology, Stanford University, supported by National Institute of Mental Health Training Grant MH 15157-06. The authors gratefully acknowledge the able assistance of Michael Bankay and Adah Kennon in collecting and coding the data, the thoughtful commentaries of John R. Dill and Vincent Franklin, and the lengthy and profitable discussions with Betty Morrison and Mutombo Mpanya of issues considered in this chapter.

American children published in *Child Development* between 1936 and 1980. Of particular interest are shifts in research procedures that have engendered considerable debate, such as comparing Afro-American children with Euro-American children (Washington & McLoyd, 1982), confounding race and social class (Myers et al., 1979), and using non-Afro-Americans as experimenters and observers of Afro-American children (Oyemade & Rosser, 1980). Also examined are secular trends in less controversial aspects of research, such as the major dependent or criterion variable of interest, ages of the children studied, and size of the research sample. Underlying the present study is the assumption that published research defines a scientific field (Kail & Herman, 1977) and represents an archive of the paradigms of research in that field (Super, 1982).

As early as 1916, an anonymous author questioned the appropriateness of the Binet test of intelligence for Afro-American children and underscored the effects of rapport on performance (Guthrie, 1976). It was the author's contention that in view of the tendency of Afro-American children "not to let a white person know anything about him . . . it is not too much to say that the mere presence in the room of a member of the dominant race creates an atmosphere in which it is impossible to get a normal response" ("Some Suggestions," 1916, p. 202).

Prevailing invidious comparison was the target of criticism by Horace Mann Bond, the first Afro-American president of Lincoln University in Pennsylvania. In 1924 he argued that intelligence tests were useful in monitoring the differential progress of children exposed to the same curricular and pedagogical conditions but decried their use to compare the abilities of children from unequal socioeconomic backgrounds. As he put it, "To compare the crowded millions of New York's East Side with the children of some professorial family on Morningside Heights indeed involves a great contradiction; and to claim that the results of the tests given to such diverse groups, drawn from such varying strata of the social complex, are in any wise accurate, is to expose a fatuous sense of unfairness and lack of appreciation of the great environmental factors of modern urban life" (Bond, 1924, p. 64). Criticisms similar to these, running the gamut in focus from language to patterns of mother-child interaction, reached a crescendo during the early to mid-1970s (e.g., Bay Area Association of Black Psychologists, 1972; Clark, 1972; Cole & Bruner, 1971; Hall, 1974; Labov, 1970; Tulkin, 1972; Weems, 1974; Williams, 1972) with an increase in both the study of Afro-American children and the number of Afro-Americans awarded Ph.D.'s in psychology and related disciplines (Bayton, 1975; Guthrie, 1976). Perhaps the most influential of the critiques came from Cole and Bruner (1971) and Labov (1970). Labov challenged the validity of controlled experiments that purported to demonstrate that Afro-American children are impoverished in their means of verbal expression. He found that lower-income Afro-

American children who showed defensive monosyllabic behavior when tested by a white interviewer in an academic setting showed much improved performance when tested by a "regular" Afro-American interviewer in a nonacademic setting designed to be minimally threatening. He concluded (1970, p 171):

> Controlled experiments that have been offered in evidence [of verbal deprivation in Afro-American children] are misleading. The only thing that is controlled is the superficial form of the stimulus. All children are asked, "What do you think of capital punishment?" or "Tell me everything you can about this." But the speaker's interpretation of these requests, and the action he believes is appropriate in response is completely uncontrolled. One can view these test stimuli as requests for information, commands for action, or meaningless sequences of words. . . . With human subjects it is absurd to believe that identical stimuli are obtained by asking everyone the same question. Since the crucial intervening variables of interpretation and motivation are uncontrolled, most of the literature on verbal deprivation tells us nothing of the capacities of children.

Cole and Bruner (1971) applied Labov's arguments more broadly to the concept of competence and resuscitated and popularized the competence versus performance distinction in their classic article "Cultural Differences and Inferences about Psychological Processes." They argued forcefully that groups typically diagnosed as culturally deprived have the same underlying competence as those in the mainstream of the dominant culture, that differences in performance derive from the situations and contexts in which competence is expressed, and that a simple equivalence-of-test procedure is not sufficient to make inferences about the relative competence of different groups of children.

Myers et al. (1979) compiled an annotated bibliography of the literature published on Afro-American children in the major social science journals between 1927 and 1977, the introduction to which echoed and elaborated on the criticisms voiced by scholars during the past 6 decades. They contended, "If the goal is to know the child, then measures normed on non-Black children are not likely to be the best tools to achieve this end" (Myers et al., 1979, p. xv). Myers et al. were not sanguine about the capacity of future research to deepen and expand our understanding of Afro-American children so long as the hegemony of the comparative paradigm exists. In their view (Myers et al., 1979, p. xiv):

> The research on Black child development with its consistent practice of defining Black behavior exclusively in terms of White normative behavior perpetuates the mystification and idealization of the White norm. In

so doing, very little can be said about variation among Black children within the phenomenal Black reality. What, for example, is normative Black development? What factors seem to account for deviations from this norm, both positive and negative, among Black children? . . . Questions such as these are not currently being asked by researchers, nor are they likely to be explored as long as a Black-White comparison model of inquiry is used exclusively.

The theoretical importance of studying intragroup variation in minority groups is illustrated convincingly by research that indicates that differences within certain minority groups in, for example, achievement are accounted for by variables that are different from those that explain between-group differences (Gallimore, Boggs, & Jordan, 1974; Howard & Scott, 1981).

In keeping with the notion that the social construction of reality by social scientists both reflects and influences the broader social structure (Buss, 1975; Merton, 1957), we assume in the present study that changes in the study of Afro-American children reflect, in part, sociopolitical forces (e.g., the civil rights movement and the black nationalist movements), economic factors (e.g., availability of funds for certain kinds of research), and other macrostructural influences. For example, one effect of the myriad criticisms voiced during the early to mid-1970s against comparative research may have been a reduction in the conduct of this kind of research or increased efforts to eliminate threats to the internal validity of comparative research.

Child Development, only one of several outlets for research findings in the field of child development, is the focus of the present study because of its prestige, interdisciplinary focus, longevity as a serial publication, and wide dissemination among professionals in several disciplines (Peery & Adams, 1981; Super, 1982). Though publication of this journal began in 1930, we chose 1936 as the point of departure because it was in this year that *Child Development* became an official publication of the Society for Research in Child Development (SRCD), the major professional organization of research-oriented child developmentalists.

METHOD

The method section of each article published in *Child Development* between 1936 and 1980 was examined by a research assistant to identify those studies in which Afro-American children constituted at least 10% of the research sample. Excluded from the present study are (*a*) literature reviews or articles of a primarily theoretical nature that were not data based, (*b*) studies in which the subjects were mentally retarded and/or institutionalized (e.g., juvenile delinquents), and (c) studies in which the research findings related only to adults. In all but a very few cases, only one study was reported in each article. In cases of multiple-study articles, one study was randomly selected for coding. Using these criteria, a total of 215 articles/studies were identified.

To establish the reliability of the selection of articles, two randomly chosen volumes from each of nine 5-year periods (for a total of 18 vols.) were reviewed by a second research assistant. Interrater agreement, calculated as the number of articles selected by both assistants/the number of articles selected by either assistant, was .95, indicating that our selection process was very reliable.

Each article was coded for the type of study reported therein. As shown in Table 1, three types of studies were distinguished: (a) studies in which the research sample consisted exclusively of Afro-American children (race homogeneous), (b) studies in which the research sample was ethnically and/or racially mixed and Afro-American children were compared to children from a different ethnic/racial background (race comparative), and (c) studies in which Afro-American children were grouped with, but not compared to, ethnically or racially different children (race heterogeneous). Articles were coded for additional variables related to characteristics of the research sample, research topics and methods, and the nature of the discussion of the research. Selected variables are shown in Table 2.

Coders were three Afro-American females with doctoral level training. To establish the reliability of the coding procedure, 54 articles (25% of the total number of articles) distributed among all but one of the 5-year periods (1941–1945) were coded by two research assistants. Across all variables, intercoder agreement for each 5-year period ranged from .81 to 1.00 with a mean of .91. Across all years, intercoder agreement for each variable ranged from .85 to 1.00 with a mean of .92.

Data analyses consisted of calculating for each variable the proportion of articles/studies falling into each category of each variable. Because the articles included in this study represent virtually the entire population of data-based articles published about normal Afro-American children in *Child Development* between 1936 and 1980, these proportions are regarded as descriptive parameters that obviate the use of inferential statistics (Games, 1967).

RESULTS

The Waxing and Waning of Research Interest in Afro-American Children

The total number of studies per year was extremely low prior to mid-1960, necessitating the pooling of articles across several of the early years.

TABLE 1

FREQUENCY OF RACE-HOMOGENEOUS, RACE-COMPARATIVE, AND RACE-
HETEROGENEOUS STUDIES IN FOUR PUBLICATION PERIODS

YEAR	TYPE OF STUDY			
	Race Homogeneous	Race Comparative	Race Heterogeneous	TOTAL
FIRST PUBLICATION PERIOD				
1936–1965 ..	9 (.27)	14 (.42)	10 (.30)	33
SECOND PUBLICATION PERIOD				
1966	1	1	0	2
1967	2	4	1	7
1968	0	7	1	8
1969	1	7	3	11
1970	4	5	2	11
Subtotal ...	8 (.21)	24 (.61)	7 (.18)	39
THIRD PUBLICATION PERIOD				
1971	8	16	10	34
1972	4	6	4	14
1973	2	6	5	13
1974	5	7	4	16
1975	5	4	5	14
Subtotal ...	24 (.26)	39 (.43)	28 (.31)	91
FOURTH PUBLICATION PERIOD				
1976	2	10	1	13
1977	4	4	3	11
1978	3	2	2	7
1979	1	5	2	8
1980	4	4	5	13
Subtotal ...	14 (.27)	25 (.48)	13 (.25)	52
Total ...	55	102	58	215

NOTE.—Numbers in parentheses represent percent of total studies.

The articles were grouped into four periods of publication: (a) 1936–1965, (b) 1966–1970, (c) 1971–1975, and (d) 1976–1980. The first publication period, then, covers a span of 30 years, while the second, third, and fourth publication periods each cover a total of 5 years. Table 1 shows the annual frequency of each type of study beginning in 1969 and the total frequency and proportion of each type of study within each publication period. It can

83

TABLE 2

RELATIVE FREQUENCIES FOR EACH VARIABLE USED TO CHARACTERIZE
RACE-HOMOGENEOUS AND RACE-COMPARATIVE STUDIES/ARTICLES IN *CHILD DEVELOPMENT*
IN FOUR PUBLICATION PERIODS

	PUBLICATION PERIOD				TOTAL FREQUENCY	PROPORTION OF TOTAL POPULATION
VARIABLE	1936–65	1966–70	1971–75	1976–80		
	CHARACTERISTICS OF THE SAMPLE					
Age:						
Infants/toddlers	.13	.06	.11	.31	24	.15
Preschool	.22	.41	.51	.26	60	.38
Elementary	.26	.38	.24	.21	41	.26
Junior/senior high	.09	.03	.03	.07	8	.05
Mixed	.30	.13	.11	.15	24	.15
Social class:						
Low	.39	.53	.57	.51	82	.52
Middle	.00	.03	.08	.03	7	.05
Both	.31	.25	.21	.18	35	.22
Unspecified	.30	.19	.14	.28	33	.21
Residence:						
Urban	.52	.59	.71	.51	96	.61
Small city/rural	.17	.16	.13	.28	27	.18
Mixed	.04	.03	.00	.08	5	.03
Unspecified	.26	.22	.16	.13	28	.18
Size of sample:						
Less than 40	.22	.28	.48	.28	55	.35
40–60	.09	.19	.25	.28	35	.22
60–100	.22	.28	.19	.15	32	.20
More than 100	.48	.24	.08	.28	35	.22
	RESEARCH TOPICS AND METHODS					
Major dependent variable:						
Physical development	.30	.16	.05	.03	16	.10
Cognitive development	.30	.44	.57	.59	80	.51
Social development	.39	.41	.38	.38	61	.39
Assessment of major dependent/criterion variable						
Test/interview	.70	.91	.71	.51	110	.70
Records/reports	.13	.06	.03	.03	8	.05
Naturalistic observation	.00	.03	.14	.13	15	.10
Multiple methods	.13	.00	.11	.31	22	.14
Other	.04	.00	.00	.03	2	.01
Race of experimenter/ observer:						
Afro-American	.11	.10	.13	.03	14	.09
Non-Afro-American	.11	.14	.14	.15	21	.14
Both (manipulated)	.00	.00	.08	.08	8	.05
Unspecified	.79	.75	.65	.74	106	.71
Confounding of race and social class in race-comparative study:						
Yes	.29	.29	.15	.24	23	.23
No	.29	.54	.67	.36	52	.51
Social class of one or both groups unspecified	.43	.17	.18	.40	27	.26

TABLE 2 (*Continued*)

VARIABLE	PUBLICATION PERIOD				TOTAL FREQUENCY	PROPORTION OF TOTAL POPULATION
	1936–65	1966–70	1971–75	1976–80		
	VALIDITY ISSUES AND IMPLICATIONS					
Caution against overgeneralization:						
Yes	.17	.09	.25	.13	28	.17
No	.83	.91	.75	.87	129	.82
Comment on generalizability of findings to non-Afro- American children:						
Yes	.38	.25	.71	.47	29	.54
No	.62	.75	.29	.53	27	.46
Comment on threats to validity of findings:						
Yes	.44	.41	.52	.36	70	.45
No	.56	.59	.48	.64	87	.55
Comment on educational implications:						
Yes	.30	.28	.52	.39	64	.41
No	.70	.72	.48	.61	93	.59
Comment on social policy implications:						
Yes	.26	.09	.30	.20	36	.23
No	.74	.91	.70	.80	121	.77

be seen that the frequency of all three types of studies peaked during the third publication period, a trend largely due to the number of articles published in 1971.

Turning to shifts across publication periods in the proportion of each type of study, Table 1 shows that there was a sharp increase from the first to the second publication period in the proportion of race-comparative studies, followed by a decline in the third and fourth publication periods. There was a corresponding decline in the proportion of race-heterogeneous studies from the first to the second publication period. The proportion of race-homogeneous studies remained fairly stable over the four periods.

Within each publication period, the proportion of race-comparative studies was almost twice that of race-homogeneous studies. In 85 of the 102 race-comparative studies, Afro-American children were compared solely to Euro-American children, while in the remaining 17, they were compared to both Euro-American children and ethnic minority children (typically Puerto Rican or Mexican-American). Thus a question posed by all race-comparative studies was how Afro-American children differed from Euro-American children.

Characteristics of the Samples

In order to assess changes in the characteristics of the subjects studied by researchers, a proportion was computed for each category of each variable of interest within each publication period by dividing the number of studies in the category by the total number of studies published within the respective publication period. The proportions for selected variables are shown in Table 2. In these analyses, we combine race-homogeneous and race-comparative studies ($N = 157$) and exclude race-heterogeneous studies. This is done because, compared to race-homogeneous and race-comparative studies, race-heterogeneous studies provide knowledge that is less particularistic, at least with regard to race and ethnicity. They neither describe normative behavior in Afro-American children per se nor, by definition, demonstrate how the behavior of Afro-American children compares to that of children from other racial or ethnic backgrounds. A related rationale for the exclusion of these studies is our belief that scholars are unlikely to look to or draw from them in their search for knowledge about Afro-American children.

As shown in Table 2, there were gradual increases over the first three publication periods and declines in the fourth publication period in the proportion of studies that focused on Afro-American children who were preschool age, from low-income backgrounds, and living in an urban setting. From the third to the fourth publication period, there were sharp increases in the study of infants and toddlers (24 months and under) and in the study of Afro-American children residing in small cities with a population of, roughly, less than 100,000. Both study of research samples that totaled more than 100 Afro-American children and failure to specify the socioeconomic status of the Afro-American children studied declined over the first three publication periods but increased substantially in the fourth.

Specification in the abstract that race or ethnicity was a variable of interest or that some or all of the research subjects were Afro-American declined consistently over the four publication periods (.83, .72, .56, and .46). There were no articles in which race- or ethnicity-related information was specified in the title but not in the abstract. Excluded from analyses of abstracts are studies published during or prior to 1963 ($N = 15$), as the publication format of *Child Development* did not include abstracts until 1964.

Research Topics and Methods

We found a consistent and dramatic decline over the four publication periods in the study of physical development and a corresponding increase in the study of cognitive development. The study of social development remained relatively stable over the four periods. Interest in whether the major dependent or criterion variable was age related dropped from the first to the second publication period but increased consistently thereafter (.69, .44, .48, and .72). Among those studies that focused on age differences, there has been a consistent decline in the use of the cross-sectional method (.81, .71, .67, and .57) and an increase in the use of the longitudinal method (.19, .29, .33, and .43).

While study of social class as a determinant of the behavior of Afro-American children remained relatively stable over the four periods (.17, .25, .24, and .15), study of situational determinants (e.g., task, environment, and treatment) increased sharply over the first three periods and declined precipitously in the fourth (.35, .41, .73, and .41).

Turning more directly to shifts in research methodology, as shown in Table 2, administration of tests and interviews to assess the major dependent or outcome variable increased sharply from the first to the second period but declined over the subsequent periods. The relative frequency of naturalistic observation, while generally low, increased over the first three periods. Use of multiple methods of inquiry almost tripled between the third and fourth publication periods.

It can be seen in Table 2 that specification of the race of the experimenter/observer was a rare occurrence. On the basis of the few studies in which this information was provided, our findings indicate that use of Afro-Americans as experimenters/observers, while consistently low throughout the publication periods, peaked during the third period. Also there was a slight decline during the first three publication periods in failure to specify the race of the experimenter/observer, followed by a small increase in the fourth period. Excluded from these analyses are eight studies based on archival records in which researchers neither observed nor had direct contact with children.

Perspectives on Afro-American Children, Validity Issues, and Suggested Implications of Research

The proportion of studies in which Afro-Americans were viewed explicitly as deficient in the behaviors of interest increased sharply from the first to the second publication period but declined thereafter (.26, .44, .29, and .33). Study of Afro-American children in largely nonjudgmental terms (i.e., emphasizing neither competencies nor deficits) remained steady during the first three periods and increased substantially in the fourth (.35, .31, .33, and .56).

While generally low during all the publication periods, caution against overgeneralization of the findings to the entire population of Afro-American children and to non-Afro-American children (race-homogeneous studies), delineation of factors that may have threatened the validity of the findings, and comment on the educational and social policy implications of the research in question all peaked in the third publication period.

The relative frequency with which studies were supported by research grants from various sources (e.g., federal agency, private foundation, and university) increased substantially from the first to the second publication period, held steady in the third period, but dropped in the fourth (.48, .81, .81, and .69).

DISCUSSION

At least some of the changes found in the present study are not unique to the study of Afro-American children. Super (1982) analyzed 10 randomly chosen articles in *Child Development* in each year between 1930 and 1979. Though the span of years examined was different from that in the present study, Super found, as we did, that research interest declined in physical development, increased in cognitive development, and remained relatively stable in socioemotional development. However, contrary to the present findings, Super found that naturalistic observation stabilized between 1965 and 1979. Further comparative analysis of the findings of the two studies is not possible because of differences in the categorization of common variables.

Our findings indicate that the most notable changes in the study of Afro-American children occurred during the third publication period, that is, between 1971 and 1975. It will be recalled that, of the four publication periods, the relative frequency with which the following occurred was highest in the third period: (*a*) study of preschoolers, (*b*) study of children from urban environments, (*c*) study of the effects of environmental factors on behavior, (*d*) control of social class in race-comparative studies, (*e*) use of an Afro-American as experimenter/observer, (*f*) identification and discussion of factors that potentially threatened the internal validity of the reported findings, (*g*) discussion of the external validity of the findings, and (*h*) discussion of the educational and social policy implications of the research. In addition, the frequency of all three types of studies peaked during the third period.

Of the four publication periods, the relative frequency with which the following occurred was lowest in the third period: (*a*) failure to specify the race of the experimenter/observer and (*b*) failure to specify the socioeconomic status of the Afro-American children studied.

Several of these changes no doubt reflect real changes in research practices and values within the discipline of psychology, whereas others may be epiphenomena caused by changes in the editorial policies (and values) of

Child Development. In either case, it is our belief that these positive changes that marked the period between 1971 and 1975 are related to several social and political changes in American society (extrascientific forces) and to forces within the discipline of psychology itself (intrascientific forces).

The most obvious of these influences is the Head Start Program, established in 1965 as part of President Johnson's War on Poverty. Head Start had as one of its goals the "inoculation" of poor children against the adverse effects of poverty and racial discrimination on social and intellectual development by insuring that they had mastered the educational prerequisites necessary to take advantage of formal, traditional schooling. Environmentalism was a cornerstone of Head Start and, indeed, had become the "zeitgeist" during the 1960s, according to Zigler and Anderson (1979). These researchers contended that "the public hailed the construction of a solid foundation for learning in preschool children as the solution to poverty and ignorance. . . . Great expectations and promises were based on the view that the young child was a plastic material to be molded quickly and permanently by the proper school environment. . . . For policymakers, legislators, and the public the theory had a common-sense appeal" (Zigler & Anderson, 1979, pp. 7–9).

Two scholars played a key role in the 1960s in increasing awareness of the role of the child's environment on intellectual growth and affirming the social policy initiatives that resulted in Head Start (Steiner, 1976; Zigler & Anderson, 1979). Bloom (1964) made the argument in *Stability and Change in Human Characteristics* that intellectual growth occurs most rapidly during the first 4 or 5 years of life. Thus the critical time to enrich the child's environment should be during the preschool years. Hunt (1961), in his book *Intelligence and Experience,* challenged the beliefs in fixed intelligence and predetermined development and emphasized the ways in which the child's environment influences intellectual growth.

With the establishment of Head Start and other antipoverty programs came vast sums of money from federal agencies and private foundations for the conduct of scholarly research consistent with the philosophy undergirding these initiatives. These developments, we believe, resulted in the increase between 1971 and 1975 in the frequency of studies of Afro-Americans and in the proportion of these studies that focused on preschoolers and children from urban environments and sought to demonstrate the effects of environmental factors on the behavior of these children. Because of the inevitable lag between the time ideas for research are spawned and findings finally appear in publication, it is understandable that the new research on Afro-Americans did not appear in the pages of *Child Development* until the third publication period (1971–1975).

The decline between 1971 and 1980 in the explicit espousal by *Child Development* authors of a deficit model of the behaviors of Afro-American children and the increased attention given to validity issues between 1971 and 1975 appear to be linked to two developments, namely, the publication of two iconoclastic papers that rendered decisive criticisms of prevailing research on Afro-Americans and set new research priorities (Cole & Bruner, 1971; Labov, 1970) and the rise of black nationalism between 1965 and 1970. The calls by Labov and by Cole and Bruner for the conduct of research in environments conducive to the display of intellectual and social skills by Afro-American and other minority children preceded a barrage of similar criticisms (e.g., Clark, 1972; Hall, 1974; Tulkin, 1972; Williams, 1972).

Around 1965, following the successful desegregation of places of public accommodation and the enfranchisement of millions of Afro-Americans in the South, the appeal of the nonviolent, integrationist ideology of the civil rights movement began to wane and give way to black nationalism (Brisbane, 1974). Various groups called for black separation or emigration to Africa, affirmed their African heritage (e.g., dress, customs, and names), and proclaimed the legitimacy and richness of Afro-American culture (Brisbane, 1974; Lester, 1971).

The reverberations of this movement were to be felt in the halls of academe, where there emerged a demand for inclusion in the curricula of predominantly white colleges and universities courses in Afro-American history, culture, and behavior. By 1970 black studies programs had been established at Yale, Harvard, Cornell, Columbia, and the University of Michigan, and by 1972 more than 600 colleges and universities were offering black studies courses (Brisbane, 1974). The veneration of Afro-American culture during this period may have served as an antidote to the cultural imperialism and calm ethnocentrism that hitherto appeared to inform so much of the research on Afro-Americans conducted by Euro-Americans. It is interesting that the lessening of expressed concern between the third period (1971–1975) and the fourth period (1976–1980) about validity and methodological issues coincided with a decline in social and political activism among Afro-Americans.

Our findings indicate that interest in how Afro-American children differed from Euro-American children remained conspicuously high in each publication period. Race-comparative studies that involve Afro-Americans have been criticized not so much because of their comparative perspective per se but because of the restricted nature of the information they provide and the characteristic interpretation of comparative data. Specifically, it has been argued that, in general, these studies (a) point to the ways in which Afro-American children do not behave rather than how they do behave, resulting in superficial understanding of individual differences and their determinants among Afro-Americans and data that are limited in their informative value and virtually useless in generating theory (Howard &

Scott, 1981), (b) foster indirectly the view that Afro-American children generally are abnormal, incompetent, and changeworthy since differences between Afro-American and Euro-American children are typically interpreted, if not by the author, by a significant portion of the readers, as deficiencies or pathologies in the former rather than in cultural relativistic or systemic terms (Hall, 1974; Myers et al., 1979; Washington & McLoyd, 1982), and (c) promote person-blame interpretations of social problems rather than thoughtful treatments of the roles of situational and systemic factors since they emphasize the race of the subjects or personal characteristics associated with race (Caplan & Nelson, 1973). These putative characteristics are not inherent to race-comparative studies themselves but appear to derive from the stigmatized and marginal existence of Afro-Americans in American society.

Riegel (1972) argued that the current comparative model that dominates research in psychology was nurtured by the economic and political ideologies within which developmental psychology developed in England and the United States during the second half of the nineteenth century and the early twentieth century. According to Riegel, Social Darwinists' view of human development as a "process of continuous competition and selection whose direction and goals are represented by the 'successful' survivors here and now" gained widespread acceptance in nineteenth-century England in part because it was in keeping with the politicoeconomic ideals of a free-competitive trade system. Because of the fit between his activities and societal demands, the "white, middle-class adult most likely engaged in manufacturing or business enterprises" was thought, at that time, to be the "successful" survivor and thus the standard ideal (Riegel, 1972, p. 130). One result of the strong emphasis on competition was that the young, the old, the deviant, and, generally, the "different" were placed in inferior positions and evaluated negatively. This "capitalistic" orientation found its way into the emerging discipline of child psychology in the United States. A surge of early descriptive studies of child development contributed to establishing trends and standards with which the performance of the "different" could be compared and found wanting in comparison with the standard ideal, that is, white, middle-class adults.

In contrast, the "mercantilistic-socialistic" orientation of Continental Europe, according to Riegel (1972), fostered a relative disregard for competition between the classes that was due in part to the fact that the development of manufacturing was largely initiated and supervised by the state rather than by individuals. An ethos appreciative of multicultural and multigenerational differences resulted, best reflected in the work of Rousseau, Piaget, and Vygotsky.

The present study found a steady decline in the tendency to report in the abstract that the subjects included Afro-American children or that race or ethnicity was a variable of interest. Thus accessing information in *Child Development* about Afro-American children has become increasingly difficult. While race-related information was provided in the abstracts of almost all the relevant articles published between 1964 and 1970, it was provided in less than half the articles published between 1976 and 1980. This suggests that scholars who rely on the abstracts of *Child Development* articles to locate recent research on Afro-American children may commit significant errors of omission. Even more articles may be missed by scholars who rely on *Child Development Abstracts and Bibliography,* as the abstracts published in the latter are often abridged versions of the authors' abstracts that appeared in *Child Development.*

VI. "FASTING GIRLS": REFLECTIONS ON WRITING THE HISTORY OF ANOREXIA NERVOSA

JOAN JACOBS BRUMBERG

Cornell University

Over the past decade, with surprising frequency, adolescent girls have been starving themselves to death. Anorexia nervosa, a disease characterized by self-imposed fasting, an implacable attitude toward eating, extreme weight loss, and social isolation, is said to have reached "epidemic" proportions in the United States in the 1980s, particularly among female adolescents, who constitute somewhere between 86% and 95% of the clinical cases.[1] Of these adolescents, an overwhelming portion come from intact nuclear families rather than from single-parent families, and almost all are white and relatively affluent: there are few black anorectics. In effect, anorexia nervosa sets starvation in the culture of plenty rather than in the culture of poverty.

The actual proportions of this "epidemic" are still unclear, although the number of reported cases and the attention given to the disorder appear to be escalating. A variety of different sources point to between 150,000 and 500,000 anorectics in the United States. Among 16–18-year-old girls, the incidence may be as high as one out of every 100. Death from the disease in the United States may approach 20%.[2] Not surprisingly, families facing the

---

[1] "Epidemic" is used easily by journalists who cover the disease. The clinical literature (Bruch, 1982; Crisp, 1976; Duddle, 1973) reports that anorexia nervosa is spreading through the social classes and into a higher age group, that is, to college women and young adults. Both the prevalence and incidence of the disease are still largely undetermined because of a lack of standardization in diagnostic criteria and different levels (formal and informal) of identification. For differences in criteria, cf. Feighner et al. (1972) with the 3d ed. of the *Diagnostic and Statistical Manual of Mental Disorders* (American Psychiatric Association, 1980).

[2] These figures are drawn from references cited in n. 1 above and from literature disseminated by the national associations for study of the disease (see Bruch, 1973). Popu-

pain and the danger of self-starvation in their daughters coalesced, in the late 1970s, to provide mutual support and self-help in the form of the National Association of Anorexia Nervosa and Associated Disorders (ANAD), headquartered in suburban Highland Park, Illinois, and the American Anorexia Nervosa Association, with similar social origins in Teaneck, New Jersey. (There are two other regional anorectic support groups, the National Anorectic Aid Society in Columbus, Ohio, and the Association for Anorexia Nervosa and Related Eating Disorders in Eugene, Oregon.)

Whatever the dimensions of its increase, anorexia nervosa has come to occupy a central place in our thinking about adolescence in contemporary America, primarily as a result of media coverage. Girls who do not eat pique curiosity and, therefore, make good copy. In the last few years, a number of personal testimonies to experience with the disease have attained wide readership: in particular, novelist Sheila MacLeod's detailed account of her own anorexic girlhood, *The Art of Starvation* (1982), and Cherry Boone O'Neill's intimate autobiographical story, *Starving for Attention* (1982). Magazines geared to the female adolescent subculture frequently discuss the issue. For example, *Seventeen* (Wood, 1981) featured inquiries by girls about what constituted the normal boundaries of dieting; "my get-thin-quick scheme's out of control" was the headline. Given popular interest in the subject, Scribner's, in 1982, published a self-help book, *Treating and Overcoming Anorexia,* by Montefiore Hospital psychiatrist Steven Levenkron. In 1981, ABC television offered a feature-length, made-for-television movie, *The Best Little Girl in the World,* based on Levenkron's earlier fictional account (1978) of anorexia, which was published by a mass-market house. Apparently, ABC felt that there was sufficient familiarity with the disorder to justify no explanation in the advertisements about either the symptoms or the etiology of the disease: the film was billed, simply, "as a drama of anorexia nervosa."

In the 1980s we use "anorectic" much as we have used "syphilitic," "epileptic," or "diabetic" to mark an individual in a particular way. Our semantic designations, of course, carry social as well as epidemiological information. "Anorexic" has clearly become common parlance, used as hyperbole in nonclinical settings to describe a particular female disinclination toward food. This disinclination is not socially tabooed; in fact, American women—who as a group are chronically unhappy with their weight—joke easily with one another about how they wish they could be "more anorexic." Studies by Herman and Polivy (1975) and Rodin, Silberstein, and Streigel-Moore (1983) confirm that American women demonstrate persistent concern about weight. "Saturday Night Live," a popular late-night television

---

lar literature generally puts the death rate at 15%–20%, while clinical studies (Schwartz & Thompson, 1981) set the mortality rate at 6%.

program, regularly includes satiric remarks about the "anorectic's cookbook," and the *Star,* a popular tabloid, speculates that Diana, the 22-year-old Princess of Wales, has "become anorexic." Only when we see pictures of the emaciated bodies of young women who have lost all their subcutaneous fat do we react with disgust. But it is the aesthetics of this deathlike body that repels us, not the pattern of overzealous dieting.

In American popular culture, anorexia nervosa is beginning to be linked to the lives of glamorous female personalities. Jane Fonda, for example, has admitted to periods of starvation and purging in her early career. When pop singer Karen Carpenter died last winter, apparently as a result of cardiac arrhythmia associated with low serum potassium—one consequence of prolonged starvation—anorexia nervosa was revealed as part of the secret life of her stardom (Levin, 1983). In general, it seems that knowledge about the disease, garnered through popular culture sources, may be implicated in generating what Hilde Bruch (1982) called "me too anorectics" or mimetic behavior that erroneously links the process of starvation to glamor rather than pain. What we may be facing is a transformation peculiar to mass culture: the shift of a predominantly psychosomatic disorder into the category of a communicable disease. Thus in determining the prevalence of anorexia nervosa we must remain cognizant of the fact that the characteristic behavior—not eating—can occur on a number of different levels ranging from chronic dieting to death by starvation. As a result, anorexia nervosa presents a complicated problem in psychiatric epidemiology: the contemporary efflorescence of the disease could be the result of the mimetic behaviors of patients, of new diagnostic techniques or preferences among doctors, or of conditions or states of tension in this society that predispose adolescent women to this particular psychopathology.

What is the history of the disease entity known as anorexia nervosa? That question has a long and involved answer precisely because disease itself is a cultural artifact, defined and redefined over time and, as a result, illustrative of fundamental historical transformations. Consequently, when I am asked the question, Is anorexia nervosa a new disease? my response must be an ambiguous yes and no. I will do my best here to explain the ambiguity of my answer as I argue some tentative suggestions about how to conceptualize the long history of "fasting girls." As you will see, my research focuses on the social and cultural processes by which anorexia nervosa became a disease and not on the psychodynamic qualities of individual cases.

First, the modern clinical term "anorexia nervosa" should be used to designate only a disease of modernity. The naming of the disease occurred in the 1870s. Anorexia nervosa, like other diseases, incorporates both symptoms and cause. The primary symptom—voluntary emaciation or fasting—is not particularly modern; I will say more about this in a moment. However, the cause of anorexia nervosa is generally understood to be rooted in the psychopathogenic pressures or tensions of contemporary culture and middle-class family life rather than in religious or political ideals. According to the contemporary therapeutic establishment, the fast provides the anorectic with a strategy aimed at establishing autonomy and resolving unbearable conflicts related to individual history and personality, age and gender, family, class, and society. In other words, anorexia nervosa denotes a complex disease entity, a modern psychosomatic syndrome that constitutes a cruel irony in this culture of chronic consumption.

Second, while there is a certain pattern of symptomatic continuity in the history of women in the Western world, we should avoid easy generalizations about the continuity of the modern disease entity, anorexia nervosa, or women's "nature." Just because a behavior occurs across cultures—or transhistorically—does not necessarily mean that the behavior is rooted in the organism. For example, the symptom of not eating or fasting behavior in women and girls has obviously been around for a very long time. Work by historian Caroline Walker Bynum (1982, 1984) demonstrates that in the High Middle Ages (the thirteenth through the sixteenth centuries) the lives of women saints were characterized by extensive fasting and passionate devotion to the eucharist (taking the wafer and the wine, a symbol of the body and blood of Christ). Moreover, where writings by these women survive, they contain pervasive images of eating, drinking, and food—much as the twentieth-century anorectic is food obsessed, counting calories, and structuring her life around nonmeals and strenuous exercise. Living with food deprivation was the particular skill of female saints; in fact, Bynum maintains that "almost all saints who were completely unable to eat or who survived for years on the Eucharist alone were women. The most famous of these women is, of course, Catherine of Siena, who, like Cherry Boone, refused commensality—that is, eating at the family table. Just as the anorectic loses control of her behavior and often cannot eat even when she wants to, some of the medieval women occasionally claimed that their inability to eat was not a religious practice precisely because it became involuntary.

Examples of marathon fasting can also be found in the sixteenth and seventeenth centuries in both Catholic and Protestant countries. In 1668, Thomas Hobbes (cited in Gee, 1908) reported seeing a young female faster at Over Haddon; her "belly touches her backbone," he observed, and her talk was "most heavenly." My own research on what were called "miraculous maids" suggests that scores of young women, most often in young adulthood, undertook fasts that were extolled in vernacular folk literature as proof of divine providence. To live without the signs of eating constituted a miracle. Typically, the young woman claimed to be eating nothing at all or existing simply on the "juice of a roasted raisin" or on water brushed on her lips with a feather. Some reports included notations that the young women seemed to exist without sleep or rest as well as without food, suggesting the hyperactivity associated with the modern anorectic. But foremost among the formulaic elements in these reports was the principle that the faster did not die, despite the material facts of inanition and emaciation over periods of time ranging from months to decades. Jane Stretton, for example, allegedly went without sustenance for 9 months, while Katerin Cooper's fast lasted 9 years and Eva Fleigen's 14 (Brumberg, 1985). Clearly, the fasts sustained by these women were not total or death would have been the result. Instead, they appear to have survived over long periods by eating only tiny portions of substances with enough nutritional value to sustain life, suggesting that the "miraculous maids" may have shared with the anorectic a certain pattern of covert eating.

Although fasting, the preoccupation with food, secret eating, and hyperactivity all suggest anorexia nervosa, I believe that the symptomatic continuities can be misleading. Behavior that looks similar across time and cultures can have vastly different origins and meanings. Thus to call Catherine of Siena an anorectic—that is, to use a contemporary psychosomatic model to explain her behavior—is to distort her psychological orientation, misread her actions as she understood them, and misrepresent the context in which she lived. In medieval and early modern Europe, marathon fasting and food deprivation were clearly not regarded as disease. Rather, fasting was an instrument of spirituality and a demonstration of the providence of God. Ultimately, this view of the faster as an agency for God's omnipotence was reflected in the "therapeutics" of that day: female ascetics and "miraculous maids" were treated with awe rather than called sick.

It is the task of the historian interested in social and cultural history to maintain connection with the historical moment in order to understand people and their behavior on their own terms. As a result, I have chosen to avoid psychohistory in its most traditional format; that is, where symptomatic continuities do exist, I have tried to let the facts of culture speak for themselves rather than follow lines of interpretation based on establishing an artificial congruence between a psychological model, derived from the contemporary world, and fragmentary historical evidence, garnered from the "world we have lost."[3]

Continuity in physiological symptoms should not, however, surprise us,

---

[3] There is a different historical approach to the subject. Demos (1982) deftly uses psychoanalytic models to explain aspects of seventeenth-century behavior. He uses a common piece of evidence—the inability to eat over long periods of time—to link anorexia nervosa to the behavior of seventeenth-century witches and suggests that seventeenth-century witchcraft shared with anorexia nervosa a narcissistic pathology that motivated challenges to authority. Bell (1985), Morgan (1977), and Skrabanek (1983) argue that anorexia-like behaviors in past time are anorexia nervosa. Bell suggests a psychological continuity through time: he uses the term "holy anorexia" to denote religiously inspired fasting.

no matter what the motivation for the fast. Here the natural program is predictable: when the human body is consistently deprived of food, it will have certain hard-and-fast consequences for the organism. As a result, the most interesting question posed by the continuity I describe has to do not with the biology of the fast but with the decisions that led to it, in other words, with behavior and with exogenetic choices basic to culture. Rather than locate a modern disease entity in past time, I suggest that we place anorexia nervosa on a wide and multifaceted continuum that represents the history of women and their eating disorders. I might frame the question in this way. Why is it that women and girls in certain cultural systems become susceptible to particular forms of exaggerated behavior centering on food? Only by putting the question in this way can we decode the fast; only by putting the question in this way do we allow for consideration of the crucial interaction between the developing person, her gender and family environment, the informal and formal settings in which she functions, and the economic and ideological forces that shape her world. Clearly, this kind of investigation must be informed by anthropological insights and cross-cultural data beyond the scope of my discussion here.

Third, because diseases are defined and redefined in response to scientific knowledge, the needs of patients and doctors, and the larger social setting, we can expect to see oscillations in both the symptoms and the cause of the same disease over time. As Rosenberg (1962) explained in his pioneering study of cholera in nineteenth-century New York City: "A disease is no absolute physical entity but a complex intellectual construction, an amalgam of biological state and social definition." This is true for diseases that are primarily somatic as well as psychological in origin (Sontag, 1977).

Still other diseases have a finite biography. Chlorosis, a popular form of iron-deficiency anemia in the late nineteenth century, is now regarded as an anachronistic diagnostic category. In the nineteenth century, chlorosis was understood to exist only in the female adolescent: the constellation of symptoms included lethargy, dyspepsia, difficult breathing, and some peculiarities of diet. The cure for chlorosis was both medical and social: as physicians came to understand the process of blood formation, they correctly prescribed large doses of iron, but they also prescribed marriage. Few are willing to link the demise of chlorosis to self-conscious medical achievement. In fact, chlorosis lost its hold on female adolescents, their families, and Victorian physicians for a variety of reasons related, in large part, to cultural transformations (Brumberg, 1982). Still other "diseases" have been transformed by developments in psychiatry that, of course, mirror social change. In 1880, for example, masturbation was treated as disease (Englehardt, 1974); in the 1980s it can be recommended as therapy.

In considering the responsiveness of disease to cultural settings we must look beyond the doctors, diagnoses, and therapies to the patients themselves. People express both physical pain and psychic discomfort in myriad ways, depending on their age, their class, their ethnic origins, their worldview, and a host of other cultural variables (Devereux, 1979; Kleinman, 1980; Streltzer & Wade, 1981). Therefore in writing the history of disease we should expect to see the disease "present" differently, both in terms of actual physical symptoms and in terms of predisposing psychological factors. For example, in the nineteenth century, the physical symptoms of hysteria, largely regarded as a disease of women caused by a structural defect in the brain or nervous system, included dramatic seizures of the limbs, paralysis, and loss of sight—symptoms that on presentation were labeled "hystero-epilepsy" (Goldstein, 1982). Today, these physical symptoms are rarely seen in hysterical patients; when they are, they are presented only by isolated, rural, unsophisticated patients whose worldview appears to interact, in some yet undefined way, with this particular set of physical manifestations.[4] It also appears that cancer, the dreaded megadisease of our time, may present differently, if one accepts the notion of psychological predisposition. In the nineteenth century, the typical cancer patient described a life overcrowded with family and friends and burdened by work and obligations that were part of his or her social network. In contrast, the contemporary cancer patient reports a form of modern despair and alienation: loneliness since childhood and social isolation as an adult (Kowal, 1955).

Just as we accept that certain psychopathologies characterize certain populations and historical epochs, we must be willing to consider how the same organic disorder may be experienced differently in diverse cultures and across time. In the sentimental and doleful Victorian phenomenon of "wasting" (phthisis), girls clearly experienced emaciation in a different way than the modern anorectic who pursues simultaneous emaciation and hyperactivity. Thus the psychological orientation and *mentalité* of the patient are crucial in determining the configuration of any of the "starving" diseases that we place on our multifaceted continuum of girlhood eating disorders.

Fourth, the study of the history of anorexia nervosa reveals how competing models of a disease can exist simultaneously. In the late 1860s, "fasting girls" became a subject of popular and medical concern in the Anglo-American world (Morgan, 1977). In this period, both American and British newspaper audiences were presented with popular brouhahas centering on the voluntary emaciation of girls. On both sides of the Atlantic, readers, as

---

[4] My information on the declining presentation of the symptoms associated with hystero-epilepsy came originally from conversations with Dr. Ellen Bassuk, associate professor of psychiatry, Harvard Medical School. Tseng and McDermott (1981) confirm the contemporary decline of hysterical reactions of disassociation or conversion prevalent in the nineteenth century.

well as medical men and ministers, debated the authenticity of the claims proposed by Sarah Jacob, "the Welsh Fasting Girl," and Molly Fancher, "the Brooklyn Enigma." Each of the women independently asserted her ability to "live without food," while family members and clergy substantiated these claims by providing the press and medical authorities with the physiological details of the fast. Nineteenth-century "fasting girls" were visited by the curious and by hopeful religious pilgrims anxious to absorb something of the miraculous: in this sense, the "fasting girls" represent an idiosyncratic remnant of an older piety and belief (Brumberg, 1985).

What is significant for our purposes is how physicians interpreted their voluntary emaciation. Some British doctors regarded Sarah Jacob's claim to total abstinence as a simple fraud and, therefore, an affront to science: this group maintained that she had to be a secret eater, a "night feeder," who sustained life by covertly ingesting tidbits of food. Consequently, they called for a watch, with empirical standards, which deprived the girl of all food and, not surprisingly, killed her within 10 days because she was already severely undernourished. Some British doctors attributed Sarah Jacob's condition to girlhood hysteria, provoked by religious enthusiasm and her celebrity status. Robert Fowler, a London physician of some renown, called it a simulative hysteria, in which the girl feigned an inability to eat, but he also considered that she might have suffered from a manifestation of hysteria known as *globus hystericus*, "a ball in the throat," generated by her frame of mind.

In the United States, William A. Hammond, a former surgeon general, a founder of the New York Neurological Society, and the author of an influential textbook on nervous diseases, decried popular belief in Jacob and Fancher in a series of articles for metropolitan New York dailies and in a book entitled *Fasting Girls: Their Physiology and Their Pathology* (1879). It was Fancher, a clairvoyant claiming abstinence for over a decade, that raised Hammond's most intense ire. He called most of history's female religious figures "theomaniacs" and used the subject of fasting girls for an all-out attack on those religions he considered to be based on emotion—in other words, Catholicism, evangelical Protestantism, and Spiritualism. Hammond told his readers in an earlier book that "the Outpouring of the Spirit of God is too often, to the physician's perception, only another name for epilepsy, chorea, catalepsy, ecstacy or insanity" (1876, p. vi). All these were nervous diseases that, according to Hammond, had somatic origins. Thus the fasting of Catherine of Siena and of Jacob, Fancher, and others was understood by Hammond as an accoutrement of female hysteria that, in turn, was generated by some dysfunction of the brain and spinal cord.

The actual naming of anorexia nervosa as a clinical entity occurred at approximately the same time. Recall that Fowler developed his analysis of the Jacob case in 1870; Hammond wrote his book in 1879. Sir William Gull

(1873) provided the first English-language definition of anorexia nervosa; he named the self-starvation syndrome and linked it to young women between 16 and 23 years of age. Gull's primary interest was in distinguishing the wasting associated with organic diseases from that which accompanied hysterical loss of appetite. He said little about anorexia nervosa in terms of its psychodynamics. Attributing lack of appetite to a "morbid mental state," Gull went on to assert that "the young women at the ages named are especially obnoxious [susceptible] to mental perversity." The French psychiatrist Charles Lasègue (1873) also reported on the existence of a self-starvation syndrome in girls between the ages of 15 and 20; he called the condition hysterical anorexia. Lasègue, in particular, noted the difficult relation between anorectics and their parents but went on to elaborate how the girl obsessively pursued a peculiar and inadequate diet—such as pickled cucumbers in café au lait—despite the threats and entreaties of her anxious parents. "The family has but two methods at its service which it always exhausts," he wrote, "entreaties and menaces. . . . The delicacies of the table are multiplied in the hope of stimulating the appetite, but the more solicitude increases the more the appetite diminishes" (Lasègue, 1873, pp. 265–266). Lasègue, who emphasized the psychological dynamics of the family in his description of the stages of the disease, noted that the anorectic was "not ill pleased with her condition," although her parents were distracted and preoccupied by her noneating. Lasègue's report clearly linked the emergence of anorexia nervosa to the intensification of family life among the Victorian middle class.

Thus by 1875 fasting behavior had moved from the realm of female spirituality to the clinical world of disease. In the 1870s, doctors such as Fowler and Hammond were still utilizing the historic connection between fasting and piety to understand the sensational claims and anomalous behavior of Sarah Jacob and Mollie Fancher. In fact, they were probably right in assessing Jacob and Fancher as religious delusionaries: both women were apparently motivated by zealous belief of one kind or another, and both received the accolades (and the financial support) of their respective religious communities. However, by the 1870s marathon fasting or voluntary starvation clearly had its secular and private expression as well. Neither Gull nor Lasègue mentioned religious piety in discussing the etiology of the disease. Rather they implicate the nuclear family—especially the middle- and upper-class family—able to pander to the eccentric dietary tastes of a demanding adolescent daughter. By 1881 anorexia nervosa was accepted as a clinical designation and was used in the professional literature. A case reported in that year, from London, involved a 14-year-old who, the doctor said, "never spoke to her mother except in tones of the greatest violence" (Dowse, 1881, p. 827).

I can only suggest here that the change from spirituality to disease reflects a much larger transformation in society, conveniently labeled "secularization" by historians. In terms of people, secularization implies a declining preference for religious explanations of the universe, of one's own actions, and of health or ill health. The modern concept of anorexia nervosa was tied also to the evolution of the late nineteenth-century bourgeoisie and to the place that daughters assumed in that particular family constellation. In this setting, interactions between family members were intense and social expectations high; family meals meant that either overeating or noneating by any member of the family was subject to the scrutiny of others, calling for attention and discussion. Simultaneously, the growing cultural authority of doctors, as opposed to ministers, meant that any extraordinary eating behavior was "medicalized." Nineteenth-century developments—secularization, middle-class formation, and the professionalization of medicine—were all preconditions for the emergence of anorexia nervosa as a disease entity with a distinct and workable nosology. In this respect, anorexia nervosa is a historically specific diagnosis at the same time that it suggests enormous continuity in human behavior.

In the twentieth century, the explanatory etiology of anorexia nervosa has moved, intermittently, in and out of the psychosomatic camp. Interpretations of the origins of the disease have clearly undergone a number of evolutions related to developments in laboratory medicine, to changing theories of human development, and to the prevalence of the disorder (Lucas, 1981). Throughout the twentieth century there have been physicians anxious to uncover a physiological cause for the bizarre starving disease; persistently, there is debate over what is the cause and what is the consequence of severe emaciation.

Traditional psychoanalysis chose to focus on the oral component of the disorder and its symbolic significance. Building on the work of Dr. James J. Putnam, professor of neurology at Harvard and the first American physician to embrace psychoanalysis, twentieth-century physicians have stressed the connection between eating and sexuality. In 1939, the first year of its operation, the *Journal of Psychosomatic Medicine* presented a dozen cases of anorexia nervosa, all of which were allegedly precipitated by either inappropriate sexuality (e.g., seeing parents having intercourse or being touched by a stranger on the breast or genitals) or failure in love (e.g., rejection by a young man following sexual intimacies) (Kahman, Richardson, & Kipley, 1939; Pardee, 1939; Waller, Kaufman, & Deutsch, 1940). This psychoneurotic model clearly regarded starvation as a defense against love relations: eating, according to theory, represented impregnation, and obesity symbolized pregnancy. In essence, a poor heterosexual adjustment provided the explanatory etiology for anorexia nervosa.

In the 1920s and 1930s, medical concern with endocrine disturbance led many physicians to an alternative explanation. In particular, those following the lead of German endocrinology came to regard anorexia nervosa as Simmond's disease (Simmonds, 1914), a dysfunction of the pituitary gland. Atrophy of the anterior lobe of the pituitary caused emaciation, loss of hair, sensitivity to cold, low blood pressure, amenorrhea, and "lack of libido"—all symptoms associated with anorexia nervosa. According to Bruch, after the discovery of Simmond's disease, "any case of malnutrition was attributed to some endocrine disturbance" (Bruch, 1973, p. 214). Thus we can understand why an American physician, in 1933, was giving 1 cc of anterior pituitary *daily* to a 17-year-old girl whose weight had dropped to 48 pounds as a result of "cathartic addiction" in the form of 15 Feen-a-Mint tablets and three enemas every day (Striker, 1933). Although the psychogenic models tended to predominate, concepts of the endocrine origin of anorexia nervosa continued into the 1950s (White & Moehlig, 1950).

Today, in the 1980s, young women experiencing anorexia nervosa are treated with methods that include various forms of insight-oriented psychotherapy and behavior modification. These therapies reflect greater concern with the personality and development of the patient and her family than did the psychoanalytic approach with its emphasis on the symbolic significance of noneating. Many anorectic patients are seen by multidisciplinary teams of psychiatrists, psychologists, nurses, nutritionists, and social workers that staff special eating disorders units in major research hospitals. While some anorectics are never hospitalized, the girl and her parents may receive outpatient therapy on a regular basis; other anorectics are hospitalized because they have dropped below critical weight. Then they may be subjected to a rigid schedule of forced feeding, weighing, psychotherapy, and nutritional rehabilitation. Some physicians prescribe antianxiety and antidepressant drugs for the anorectic; occasionally, a doctor will justify use of an antipsychotic drug as a way of diminishing the hold of a distorted body image. All in all, these therapeutic regimens—developed largely in response to the current epidemic—lack commitment to any particular explanatory model. Rather, because anorexia nervosa is still so mysterious and difficult to treat, physicians—even psychoanalysts—are looking for an innate predisposition to the disease, perhaps even a biochemical explanation, the characteristic panacea of our age.

In the current search for an organic explanation, a number of theories have been tried, including hypothalamic dysfunction, diabetes mellitus, gonadal dysgenesis (especially Turner's syndrome), and heritability (Brooks, 1984; Dougherty, Rockwell, Sutton, & Ellingwood, 1983; Gwirtsman, Roy-Byrne, Yager, & Gerner, 1983; Miles & Wright, 1984; Vandereycken & Pierloot, 1981). At the moment, an explanatory model with some currency is alexithymia (Sifneos, 1973), a term that means, literally, "without words for emotions." Alexithymia is actually an amorphous constellation of behaviors. Sifneos characterizes the alexithymic person as one who has difficulty de-

103

scribing emotional states and who has a limited ability to use fantasy. Patients like this often have psychosomatic illnesses and tend to do poorly in traditional dynamic psychotherapy. Alexithymia could be the manifestation of defense mechanisms (such as repression and denial), it could be the result of a developmental disorder or a failure in an early learning process that leads to a subsequent inability to verbalize, or it could be the result of a neurophysiologial dysfunction. The last of these is generally described as a lesion or defect in the limbic system of the brain, which means, in effect, that the individual suffers from inadequate connections between the subcortical limbic system (the substrate of emotions) and the overlying neocortex (the substrate of language and associations) (Lesser, 1981).

When the anorectic is cast as an alexithymic, she is treated as an individual whose emotional output is impaired by neurophysiological dysfunction. Her lack of emotion, her "dullness," is regarded as an organic disorder rather than an emotional state generated either by her environment or by the depressive effects of starvation. Nature, in this biomedical view, rather than nurture, determines anorexia nervosa. Just why it is that this neurological disturbance has emerged as so troublesome in the past 2 decades, why it strikes adolescent females disproportionately, and why it is expressed in a dramatic but encoded form of eating behavior (the fast) are questions left unanswered by those who link anorexia nervosa solely to neurophysiology or other forms of biomedical disorder.

In sum, I am arguing for a conception of anorexia nervosa that incorporates culture as well as biomedical and psychological models. I am not suggesting simply that culture causes anorexia nervosa—that is, that modern advertising single-handedly generates the compulsion to starve. Culture, like cognition or socialization, must be conceived as a many-layered process; the cultural factors that put contemporary adolescents "at risk" for anorexia nervosa are multidimensional but relatively unexplored. What I am proposing is a more complex historical view of the meaning of diseases and disorders, how these conditions are perceived, why explanations of illness change, and what diseases tell us about particular segments of the population and societies as a whole. Only in an enlarged research context that considers meaning as well as behavior will we be able to understand how anorexia nervosa is experienced and why it has become the characteristic disorder of the female adolescent in our day.

PART 3
HISTORY OF THE SOCIETY FOR RESEARCH IN CHILD DEVELOPMENT

HISTORY OF THE SOCIETY FOR RESEARCH IN CHILD DEVELOPMENT: INTRODUCTION TO PART 3

The histories of the founding of the Society for Research in Child Development (SRCD), by Smuts, and of its early years, by Rheingold, are based mainly on primary sources available only in archives. They are not typical histories of a professional organization for two reasons. First, SRCD's diverse membership and its interest in application as well as in basic research distinguish it from most scholarly organizations. The tensions created by disagreement among scholars from widely different backgrounds on how to achieve complex goals provide a drama lacking in organizations with a more homogeneous membership and simpler aims. Another source of drama is SRCD's faltering fortunes during the depression and war that provided the backdrop for its first 2 decades.

A. B. S.
J. W. H.

VII. THE NATIONAL RESEARCH COUNCIL COMMITTEE ON CHILD DEVELOPMENT AND THE FOUNDING OF THE SOCIETY FOR RESEARCH IN CHILD DEVELOPMENT, 1925–1933

ALICE BOARDMAN SMUTS

University of Michigan

To understand the origins of the Society for Research in Child Development (SRCD) we must begin not with its official organization in 1933 but with the founding of the Committee on Child Development (CCD) in 1924 by the National Research Council (NRC). The SRCD evolved directly from this committee and for 15 years continued to receive its support, becoming autonomous only in 1948.

The NRC, a part of the National Academy of Sciences, was itself only 9 years old when it established the committee. It was founded in 1916 by reformers within the academy to make that ineffectual organization more responsive to the nation's defense needs and to create a permanent central-ized scientific organization that would stimulate and coordinate the research activities of government, industry, and academe (Dupree, 1957).

I am indebted to Hamilton Cravens, Lauren J. Harris, Robert R. Sears, and Lois M. Stolz for helpful suggestions. The research was supported in part by a grant from the William T. Grant Foundation. I also wish to thank Manfred Waserman, then curator of modern manuscripts, History of Medicine Division, National Library of Medicine, and David J. E. Saumweber, deputy archivist, National Academy of Sciences, for their assis-tance in locating and sending me materials. Most of the unpublished sources that I have used that concern the Committee on Child Development (CCD) are in the National Academy of Sciences (NAS) Archives. These sources have not been included in Sec. II of the reference list, where much of the unpublished material used in the *Monograph* can be found, but sufficient information is given in the text to enable other researchers to locate them. Unpublished sources from the Rockefeller Archive Center (RAC) and from the NLM have been included in Sec. II of the reference list and are identified by the letters "NP" (not published) following the date. For additional information on all these collections and also on the unpublished CCD conference proceedings, see the bibliographical essay in Sec. II of the reference list. It may be helpful to other scholars wishing to review these

THE SOCIAL AND SCIENTIFIC SETTING

Several significant developments help to explain why NRC established the CCD at this time. During the first 2 decades of the century, a series of great foundations were established that were unprecedented in the size of the fortunes they would give away and in the efficiency of their management. Instead of continuing nineteenth-century programs to help the poor and unfortunate, they adopted the bold new goal of preventing social ills. The instrument of reform was to be the new social and behavioral sciences (Bremner, 1960; Coben, 1979; Curti, 1958).

The social sciences established themselves in the universities before the war; their application during the war seemed to demonstrate their usefulness to society. During the 1920s, many believed that social science research and education would transform social practices as dramatically as physical science and technology had transformed the physical environment and industry (May, 1954). The Division of Anthropology and Psychology, established within NRC in 1919, was one sign of the ascendancy of the social sciences; the CCD came under its auspices.

During the 1920s, even when the sponsor of scientific programs was an official or affiliated agency of government, funding usually came from the private sector. All the support for the NRC and its committees during the 1920s and most of the money for the 1929–1930 White House Conference for Child Health and Protection (1930 WHC) came from philanthropy.

Philanthropic support shifted during the 1920s from adult programs to programs for children (Coffman, 1936, p. 48). This shift was a reflection of the strength and exuberance of the postwar child welfare movement. Unlike many other prewar progressive reform movements, which perished or declined after the war, the crusade for children became broader and bolder and adopted the exalted aim of improving the lives not only of disadvantaged children but of *all* children (Chambers, 1963, pp. 13–14). President Wilson's establishment of Children's Year, President Harding's support of the Maternal and Child Health Act of 1921, and President Hoover's active

---

materials to know that, with the exception of correspondence and reports relating to policy conflicts over CCD functions during and after the period of Todd's chairmanship and excepting also the minutes of the division's meeting on December 17, 1932, most of the sources attributed to the NAS Archives may also be found in the RAC. Many, but not all, of the sources on SRCD up to 1948 may be found in the NAS Archives as well as in the SRCD Archive Collection of NLM. The following abbreviations have been used throughout this paper: NAS (National Academy of Sciences), NRC (National Research Council), the division (NRC Division of Anthropology and Psychology), CCD (NRC Committee on Child Development), and LSRM and GEB (Rockefeller Foundation's Laura Spelman Rockefeller Memorial Fund and General Education Board).

role in the 1930 WHC were not just baby kissing but a reflection of the prevailing belief that the reconstruction of society must begin with the child. Two developments in particular contributed to this intensified concern for children: the revelation that over half the military recruits examined had physical defects that were attributable to unwholesome conditions in early childhood and the new psychological emphasis on early childhood experiences as crucial influences on later life (Abbott, 1923; Burnham, 1968).

It was apparent that child welfare activities were fast outstripping the research on which they should be based. G. Stanley Hall had led a child study movement in the 1890s, which gained great popular support. At that time, however, most scientists were indifferent to or scornful of the study of children. Harvard psychologist Hugo Münsterberg responded to the movement by proclaiming that he would love his children but never study them (Hall, 1923, p. 392). Hall, that master institution builder, founder of the American Psychological Association and four psychological journals, was unable to establish a single enduring child research organization, although he tried until 1910 (Hall, 1923, p. 583). He created enthusiasm for child study among parents and teachers and stimulated many scientists to study children, but he alienated other scientists, who regarded his theory and method as unscientific (Siegel & White, 1982). His worst sin was his encouragement of lay participation in scientific investigation (Ross, 1972, p. 341).

At the time of the Armistice, in 1918, scientific study of children was in a sorry state. Most scientists who studied children were generalists who occasionally investigated childhood. Harold Jones (1956, p. 239) reported that a 1918 survey revealed only three psychologists and two psychiatrists with a primary interest in children. The first institute of child development, the Iowa Child Welfare Research Station, had just been established (Bradbury & Stoddard, 1933; Cravens, 1979, 1985). Gesell had opened the Yale Psycho-Clinic in 1911 but had not yet begun his study of normal child development. Watson and Rayner would not publish their famous study on children's fears until 1920. It was not even known how many babies were born each year in the United States; birth registration became nationwide only in 1933. Myrtle McGraw (Senn, 1972bNP, p. 3) got her sample of babies for her thesis research in Tallahassee, Florida, in 1927 by looking for diapers on clotheslines. Only two major and a few minor child guidance clinics were operating. Systematic, institutionalized study of children's growth and development was not even in sight.

The postwar trends I have described—philanthropic patronage of science, the takeoff of the social sciences, and the growing gap between child welfare programs and child research programs—converged in the new policies of the Laura Spelman Rockefeller Memorial Fund (LSRM) formulated during 1923 and 1924. The LSRM had been established in 1918 with an endowment of $74 million by John D. Rockefeller in memory of his wife. Its goal was to advance the charitable work she had undertaken to "further the welfare of women and children." In 1923 the foundation directors voted to change this goal to the "application of the social sciences for the purpose of reform," a program advocated by Beardsley Ruml, appointed director of LSRM in 1922 (Fosdick, 1952, pp. 192–195). Ruml and Lawrence K. Frank, a program officer of LSRM, became the architects and Frank the chief executor of its programs for child development research and parent education. To Frank (1939NP, p. 1), child development research was "preventive politics . . . a significant break with the [fatalistic] attitudes of the past . . . the most effective method for dealing with our social difficulties" and the way by which "at last man may take charge of his own destiny."

By 1924 LSRM (Senn, 1963NP) had established the first Rockefeller child development institute, at Teachers College, Columbia University, and arranged a grant to the Iowa Child Welfare Research Station to expand its program. In the next 3 years three additional major Rockefeller institutes (Minnesota, Berkeley, and Toronto) were founded, and Gesell's clinic, renamed the Yale Clinic of Child Development, was given a 5-year grant. The LSRM also supported the revitalization and professionalization of the parent education movement (Schlossman, 1976, 1981). The LSRM programs could not succeed, however, unless child development became a viable and respectable scientific enterprise. The CCD was created by NRC to help achieve this purpose.

THE FOUNDING OF THE COMMITTEE ON CHILD DEVELOPMENT

The NRC's Division of Anthropology and Psychology had established the Committee on Child Welfare in April 1920 for the purpose of advising government agencies concerned with children. Bird Baldwin, director of the Iowa Station, was appointed chairman in 1922. The committee had no funds, however, and remained inactive (McLean, 1954). Fortunately for LSRM, the chair of the division in 1924–1925 was Robert S. Woodworth, an eminent Columbia University psychologist.

Although his own research was not on children, Woodworth's commitment to establishing a science of child development was as strong as anyone's. Assured of LSRM's financial support (R. S. Woodworth to B. Baldwin, August 10, 1925), he devoted most of his time and energy during his year as chair of the division to preparations for the new committee (CCD conference proceedings, 1925, p. 10).

The Committee on Child Development (CCD), which replaced the Child Welfare Committee, not only had a new name but also lacked most of the parent education functions of its predecessor. By 1928 a separate parent education organization was established by LSRM with headquarters in New York rather than Washington.

Throughout the life of CCD great care was taken to maintain this strategy of confining its function to research and assuring that its scientific status was not tainted by association with child welfare or parent education activities. At the first CCD conference Bird Baldwin (CCD conference proceedings, 1925, p. 13) said, "We are concerned with a scientific analysis of the fundamental scientific problems underlying childhood rather than with formulating remedial measures or outlining methods of training." The Rockefeller institutes had twin goals: the fostering of child development research and parent education. Not so the committee. Frank (1932NP) advised Chairman T. Wingate Todd to portray CCD in a grant proposal as "as rigidly a scientific enterprise as possible and minimize references to child welfare implications and obligations."

The CCD was officially established by the division on June 20, 1925, with Baldwin as chairman and Woodworth and John Anderson, director of the Minnesota institute, as the other members. Baldwin remained chairman until his death in 1928, when Anderson succeeded him. The CCD did not begin to operate, however, until the need for it was confirmed and its functions were determined at a conference on October 23–25, 1925, cosponsored by NRC and LSRM. In preparation for the conference Woodworth (1925NP) sent 1,200 questionnaires to all members of the American Psychological Association and to a sample of members of the anthropological, physiological, biochemical, anatomical, zoological, and animal husbandry societies to determine "who was undertaking research in the physical or mental development of children or young animals" and to ask what a committee might do to aid such research. Of the 355 questionnaires returned, 129 reported work in progress.

After consulting on personnel with Frank, Baldwin, and Anderson, Woodworth (August 10, 1925) invited 30 researchers to a conference to determine whether a new committee on child development should be established under NRC auspices and to plan a long-range program. Conference members wholeheartedly approved the formation of CCD and stated succinctly that its purpose was to demonstrate that child development research was both possible and necessary.

THE FIRST PHASE OF CCD'S PROGRAM: OCTOBER 1925–MARCH 1930

On January 20, 1926, LSRM appropriated $40,000 for the CCD to carry out a three-part program during the next 4 years: the holding of biennial conferences (for which an additional $7,500 was given), the publication of bibliographies and research surveys, and an award program to support the training of investigators in child development research. A full-time executive secretary, Leslie Ray Marston, was employed in the Washington office.

Conferences were considered CCD's best instrument for achieving its primary function: the stimulation of integrated research involving many disciplines. The second conference (1927), with 51 members, tackled the problem of ways to standardize techniques so that research could be cumulative and comparable. The 1929 conference, with 48 members, was by far the most ambitious. Through reviews of trends in child development research it attempted to measure progress in the field since 1925. The two-volume *Proceedings,* autographed from typed copy, sold out immediately.

The CCD's first publication, *Child Development Abstracts and Bibliography* (1927), was designed to help investigators in one discipline become acquainted with research on children in other disciplines. It contained digests of pertinent literature scattered through 15 academic journals. By 1930 it was sent to 500 subscribers for $5.00 a year. The first *Directory of Research* (Marston, 1927) listed 417 investigators in the United States and Canada on early childhood development up to 7 years. A second edition (Hicks, 1931) listed 627 investigators.

The scholarship and fellowship program was designed to lure good people into the new field and train them. Difficulties in achieving the program's purpose are indicated by CCD recommendations: that special efforts be made to interest qualified men as well as women (Marston, 1926NP), that training be limited to research rather than parent education or other service activities, that preference be shifted from pre- to postdoctoral candidates (minutes, February 17–18, 1928), and that half the centers proposed as training sites be rejected because their programs were not sufficiently well-rounded (Committee on Child Development of the National Research Council, 1929bNP). From 551 applicants, 116 were awarded scholarships and 14 fellowships. Although CCD recommended continuation (Committee on Child Development of the National Research Council, 1929aNP), the program was terminated in 1930.

PROBLEMS AND GOALS

One is struck by the extent to which the CCD conference proceedings (1925, 1927, 1929, 1933) reflect concerns and aspirations with which SRCD still struggles today (Rheingold, in this vol.; Super, 1982). Chief among them was how to achieve an integrated science of child development and to work out the proper relation between research and practice. "Child development," Frank insisted (Senn, 1963NP, pp. 10–16), was not a new term for child psychology but an interdisciplinary endeavor. All investigators in the

113

basic sciences represented in the study of children must be motivated not to use the child as a tool to contribute to the advancement of a particular discipline (to substitute children for rats, as some put it) but to integrate their findings with those of others for the purpose of understanding children.

The membership and content of the conferences and the range of subjects covered in the publications demonstrated CCD's commitment to cover and draw together as many disciplines as possible. The first conference, in 1925, was organized into six committees: animal behavior in relation to child development, physical growth, nutrition, medical care, psychology, and mental hygiene (which in those days encompassed child psychiatry). The focus of the second conference was on the kinds of methods that could lead to the integration of fragmented knowledge. Frank's paper (CCD conference proceedings, 1927, pp. 115–119) is important as the first expression of his thinking on "the problem of child development as a focus for scientific research." Marston regretfully reported that only 5% of the investigators listed in the *Directory of Research* (Marston, 1927) attempted to relate findings in one field to those in another. Conference members were particularly concerned with how to get mathematicians "to understand our problems"; they voted to strive for a closer relationship with mathematicians and statisticians (CCD conference proceedings, 1927, pp. 119–123).

There were other indications of the desire to encompass many disciplines. The CCD was enlarged in October 1927 to include a pediatrician, Martha Eliot; a biochemist, E. V. McCollum (representing nutrition); and an anatomist, T. Wingate Todd. Dental literature was added to the *Abstracts* 2 years later.

The other chief concern in these early years—the relation between research and practice—was discussed by Woodworth (CCD conference proceedings, 1925, p. 3) in his opening address to the first conference. It was a reassuring message to those who feared that current knowledge was an inadequate guide to the thriving child welfare movement. He insisted that fundamental research be recognized and supported as an essential part of the whole child welfare movement. But, he added, "practical endeavor is certain to go on without waiting for a thorough scientific grounding. . . . Nor, if we could, would we desire to call a halt on all practical endeavor until our scientific explorers were able to assure us that the whole territory . . . was thoroughly mapped. . . . Our inevitable blunders will be valuable and even necessary as clues to the investigator. Research and practice will react each upon the other."

At the second conference, Marston (CCD conference proceedings, 1927, p. 91) reiterated Woodworth's message: "Science itself profits by these cut-and-try attempts of society to adjust itself to its new focus on the child." They might have added that application is the point at which the interdisciplinary goal is most readily achieved. Although education and application were outside CCD's scope, they might also have acknowledged that "inevitable blunders" in application could be costly to children and parents as well as valuable to the investigator. That is why Frank and Ruml sought, unsuccessfully, to maintain some control over the contents of *Parents' Magazine* (Schlossman, in this vol.).

THE SECOND PHASE: APRIL 1930–JUNE 1933

Trends in American society had favored the creation of CCD. By the early 1930s, however, new circumstances hindered its progress. The stock market crash in October 1929 and the subsequent depression not only reduced the funds available for research but also undermined the utopian optimism about the potential for social improvement that prosperity had fostered. The urgent needs of unemployed adults distracted the nation from its preoccupation with children. At the same time, the Rockefeller Foundation reorganized its programs and adopted new policies. The LSRM was dissolved in January 1929. Some of its programs were terminated; most were curtailed. The CCD's first grant expired in March 1930. Requesting $63,000 for the next 6 years, it received only $22,500 for a little more than 2 years, the grant ending in June 1932 (CCD, memorandum to Rockefeller Foundation, September 10, 1931).

By the time CCD applied for its second grant a rival organization had emerged, the 1930 White House Conference (1930 WHC). Since the follow-up committee of the 1930 WHC appeared to duplicate CCD's functions, the need for CCD was questioned. The 1930 WHC, reflecting the importance assigned to children and to research during this era, was vastly more ambitious than its two predecessors. The White House conferences of 1909 and 1919 had only a few hundred participants and a limited agenda, which did not include child study. The 1930 WHC, 16 months in preparation, with an attendance of 3,200 and a budget of $1.5 million, brought together specialists from many disciplines to review and evaluate research. Unlike any of the White House conferences for children before or since it organized task forces to conduct original research; one of them was directed by CCD chair John Anderson (1936). Thirty-two volumes of research reports were published. The emphasis on research during this decade was demonstrated also by the sponsor of the 1930 WHC, the Children's Bureau, which conducted more research during the 1920s than during either of the next 2 decades.

Members of CCD were active in the 1930 WHC and contributed significantly to its success. But the 1930 WHC interfered with CCD's own progress, causing it to cancel its 1931 biennial conference and publication of a new review journal (J. A. Hicks to M. Knight, March 26, 1931).

In February 1931, the Rockefeller Foundation decided that CCD's subsequent appeals for funds should be submitted to NRC rather than to the foundation. Only if NRC approved the appeal and included it in its own appeal to the foundation would CCD be funded. Henceforth, CCD would have to sell itself to the Division Executive Committee, to the central officers of NRC, and to officials of the foundation. Conflict over CCD policy among these three groups threatened its continued existence and delayed approval of a grant until May 1933.

In March 1932 a proposal (minutes, January 31, 1932) for a 5-year program with a budget of $92,000 was rejected by the division. The following month, Anderson resigned as chair for "reasons of health" but continued as a member. To succeed him NRC appointed Todd, professor of anatomy at the Medical School of Western Reserve University, Cleveland. (George Stoddard and Mandel Sherman, both psychologists, had been added to CCD in 1931.)

The history I have been reporting and that Harriet Rheingold (in this vol.) continues is the story of a small group of researchers dedicated to the establishment of a new discipline and a new professional organization with functions and goals on which they agreed. Todd's 9 months as chairman is another story. An autocrat of amazing energy, Todd tried to force through a radically different program that he believed would secure NRC and Rockefeller support, despite the opposition of every other CCD member as well as of several NRC executives to the proposed changes in CCD policy. When thwarted, he tried to dissolve CCD and opposed the formation of SRCD. He almost succeeded. The CCD and SRCD were saved primarily by the efforts of A. T. Poffenberger, division chair in 1932–1933, and Woodworth, who replaced Todd as CCD chair only 4 months before SRCD was established. The story is fully documented by voluminous correspondence, reports, and minutes of meetings and deserves a fuller telling than I can give here.

Before his appointment was 2 weeks old or even official, Todd went into action. He sent the division two reports (May 14, 1932) that had not been approved by CCD. One proposed general changes; the other focused on transforming the *Abstracts* into a review journal. Todd (May 17, 1932) also sent a history of CCD that inaccurately described it as engaging in parent education; one proposal was that CCD sponsor a publication to popularize child development research.

Beulah Brewer, CCD secretary, and Marion Hale Britten, division secretary, recognized the implications of the historical error and the proposal and wrote about them to division chair Robert Lowie on May 20. The same day, Lowie wrote to Todd to explain why CCD had scrupulously restricted its function to research and, in light of this, questioned the proposed publication. But Todd, who never gave up easily, continued to argue for the publication. After Lowie (May 26, 1932), Britten (May 31, 1932), and A. L. Barrows (May 31, 1932), assistant secretary to NRC, wrote additional explanations of why popularization was contrary to both NRC and CCD policy, Todd (June 2, 1932) asked Lowie, "Tell me how you and Dr. Barrows would word the dubious phrases. I'm pretty sure there is no obstacle to complete agreement." The next day (June 3, 1932) he called Lowie's attention to a popular article, "Why Children Lie," in *Science News Letter* (Van de Water, 1932), the model for the proposed publication, and argued again for his proposal. Avowing agreement with the opposition while persisting in arguing for his own program was a tactic Todd used repeatedly.

Soon after becoming chairman, Todd attempted to cancel, but succeeded only in postponing, a conference that had been officially approved by the full committee the preceding January. The conference, to be held in Chicago, was to be jointly sponsored by CCD and the Committee on Personality and Culture of the Social Science Research Council. A primary goal of the conference was to draw more sociologists into CCD. A subcommittee of three (Sherman, Anderson, and Stoddard) had begun work, and participants had been invited and were preparing papers (M. Sherman to R. Lowie, May 23, 1932; J. Anderson to R. Lowie, May 31, 1932).

Finding NRC unenthusiastic about CCD proposals as well as about his own ideas on parent education, Todd tried to find out what NRC did want through meetings and correspondence with its executives, Barrows, Lowie, and, particularly, William H. Howell, NRC chair, who had discussed CCD policy with Max Mason, president of the Rockefeller Foundation. Either unfamiliar with or unsympathetic to the fundamental goal of CCD to encourage integrated research, Howell was critical of its efforts and cordial to Todd's eagerness to lead it in new directions. On July 6, he wrote to Todd, "My feelings in regard to the direction our efforts should take are expressed admirably in the program you enclose in your letter of June 24th." He invited Todd to submit a detailed proposal and all but promised that financial backing would be available.

Todd (July 8, 1932) replied to Howell, "You are quite right and President Mason is fully justified in calling a halt to the rather nebulous schemes of Committees which . . . expend their efforts and public money in the easiest manner. . . . Your letter relieves me of all uncertainty. . . . I feel free to throw all my energy into future construction, unhampered by the necessity of upholding the past."

Todd (July 30, 1932) then sent to members of CCD and the division a letter and enclosures containing proposals for his new program. He recommended abolishing the entire past program, describing it in terms that must have seemed insulting to CCD founders. He proposed (1) the termination of the *Abstracts*, calling it "a haphazard collection . . . without plan and set together without order. . . . it cannot guide the uninitiated and it is redundant for the conscientious and the informed"; (2) the closing of the Washington office and the transfer of all CCD functions to Todd's Cleveland office; and (3) the elimination of conferences from the regular budget and, again, the abandonment of the Chicago conference since "conferences are a cumbersome and tedious method of bringing together diverse disciplines."

The new program included the following. (1) The CCD itself should undertake fundamental research on "somatic development, mental growth and emotional expression in their interrelationship." (2) The initial research should be on physical development (Todd's own field). (3) For this project CCD should use its remaining balance of $6,500. (4) A subcommittee of Todd and McCollum should be authorized to draw up the program and supervise the expenditures. (5) The CCD should have the right to apply through NRC for support for local programs that could be integrated into the basic investigation of CCD.

Knight Dunlap, division chairman in 1927–1929 and a member of the Division Executive Committee, was the first to react negatively. (He had not received any material from Todd; I suspect that Sherman was his informant.) "In case the proposed action has not been reported to the office," Dunlap wrote to Britten on August 11, 1932, it "will be interpreted as follows: 1. Committee asked to approve abandonment of plans approved by Committee at previous meeting. . . . *Asked* is the euphonious word. 2. The remaining funds to be turned over to the chairman for his particular line of investigation." A "stench" will cling around the CCD chairman and the division for a long time, he warned, if "steamroller" methods are used. "Money spent for a physical meeting of the committee to settle the matter decently would be money well spent."

Poffenberger, a Columbia University psychologist who succeeded Lowie as division chair on July 1, wrote to Todd on August 12, expressing interest in and approval of his proposals and offering help, "although I am mighty new at the game." After briefings by Barrows and Woodworth, however, Poffenberger withdrew his approval. Shortly thereafter Sherman (August 13, 1932) and Stoddard (August 19, 1932) objected strongly to the implication that investigations of mental and emotional development were dependent on studies of physical development. Stoddard, opposing management of research by a subcommittee consisting of Todd and McCollum, declared that it would be "a subversion" of the plain intent of NRC to have CCD "act as a unit . . . and would make other members of the committee figureheads."

In a second letter to CCD members Todd (August 24, 1932) so flagrantly exceeded his authority that CCD members were outraged, executives of NRC were shocked and bewildered, and members of both groups were aroused to preventive action.

Recipients of the letter found two parts of it extremely objectionable.

One was Todd's reference to his proposed program as a "mandate," implying its approval by NRC. The other was Todd's statement that CCD memberships had terminated on June 30 "but are renewable at the chairman's discretion. If you are willing to accept the conditions of the mandate," he told the members, "notify me. If the conditions are unacceptable consider carefully, in the interests of child development, your responsibility in remaining on the Committee."

Poffenberger (August 31, 1932) quickly asked Barrows to clear up certain matters. Had CCD members been legally reappointed by the division? Had NRC, through Howell or otherwise, issued a mandate to CCD or its chairman? If CCD undertook the proposed research program, it might be looked on as just another Rockefeller child development institute. Had conditions so changed that the foundation now preferred to support another institute rather than an organization to encourage coordinated research? Was the continuation of the existing institutes in doubt?

Barrows (September 2, 1932) replied promptly. Both CCD and its subcommittees had been properly authorized. He did not know the origin of the idea of giving the members the option of continuing or retiring. Howell was trying not to dictate CCD policy but to bridge the gap between Lowie's and Poffenberger's terms of office. Howell also wished to give Todd the benefit of his discussions with Mason of Rockefeller. The NRC's function, in Barrow's opinion, was to advise the foundation rather than merely to accept a plan suggested to them. The CCD's function was to assess the situation in the field and decide what was needed, more research centers or new means of coordinating research.

In a 6-hour meeting with Poffenberger, Woodworth discussed CCD history, interpreting goals and procedures in light of this historical context. In a letter (August 30, 1932) summarizing the discussion, he pointed out to Poffenberger that CCD had been denied funds for specific research projects because LSRM was making large research grants to the institutes and "it seemed superfluous to grant a small additional sum to be allotted through . . . the Committee." Moreover, both LSRM and CCD were dedicated to promoting an interdisciplinary approach to the study of children, and the funding of specific investigations "would be positively objectionable since it would tend towards isolation rather than coordination." Still another reason for not allowing CCD to control research funds, Woodworth said, was to dispel fears that NRC "would carry over from war time a militaristic attitude toward the workers and assume to assign them their tasks. . . . The Council's aim was said to be thoroughly democratic—to follow the lead of the active research men, establish contacts between them and let them coordinate their own efforts." Baldwin (CCD conference proceedings, 1925, p. 12) and A. V. Kidder (CCD conference proceedings, 1927, p. 1) had expressed these same themes at the first and second CCD conferences.

Woodworth (August 30, 1932) also wrote to Todd that he opposed all Todd's proposals. Funds granted for other purposes "cannot be legally appropriated for specific research." Only CCD, in session, could change the plan. If acceptance of CCD membership meant willingness to commit oneself in advance to a certain policy, then "in self respect I must decline." It would be "absurd for our small Committee to feel ourselves responsible for the general direction of child development investigation." He would not consider for a moment membership on any committee that had that responsibility and was sure that NRC "would never permit us to publish any such declaration of dominance."

Even before Todd had sent his August 24 letter, Barrows (August 15, 1932) pointed out to Poffenberger the radical nature of Todd's proposals and secured his agreement on the need for an early joint meeting of the division and CCD to resolve differences and clear the way for a new CCD proposal that NRC could submit to Rockefeller. Barrows (August 15, 1932) and Poffenberger (August 23, 1932) wrote to invite Todd and CCD members to meet with the division for this purpose on September 10. Todd replied (August 26, 1932) that he would be delighted to attend the meeting himself but would not invite other CCD members because that would be too costly, because members were unprepared and would be embarrassed to thrash out their differences before the division, and because NRC and the division should approve a plan prior to its submission to CCD.

Reading the exchange of correspondence between Todd and members of CCD, the division, and NRC is like being in never-never land. From mid-August until early November, despite the number and urgency of the demands on Todd to call a meeting of CCD, he pleasantly and cheerfully but firmly refused. Apparently undaunted by any of the opposition to his proposals, Todd wrote to Frank (1932NP) and to Poffenberger (August 25, 1932) of the "thrilling" and "merry" time he was having and of his expectation that his committee soon would support him. Barrows (August 22, 1932) confessed to Poffenberger that he could not harmonize Todd's optimism with the angry opposition expressed by Sherman and others. In his cheerful reply to Woodworth's negative letter, Todd (September 7, 1932) wrote that Woodworth's definition of the coordinating function of CCD "not only still holds good . . . but is the clearest and most compelling definition of our purpose." This passage was followed by three pages purporting to clarify his views, which led Poffenberger (September 27, 1932) to ask Woodworth, "Did that confuse you still further?" Although Todd would not call a meeting, he did, on September 7, send copies of Woodworth's and Stoddard's letters objecting to his proposals to CCD members and on September 22 invited them to send suggestions for a grant proposal for a 5-year program.

Todd always offered many reasons for refusing to call a CCD meeting but stressed one: the need for NRC endorsement before a plan could be submitted to CCD. The real reason may have been his hope that when Howell returned from several months abroad he would again champion Todd's proposal. On his return, however, Howell wrote to Todd (October 18, 1932) that he would not discuss any plans until they had CCD approval. Typically, Todd (October 18, 1932) replied as if this was what he had wanted all along. Howell's letter had provided "great hope and encouragement. It assures me that the Committee is free to develop its own ideas and program for the future."

The CCD finally met on November 19–20 to draw up a new grant proposal. With every member present, CCD adopted a proposal that reflected Woodworth's rather than Todd's view of its functions. The most significant part of the proposal was a plan for an independent society of child research workers that would assume all but the advisory functions of CCD. The CCD had intended to sponsor such a society sometime in the future, when the time was ripe. Now, because the outlook for its future was clouded by NRC's lack of enthusiasm, CCD members decided to move ahead with a concrete plan and a specific date, June 1933, for an organizational meeting.

Todd's minutes of this meeting, sent to the division on November 30 without CCD approval, were later approved by Stoddard and Eliot but challenged, in letters to Todd, by Woodworth (December 31, 1932) and Anderson (January 4, 1933). The disagreement was primarily over whether members had agreed to employ a full-time field secretary to be appointed by the chairman and to transform the *Abstracts* into a review journal immediately.

The Division Executive Committee (Poffenberger, Dunlap, C. E. Guthe, Ralph Linton, and Lowie absent) met on December 17. The first item on the agenda was the status of CCD and its grant proposal. The executive committee approved the establishment of a national child development society with a budget of $6,500 a year for 3 years. (CCD had requested $9,100 for each of 6 years.) It agreed to the Chicago conference but not to the proposal for a field secretary. In order to fulfill obligations to subscribers it insisted that the *Abstracts* be published through 1933 and, if changed, be converted gradually into a résumé service, not a review journal (Division Executive Committee, minutes, December 17, 1932).

On January 3, 1933, Poffenberger wrote to Todd reporting the division's decisions. Todd's angry reply to Poffenberger by day letter on January 6 declared that "authoritative advice" he had received in October suggested that his role as chair was to provide "an effective termination" and "decent interment" of CCD. He had asked permission "to make one more effort," but added, "I am now ready to carry out these duties." He informed Poffenberger that he had discharged the Washington stenographer, disbanded the subcommittee on the *Abstracts,* and canceled subscriptions. "Abstracts are now dead. . . . Executive Committee action is therefore futile." Todd (January 6, 1933) also sent a report, which defended his leadership, and concluded by recommending that CCD be dissolved. Three days later he wrote to Frank (1933NP), "The Society for Research in Child Development is unnecessary at this juncture. What we need is consolidation and not expansion."[1]

After conferring with Dunlap, Woodworth, and Howell, Poffenberger (January 9, 1933) replied that he did not know the source of Todd's "authoritative advice" but that CCD could be terminated only by NRC, not by its chairman. The CCD's work in the Washington office would continue at least until June 1933. The *Abstracts* was not dead; the December number would be issued, the *Abstracts* subcommittee reappointed, and subscriptions reinstated. Since Todd had said he could not carry out the duties of chairman without funds,[2] Poffenberger suggested that he "might wish to withdraw at once" (January 9, 1933). Todd (January 9, 1933) wired back that urgent local affairs demanded his attention, but he would reply at the earliest possible opportunity.

When he had not heard from Todd by January 20 Poffenberger wrote to all CCD members asking whether CCD should be dissolved and immediately reconstituted without Todd. Poffenberger was not dissuaded from this course of action by a letter Todd sent on the same day offering to meet with him "to analyze the situation dispassionately." The CCD members approved Poffenberger's idea unanimously (E. V. McCollum to A. T. Poffenberger, January 21, 1933; G. Stoddard & M. Sherman to A. T. Poffenberger, January 23, 1933; J. Anderson to A. T. Poffenberger, January 24, 1933; R. S. Woodworth to A. T. Poffenberger, January 26, 1933; M. M. Eliot, personal communication with A. T. Poffenberger, February 1, 1933; and M. M. Eliot to A. T. Poffenberger, February 13, 1933). Division executives also approved. On February 14, NRC's executive board dissolved CCD and immediately reappointed all its members, except Todd.

---

[1] Todd's letters to Frank (1932NP, 1933NP) express his belief that he had Frank's wholehearted support. He told Frank that he had not divulged that Frank was the source of the "authoritative advice" that guided his actions. Frank's replies are ambiguous, neither affirming nor questioning Todd's view of Frank's attitudes and role in these events.

[2] Poffenberger was referring to another long dispute between Todd and the division over money Todd believed the division owed him for services and expenses incurred in connection with his work as chairman of CCD (M. H. Britten to T. W. Todd, June 16, 23, 1932; T. W. Todd to M. H. Britten, June 21, August 19, 1932; T. W. Todd to A. L. Barrows, August 19, October 5, 13, 1932; A. L. Barrows to T. W. Todd, October 11, 1932; W. H. Howell to T. W. Todd, October 10, 1932; T. W. Todd to W. H. Howell, October 13, 1932). At the December 17 meeting, division executives had again refused to authorize reimbursement. A full account of this dispute would require another long article, as would an account of the dispute over the continuation and content of the *Abstracts*.

Poffenberger notified Todd by letter on February 15, and Todd responded on February 17 by sending Poffenberger a report prepared before he had received Poffenberger's letter. The report summarized the "progress" of CCD under Todd's leadership and recommended that CCD be dissolved because the impetus of the 1930 WHC rendered the supervision of NRC unnecessary. An accompanying letter said, "I am sure that your feeling of relief must equal my own that the final stages of this discussion have been passed through with such ease." Thus Todd remained in character until the end. Less than 6 years later he died at the age of 53.

Poffenberger wrote Woodworth on February 15 that he had seriously considered Woodworth's suggestion that he become chairman but that he could not accept because he believed that CCD needed Woodworth's guidance. (Poffenberger did help the new society as chair of the subcommittee on the *Abstracts*.) As the crisis deepened, communication between the two men increased. The tone of the letters and the change from "Dr. Poffenberger" to "Dear Poff" reflect a growing intimacy and trust that may have contributed to their collaboration in saving CCD and launching SRCD.

Since the organizational meeting of the new society was set for June 24, only 4 months away, the two men faced a formidable task, handicapped by lack of time and money and the damage done to CCD's reputation during Todd's term of office. Lack of esteem for CCD was reflected in Ruml's comment that he had heard that CCD was "blowing up" and was devoted to "physical studies" (M. Sherman to A. T. Poffenberger, January 19, 1933). When Woodworth sought Frank's support for a CCD grant, Frank, now with the General Education Board (GEB) of the Rockefeller Foundation, asked him whether research workers really wanted CCD continued (R. S. Woodworth to A. T. Poffenberger, March 16, 1933).

After much preparation and negotiation Poffenberger and Woodworth secured approval of a CCD grant proposal from the division, NRC, and NAS, only to be informed that Rockefeller had changed its mind about having CCD's appeal incorporated in NRC's budget. The foundation suggested, instead, that CCD apply separately to GEB (M. Mason to W. H. Howell, April 4, 1933; R. S. Woodworth to A. T. Poffenberger, April 8, 1933). A request for $18,900 for 3 years was submitted to GEB on April 8. A grant of $12,600 for 2 years was approved on May 19, accompanied by the dismal message that no further appropriation would be made by GEB to NRC for "the purpose stated" (W. W. Brierly to W. H. Howell, May 19, 1933). In fact, GEB did support CCD and SRCD publications and projects for many years. At the time of SRCD's first biennial meeting, however, Woodworth (Society for Research in Child Development, 1934NP, p. 40) did not expect Rockefeller support to continue.

Almost 100 researchers met to launch the new society and to attend the fourth CCD conference in June 1933. Located in Chicago, with many anthropologists and sociologists participating and with emphasis on the social development of the child, the meeting was essentially the conference Todd had tried to cancel. At the business meeting on June 23, CCD voted to have a report of its SRCD organizing committee substituted for Todd's minutes of the November 1932 CCD meeting because of doubts as to their accuracy. Sociologist Robert S. Lynd and pediatrician Kenneth D. Blackfan were elected to membership, and SRCD also was invited to nominate a member (R. S. Woodworth, SRCD minutes, June 23, 1933, p. 1).

CONCLUSION

In spite of a premature birth and a youth handicapped by the effects of depression and war, SRCD survived to become today's thriving organization of 4,000 members. Harriet Rheingold (in this vol.) describes the society's early struggles and demonstrates that its initial progress must be attributed partly to the continuing support of CCD, which with Woodworth as chairman nurtured its offspring for 15 more years.

The SRCD's early progress can also be attributed to the extraordinary expansion of child welfare and child study during the 8 years between the founding of CCD and the founding of SRCD. In this brief period, scientific study of children was transformed from sporadic, local, modestly funded activities to institutionalized, nationwide, relatively well funded research.

The growth of the child guidance movement, sponsored by the Commonwealth Fund from 1922 to 1927, paralleled that of the child development movement. Commonwealth, like Rockefeller, supported training fellowships. By 1930, 355 guidance clinics were serving 44,000 children annually (Cohen, 1980; Frank, 1933).

Two major research institutes, in addition to those founded by LSRM, were established during the 1920s—Merrill-Palmer in 1922 and Fels in 1929. During the 1930s the institute at Teacher's College closed; all others survived, although with reduced budgets. The GEB gave almost $2.4 million to child development research during the decade and created new institutes (Fosdick, 1962, pp. 260, 264) to encompass research on infants and adolescents as well as on preschoolers, an expansion recommended by CCD in 1931 (minutes, February 21, 1931). Many philanthropic organizations and individuals, following the lead of Commonwealth and Rockefeller, established new clinics and institutes during the 1930s.

After 1925, increased funding of child study came from the federal government as well as from philanthropy, chiefly through the 1930 WHC and the Children's Bureau. Under the auspices of the Maternal and Child Health Act of 1921, 3,000 child health and 700 prenatal centers were established before the act was repealed in 1929.

The increase in the number of professionals in the field and pressure from the newcomers to be allowed to attend CCD-sponsored meetings influenced the decision to establish SRCD earlier than had been anticipated (L. M. Stolz, personal communication, January 9, 1983, September 3, 1984). Another helpful factor was the discontinuance of the 1930 WHC follow-up committee, an event that Woodworth quickly used as an argument for funds for a new society (R. S. Woodworth to T. A. Arnett, April 28, 1933).

Although CCD was under strong pressure to abandon its original purposes during the trying months preceding the founding of SRCD, SRCD adheres to them to this day. As expressed at the first CCD conference in 1925 and restated in SRCD's constitution in 1934, those purposes are to stimulate and support research and to encourage cooperation among researchers in many fields. The service function, lost when the Child Welfare Committee became CCD in 1925, was restored in SRCD's constitution, which committed SRCD to support efforts toward successful application of research findings.

An integrated science of child development based on interdisciplinary research is an ideal that SRCD has not realized but has continued to work toward (Ainsworth, Anders, Caldwell, Hetherington, & Kennell, 1979; Harris, 1953). It continues to search for new procedures and programs that will prevent the dominance of any one discipline, draw in new disciples, and promote the exchange of views and information among all. During the 1930s, CCD thwarted Todd's attempt to make research on physical development paramount. Today SRCD strives to keep psychologists from capturing it. At the 1933 conference CCD sought to attract sociologists; at the fiftieth anniversary meeting SRCD tried to draw in historians.

SRCD's allegiance to its roots is also evident in its major programs, which employ the same methods CCD adopted; the holding of biennial conferences, the publication of the *Abstracts,* and the sponsorship of training fellowships.

Reflections on the continuity between CCD and SRCD lead inevitably to recognition of the crucial role of Woodworth. More than anyone, he set the course for both CCD and SRCD. Anderson (1956, p. 188) called him "the strong, silent man of our history." Woodworth has been recognized for his contributions to psychology, but not sufficiently for his service to child development.

VIII. THE FIRST TWENTY-FIVE YEARS OF THE SOCIETY FOR RESEARCH IN CHILD DEVELOPMENT

HARRIET L. RHEINGOLD

University of North Carolina at Chapel Hill

When I was invited to prepare this part of the society's history, I accepted at once, and then only gradually did it dawn on me that I would need to find some records. A few letters and many telephone calls later, I learned that seven boxes of the archives of the society had just the past summer been stored in a warehouse on the far south side of Chicago, there awaiting shipment to the National Library of Medicine. With Barbara Kahn's kind offices it nevertheless took many weeks to effect the transfer. Then in November 1982, with Manfred Waserman's many courtesies, I searched through those large unlabeled boxes to glean what I could of events during the first 25 years. Most informative were the yearly reports prepared by Robert S. Woodworth for the National Research Council on the work and financial status of the society, the minutes of business meetings, and letters to the membership from the governing council. For additional information I reviewed all the society's publications during the years of interest.

THE MAIN EVENTS

The minutes of the first meeting of the society, held in Washington in 1934, a year after its founding, convey the excitement of the new venture. There was a consciousness of purpose, of dedication, of enthusiasm, of high hopes for the then new discipline of child development and the contribution

All unpublished sources cited in this paper are from the Society for Research in Child Development Archive Collection in the National Library of Medicine, which is described more fully in the bibliographical essay in Sec. II of the reference list.

it could make to the welfare of children and the nation. There was indeed a sense of mission.

The society rapidly acquired the three journals we still have, held biennial meetings in 1936 and 1938, freely debated and defined its nature and functions, and held many interim meetings. Starting with 125 members (most of them with the status of fellows), their numbers grew rapidly so that by the 1938 biennial meeting they reached 519, an increase of approximately 400 new members in only 5 years. From the beginning, however, the cost of maintaining the society and its publications presented severe problems. The dues of $3.00, which included membership and subscriptions to the three journals, were insufficient, and only grants and favors from the National Research Council and the General Education Fund sustained the society. As a nation we were still recovering from the depression.

By 1939, war abroad and emergency measures at home began to affect the society. The journals continued, but the number of entries in the *Abstracts,* of articles in *Child Development,* and of *Monographs* began to fall. By 1941, we had acquired only 30 more members, for a total of 550, a peak not reached again until 1959, 18 years later, at the time of the twenty-fifth anniversary. In fact, in 1946 the membership had dropped to 488. Contrast that with our current membership of over 4,000! The entire 1943 volume of *Child Development* contained only 10 articles, the 1944 volume only nine, and the 1945 volume again only 10. A desperate call went out for articles, reviews—anything. Contrast that with the submission in 1980 of 859 manuscripts to *Child Development* and a rejection rate of 85% or with the April 1983 issue, which lists 51 manuscripts already accepted and awaiting publication.

Then, because of severe restrictions on travel, the biennial meetings of 1940 and 1942 could not be held. Thereafter, only small meetings occurred, usually in connection with the American Association for the Advancement of Science, and a regular biennial meeting was not held until 1946, the year after the war ended. Let me quote from Robert R. Sears's (1975, pp. 23–24) vivid account here:

World War I had helped bring child development alive. World War II nearly killed it. The reason was unexpected but simple. Most child development researchers belonged also to some discipline or profession and were masters of its skills, knowledge, and technology. They were needed in the war effort. Dentists, psychiatrists, and clinically trained psychologists were drawn into the armed services. Pediatricians were converted to psychiatrists and internal medicine. Psychologists, physiologists, anthropologists were drawn into war-relevant research or administrative work. The developmentalists left in the universities were needed to substitute for them as teachers.

127

The members' dues never were sufficient to cover the costs of the publications, even when they rose from the original $3.00 to $5.00 in 1938 and to $8.00 in 1948. On November 9, 1940, the secretary expressed his gratitude to the fellows for their voluntary contribution of $570. At this point I quote a touching note to the members 7 years later (June 23, 1947) from Carroll E. Palmer, the secretary-treasurer for many years, when the dues went up from $5.00 to $8.00: "Your $3.00 sent at once will constitute a much appreciated indication of your interest and support."

When, in 1948, it became clear that the society was running severely into debt and could not support its journals, the governing council and the National Research Council established a joint committee on publications and obtained a grant of $3,000 from the Cattell Fund. Also Robert Sears replaced Woodworth, who had been asking to be replaced for many years; the National Research Council office was closed; and the Children's Bureau agreed to assist in publishing the *Abstracts.* Thomas W. Richards was appointed editor of *Child Development* and the *Monographs,* and at last the society achieved its independence.

THE ROLE OF THE COMMITTEE ON CHILD DEVELOPMENT

It may come as a surprise to many, as it did to me, that the Committee on Child Development (a committee of the Division of Anthropology and Psychology of the National Research Council, as explained by Alice Smuts, in this vol.) not only was largely responsible for the formation of the society but also for many years functioned almost as an equal. At the first meeting of the society (proceeding of the first biennial meeting, November 3–4, 1934, p. 8), Robert S. Woodworth, who was then chairman of both the committee and the society, told the members, "The National Research Council is the fostering mother of the infant which is here taking its first steps; but, as a well-adjusted modern mother, she is not disposed to keep her child dependent but is ready and willing to see that infant walk alone." Five years later (June 5, 1934) he wrote, "We can give the Society one more year in which to consolidate its position." But as shown, the Second World War intervened, and it was not until 1948 that the infant society found itself able to walk alone.

No history of the Society would be complete without a consideration of the committee's contribution. In the first place, all members of the committee were members of the society, and they and the governing council of the society held many joint meetings. Then, beyond advice and benevolent support, the committee provided concrete support. It financially supported the *Abstracts,* which it had begun in 1927, until 1936. During those years its parent, the National Research Council, provided office space for the editing and publishing of the *Abstracts, Child Development,* and the *Monographs.* There the copy was typed for planographing, the journals mailed, membership lists kept, and monies collected and disbursed. For many years the publications carried the imprint of both the society and the National Research Council, and even as late as 1944 Woodworth labeled his yearly report as from the Committee on Child Development and its "affiliated" Society for Research in Child Development.

When Sears replaced Woodworth as chairman of the committee, he wrote to the members (December 2, 1948), "The National Research Council will continue to have a warm and active interest in the activities of its Society offspring but it feels the time has come for the youngster to get on his own feet."

Alfred H. Washburn (1950, p. 61), in his presidential address at the 1949 meeting in New York, paid tribute to the National Research Council in these words:

> This meeting in New York, December 1949, is also an historic occasion. It is the first meeting of this group as a completely autonomous Society—now, after 15 years, our Foster Mother has sent us out into the world to fend for ourselves. The debt which this Society owes to her Foster Mother, the National Research Council, is tremendous even if, like many another adolescent, she does not always exhibit her awareness of it. It seems fitting, as we take part in starting this Society on a long and useful independent career, that the retiring President should pay tribute to the wisdom, the foresight, and the very tangible assistance bestowed upon our Society during its childhood from the National Research Council through the Committee on Child Development in its Division of Anthropology and Psychology.

I have tried to do justice to the committee's, and thus the National Research Council's, support of the society and the vital role it played in the founding and nurturing of the society. I had not known of it and was deeply moved by Woodworth's devotion.

THE NATURE AND FUNCTIONS OF THE SOCIETY

Two main themes may be abstracted from the records concerning the nature and the function of the society: how to become interdisciplinary and how to ensure that knowledge about the development of children would be translated into practice for the benefit of society.

From its inception, the members recognized that child development demanded the knowledge of many disciplines, and year by year at their meetings and in their publications they wrestled with how to effect the desired integration. Should each different discipline present its findings on its research with children, or should several disciplines contribute their findings to a common problem? The programs of the meetings provide insight into how the society strove mightily to honor its avowed commitment to the interdisciplinary nature of research in child development.

At the first meeting in 1934, one of the two symposiums was devoted to the control of dental caries and the other to prenatal and neonatal development. In addition, each of 10 disciplines held separate and concurrent meetings. The disciplines were labeled "fields" and in alphabetical order ran from anatomy and anthropometry to sociology. Yet at that meeting Frank N. Freeman urged that the members not conceive of themselves as "a mere collection of specialists," that the primary purpose of the society should be to bring about "a functional relationship" between their activities, techniques, and thinking. He went on, "I am inclined to take the position . . . that there is at least potentially a field of research which we may call child development" (proceedings of the first biennial meeting, November 3–4, 1934, pp. 137, 138). (Present members, please take note of this prediction.) He also called for programs at meetings that would facilitate a common consideration of issues in child development. Other members echoed his call that future meetings be communal, and it was so moved.

At the next biennial meeting in 1936, nine communal symposiums were devoted to such general topics as the child's environment and the organism as a whole, but once again the field committees met separately, although now reduced to six: adjustment and personality, mental growth, and training and education, combined; community health; dentistry; nutrition; physiology and endocrinology; and social and cultural environment. It was at that business meeting (proceedings of the second biennial meeting, October 30, 31, and November 1, 1936) that Harold C. Stuart said,

> It is to the advantage of all that these lines of distinction be obliterated insofar as possible during the sessions of the Society. The unique opportunity which these meetings afford is to meet and associate with members of other disciplines. Section meetings interfere with the desirable ends and differ little from ordinary society meetings. They do not offer any particular opportunity either to members of the discipline concerned or to other groups. It is therefore proposed that such meetings be discontinued, and that ample time be provided on all programs for informal discussions between members from different fields. It is further proposed that in place of sections each discipline within the Society be represented by a committee.

Although field committees still existed, they held no separate meetings at the next biennial meeting in 1938. And so the program veered between more strictly disciplinary and more general interdisciplinary topics through the 1940 meeting.

Finally, in 1940 the governing council decided to discharge the present field committees but then set up still another series of field committees, now reduced to physical environment and nutrition, cultural environment and education, anatomical and physiological problems, mental and emotional problems, and developmental periods. A year later, Woodworth noted in his April 26, 1941, report to the National Research Council that "fostering the integration of the different scientific approaches to child development has not yet been fully solved." I should say so! When meetings were resumed after the war, field committees survived until 1950 but only in the masthead of the *Abstracts.*

The commitment to an integrated approach continued to exercise the society. At the 1946 biennial meeting, Florence Goodenough, chairman of the society (at that meeting, the title was changed to president as "more dignified"), spoke of the unique contribution an interdisciplinary group such as the society could make and of the importance of recognizing that children, as well as other human beings, were well-integrated organisms functioning as wholes. A similar note was struck by Alfred H. Washburn (1950) in his presidential address in 1949 in which he urged bending every effort to make the society "so happy and so fruitful a common meeting point that it may serve to foster constant cross-fertilizing between many different disciplines" (p. 63). The theme of interdisciplinary research was considered at length by Dale B. Harris (1953) in his thoughtful and searching address at the 1953 meeting entitled "Why an Interdisciplinary Society for Research in Child Development." He said that the interdisciplinary idea was certainly not dead but that we needed to achieve more integration in concerted attacks on common problems. He admitted, however, to the sense of helplessness that seems to come with broad gauge, interdisciplinary effort. Then, at the 1955 biennial meeting, in the interests of revitalizing the society and making it more adequately meet the needs of its members, the governing council charged Icie Macy Hoobler, chairman of the program committee for the 1957 biennial meeting, with selecting members from different disciplines to ensure an interdisciplinary flavor to the program.

From the records I gather a strong urge to have many common events on the program, not only to hold the membership together, but also to have them treat broad topics, interdisciplinary in nature when possible, that would stimulate thought as well as research. This theme still vexes us today. The capturing of the society by any one discipline, and specifically by psychology, was recognized very early as a threat to its original design, and as we know, the recognition still continues. We do now have an interdisciplinary affairs committee, and as recently as 1979 the lead article of the society's winter *Newsletter* was titled "Forum on Interdisciplinary Issues."

The second main theme was the endeavor to be useful to society in general and to children in particular. At the first biennial meeting in 1934, during a discussion of the purpose of the society as set forth in the constitution, George T. Palmer moved that the purpose include not only the furthering of research but also its application, and the amendment was accepted. To this day, the constitution of the society includes almost the same phrasing of its purpose.

At the 1940 meeting, the governing council considered the committee's and the society's participation in the National Defense Program, proclaimed by President Roosevelt in 1939. They discussed how they could contribute to problems of human conservation, possibly by offering their services to various governmental agencies, possibly by obtaining reviews of research at the leading child development centers. Woodworth, in his report of April 26, 1941, to the National Research Council, expanded on the matter, saying that, with regard to the emergency (there was such, months before Pearl Harbor), fitness of the juvenile population was one of the goals of a national defense program, " 'fitness' to be taken in a very inclusive sense." A few months later, in November, the committee, at the request of the society, held a conference on the emergency problems of children and youths, attended by representatives of governmental bureaus and agencies and members of the committee and the society. The conference recommended that a full-time executive secretary be established in Washington and that permission be obtained from the National Research Council to solicit funds from foundations for the secretary's salary and expenses. Unfortunately, the funds were never found and the office never established, although in 1943 the committee sponsored a conference on war and postwar child services and research.

It was at the 1946 meeting that a member of the governing council said, "We need to think of ourselves . . . as an organization which has a large and growing responsibility to translate new knowledge . . . into professional practices and living habits generally." The test, or a test of a kind, came up at the same meeting over the question of the society's publishing *A Psychology for Parents*. The proposal had originally been made to the committee by Edwin G. Boring, and the committee turned it over to the society. Boring had envisioned a 25-cent paperbound popular book like the successful *Psychology for the Fighting Man* (1943) and *Psychology for the Returning Serviceman* (Child & Van de Water, 1945), for both of which he had assumed a measure of responsibility. A special committee was appointed to consider the proposal. Except for some rough unofficial notes of debate on the topic, including a straw vote of 17 members of the council, no further mention of the proposal was found.

In 1949, when Richards assumed the editorship of *Child Development*, he expressed his opinions on policy pertaining to its publication (Richards, 1949, p. 3). He said that articles in *Child Development* should be of interest to a wide variety of disciplines, be interdisciplinary in nature, should study the child as an integrated individual with emphasis particularly on development, and, last, be "particularly significant in the light of the broad problems of the world today. It is the function of publication to bring research out of the laboratory and ivory tower . . . to reach not only scientists, but also the larger public which needs to know . . . the continuous contribution of research." Thus did he set a policy to incorporate both themes—research to be interdisciplinary as well as useful.

These two main themes aside, many others surfaced from time to time. One was the use of statistics. Larry K. Frank proposed in 1936 that a general theme at a meeting should be "Individuality as Revealed through Child Development." He complained that so many studies were directed to uniformities and central tendencies that individual variation was regarded as a scientific nuisance to be overcome by statistical analysis. Almost 50 years later, we still hear the same complaint based on the misunderstanding of statistics as the study of variation. Even earlier, at the first biennial meeting, disaffection with the use of correlation and factor analysis was strongly voiced, one member stating that any more elaborate statistical methods other than correlations were merely a form of paranoia. But Helen Koch protested that one should "not place at the feet of statistics all the difficulties that arise through limitations of human intellect" (Society for Research in Child Development, 1934NP, p. 136).

Another recurrent theme was the plea to study the child as a whole. In 1933 Charles B. Davenport wrote to Woodworth, "The child develops as a whole. It is not advantageous to consider separately his physical development, mental development, physiological development, instincts, speech, walking, etc." But 20 years later, Dale Harris in his 1953 address said, "Most of us agree that one cannot really attend to the whole child—he eludes you. . . . we recognize that we cannot attain scientific excellence as an expert on the whole child."

Concerns about longitudinal studies also arose early: witness the society's committee on long-term growth studies. Now and again members would propose that the term "human" be substituted for "child" in the name of the society and that our studies should go beyond childhood to encompass all stages of life, echoing Davenport's 1933 recommendation that the word "child" should be used in a very large sense.

All these are enduring concerns, as fresh today as they were 50 years ago.

MEETINGS OF THE SOCIETY

From its inception, the society decided to hold national meetings every 2 years, beginning with its first in 1934 at the National Research Council. It followed this plan, meeting again at the National Research Council in 1936, at the University of Chicago in 1938, and at the Harvard Medical School in 1940. Because of restrictions on travel during the war, no meetings were held in 1942 and 1944. The next biennial meeting was held in St. Louis in 1946, but so precarious were the financial affairs of the society, so pressing the problems of maintaining the journals, that, except for relatively small meetings held in conjunction with the American Association for the Advancement of Science, the next regular biennial meeting did not take place until 1953 at Yellow Springs, Ohio. Thereafter the schedule was maintained with regular meetings in 1955 at the University of Illinois, in 1957 at the University of Iowa, and in 1959, the twenty-fifth anniversary meeting, at the National Institutes of Health in Bethesda, Maryland.

When the society could not meet as a whole, the committee and the governing council of the society corresponded with each other, kept the members apprised of the state of affairs, and elected members and officers by mail. One meeting of the governing council and the committee deserves special attention. Originally, I was perplexed to find that in 1943 the council met on March 19 in Chicago and on March 20 in Washington. How was that possible? Reading farther on, I discovered that John E. Anderson, then chairman of the society, traveled by train from Minnesota to Chicago, met on March 19 with Helen Koch, Lydia Roberts, Beth Wellman, directors of the society, and Mandel Sherman of the committee (at Koch's apartment, to save money). Anderson spent the night on the train to Washington and the next morning met there with the other members of the council and the committee. Thus did the officers of the society manage to conform to the nation's demand to restrict travel and at the same time to conserve the society's funds—but not Anderson. Aside from routine business, they considered methods of recording the effect of the war on children, with special reference to the relief and rehabilitation efforts then being carried out for children abroad. Such devotion to the affairs of the society deserves special recognition, and I was filled with admiration for Anderson.

THE PUBLICATIONS OF THE SOCIETY

When the society was organized in 1933, *Child Development Abstracts and Bibliography* had been published since 1927 by the Committee on Child Development under the editorship of Leslie Ray Marston. The journal, *Child Development,* had been published since 1930 by Williams and Wilkins under the editorship of Buford Johnson, professor of psychology at Johns Hopkins University, and the *Monographs of the Society for Research in Child Development* did not exist. How did the society acquire these publications?

As for the *Abstracts,* the committee proposed that it become a joint project of the new society. But from the first biennial meeting in 1934, the *Abstracts* came under attack, and it was proposed that it be replaced by *Proceedings* that would report news of the society. The members, however, protested that the *Abstracts* were of "real value as a research aid" and declared that they were willing to add a dollar or two to their dues to maintain it. Printing the *Abstracts* always proved costly, and from time to time its demise was considered but always rejected by the members.

When Williams and Wilkins decided not to continue publishing *Child Development* after 1935, the society took it over in 1936 and published it jointly with the Committee on Child Development, still under the editorship of Buford Johnson. In that same year, the governing council and the committee decided to inaugurate a series of monographs to be funded (but only until 1938) by a grant of $5,000 from the General Education Fund.

Thus by 1936 the society had acquired the three journals of our present mature society. Now I will briefly trace their separate histories until 1959.

Child Development Abstracts and Bibliography

In 1936, listed as a publication of the society, the *Abstracts* were published six times a year, in planograph form, by the National Research Council under the editorship of Carroll E. Palmer and a board of seven members. The contents (I give details here to illustrate changes in how the field was conceptualized) were arranged by the following headings: anatomy and physical growth; physiology and biochemistry (including endocrine functions and metabolism); nutrition and diet; physical health and disease (including mortality); heredity, eugenics, and evolution (including sex and race differences); mental development and behavior (including habit and learning); intelligence (including mental deficiency); personality (including character and emotional states); special abilities and disabilities; social and economic (including family); mental hygiene and psychiatry (including delinquency and crime); education (including preschool and vocational); and tests and measurements. I found interesting the following statement at the bottom of the title page: "The Chairman will appreciate your cooperation in keeping the editorial office in touch with any new research with which you are in contact."

From 1938 through 1940 Harold Blumberg (biochemist, Johns Hopkins School of Hygiene and Public Health) was the editor, and in 1941 he was replaced by Antonio Ciocco (biometrician, United States Public Health Service). In 1942 Ciocco reduced the 13 headings to nine more general headings: morphology (anatomy, embryology, anthropometry, and somatic constitution); physiology and biochemistry (growth, endocrines, hormones, nutrition, and vitamins); clinical medicine and pathology (dentistry, immunology, and diagnostic tests); psychology (behavior, intelligence, learning, and personality); psychiatry and mental hygiene (crime and delinquency); public health and hygiene (epidemiology, morbidity, and mortality); human biology and demography (genetics, natality and fertility, population, and race and sex differences); education (class curriculum and vocational guidance); and sociology and economics (laws, family, marriage, and divorce). In 1948 Isidore Altman (statistician, United States Public Health Service) took over the editorship. In 1949 the National Research Council's assistance ceased, and the *Abstracts* were published by the society in cooperation with the Children's Bureau (and printed instead of planographed). This arrangement ended in 1953 when the society became solely responsible for the *Abstracts,* first under the editorship of T. W. Richards and then under that of William E. Martin. Martin then reconstituted the system of volunteer abstractors that had broken down and dropped the request that subscribers keep the editor informed of any new research with which they were in contact.

The last volume covered by this history, that is, the one for 1959, contained 773 abstracts of articles (listed under the same nine headings first adopted in 1942), and 21 journals were searched (albeit some were journals of abstracts). In contrast, the 1982 volume contained 2,337 references, now arranged by six still more general categories, and 209 periodicals were regularly searched.

Child Development

Published quarterly, this journal was also planographed in the National Research Council office after it became a publication of the society. During the first 4 years, the number of articles hovered around 30, except for an increase to 43 in 1937, a number not again approached until 1957. Shortly after Carroll E. Palmer became chairman of the editorial board (which contained six other members) in 1938, the number of articles declined slowly, hovering around 20, fell to nine in 1944, and then increased very gradually year by year until the end of Palmer's editorship in 1948. Then, under the editorship of Richards and later of Martin, the year-by-year increase continued to be slow, even though the 1948 volume contained 10 papers from a conference on the dissemination of knowledge about child development and the 1950 volume contained papers read at two symposiums of the 1949 biennial as well as Washburn's presidential address, the minutes of the business meeting, and the new constitution of the society.

By 1959, the last year covered in this account, the volume under the editorship of William E. Martin and a board of 10 consulting editors contained 50 research reports, totaling 554 pages. For contrast, let us consider the 1982 volume of *Child Development.* Now published six times a year, it contained 160 articles for a total of 1,634 pages, with one editor, as many as six associate editors, an editorial board of at least 120 persons, and more than 150 different ad hoc reviewers for each of the six numbers.

Monographs of the Society for Research in Child Development

The monograph series was planned for the publishing of longitudinal and especially multidisciplinary studies because, it was explained, "they do not readily fit into the existing single-discipline publications" (Palmer's memo to subscribers, January 20, 1936). Funded for the first 3 years by a grant of $5,000 from the General Education Fund, the series, under the editorship of John E. Anderson, was to contain 400 pages in each annual volume, to be divided into as many numbers as these pages would cover. The first in the series was Nancy Bayley's "The Development of Motor Abilities during the First Three Years." It was planographed, so 1,500 copies cost only $100. Carroll Palmer advised liberal free distribution for advertising purposes, and to that end he sent complimentary copies of the *Monograph* to all subscribers to *Child Development.*

A year later, Palmer would report that two *Monographs* had been issued, three were in press, and two more in process. After this valiant start, the number of *Monographs* decreased gradually. During the war years and for many years thereafter, the usual number was two, with only one in 1951. In 1959 there were, however, five. Lester W. Sontag became the editor in 1938 and continued until 1953, when first T. W. Richards and then William E. Martin assumed the post.

Now to chart our growth, let me go to the 1982 volume: it contained six *Monographs,* with one editor, one editorial associate, two editorial assistants, and 44 consulting editors.

TRIBUTES

Many persons deserve special recognition for their efforts to maintain the society during those 25 years. Among these, Robert S. Woodworth, Carroll E. Palmer, and Beulah Brewer especially stand out.

Robert S. Woodworth was often called the dean of American psychology. He taught at Columbia from 1909 to 1942, conducted basic and applied research, wrote journal articles and textbooks that went through many editions, and responded to his country's needs in many ways. He was a genial and generous person. Alice Smuts (in this vol.) has detailed his role in the society's birth, but as I have already shown, as chairman of the National Research Council's Committee on Child Development he nurtured the society for 15 years. When he retired from Columbia in 1942 at the age of 73, he also sought to relinquish his chairmanship of the committee. The times could not permit it, and he continued until 1948, at which time he was 79 years old. Parenthetically, 10 years later, when he was 89 years old, he went on to publish what I consider his best textbook, *Dynamics of Behavior* (1958). A warm appreciation of children shines through his textbooks, as it did in his work for the society. He appreciated not only children but the young in general, as this letter to Brewer after the 1940 meeting shows: "The next biennial might be planned to favor attendance by the younger members. The meeting might be held where accommodations would be cheap, and opportunity might be provided for a large number to have their say." Of him, John E. Anderson wrote, "He is the strong silent man of our history, a man famous enough outside our field, who was for us over many years a real father figure" (1956, p. 188).

Palmer was secretary-treasurer and chairman of the publications committee for 12 years, from 1936 through 1948, until the break with the National Research Council and the editorship of Richards. Palmer was a biostatistician at the Johns Hopkins School of Hygiene and Public Health, director of research of the Child Hygiene Office, surgeon in the United States Public Health Service, and in 1948 senior surgeon in the Office of Field Studies of the Tuberculosis Control Division—a very busy man indeed. It was he who was most directly concerned with overseeing the publications and the work of the National Research Council office. In 1944, in the midst of the war, when the society's foundations were still very shaky, he wrote, "We have kept going, and we do have the basic elements of a useful organization still intact. Having been intimately concerned with the vital matters of merely surviving during the war, I am not inclined to depreciate the fact that we do still exist. Perhaps this is all we can expect now—but after the war we must do better to justify our existence. . . . We have a fair membership, we have three publications . . . we have meetings—I hope we have the leadership—all the basic elements for a strong association" (R. S. Woodworth, report of the Committee on Child Development, April 22, 1944). In fact, it is fair to say that for actual work Brewer and Palmer kept the publications going, as has been said, "by sheer will"—manuscripts and money they had not.

Of the three, Beulah Brewer is the least well-known and was probably the hardest worker day by day. Although her title was only editorial assistant, she managed the whole National Research Council office devoted to the work of the committee and the society. Not only did she edit all the copy for the publications, type it or have it typed for planographing, maintain the membership and subscription lists, and mail the journals, but she also kept minutes of the work of both the committee and the society whose meetings she arranged, handled the correspondence, and, mirabile dictu, preserved the records for our use. Through them I came to know Brewer well. Some of her travails during the war years (and of course those of the society) are illustrated in the following letters:

On March 23, 1944, she wrote to Woodworth:

It has been a terrific strain the past year to keep up the publication work—personnel difficulties being our worse problem. But we have been busy every minute—apparently there is still a strong need for *Child Development*—we have lost very few of our subscriptions, and we even follow around certain members of the armed forces who are constantly going from one post to another but who always send in their new address. All this means extra work, but we have managed to do it. . . . To add to my troubles, the Council seems to be constantly making more room for different defense agencies, and my steel cases in the basement which hold various publications have had to be moved. So at the present moment it is difficult to see me for the file publications which surround me! However, our skies are still free from intruders and no bombs are in evidence, so we should be very humble and grateful for being so safe.

Two years later, Brewer was more sorely tried. In May of 1946 she wrote to Palmer, "When I think that it is almost June and not a single publication has appeared for the year 1946 (except the late 1945 journals, CD and CDA and *no* monographs) I feel like hiding my head in the sand! And the complaining and sarcastic comments we receive about publications not appearing nearly drive me mad. Let's do *something;* OR GO OUT OF BUSINESS! WE CAN'T CONTINUE TO ACCEPT MONEY AND NOT GIVE ANYTHING IN RETURN."

Beulah Brewer died suddenly late in 1947. With her passing a new structuring was required. Robert Sears replaced Woodworth as chairman of the committee, a new committee on publications was formed, the tie to the National Research Council was dissolved, and the society at last achieved independence. Although nowhere did I find an acknowledgment of her death in precipitating these events, I so believe. A great lady indeed!

CONCLUSION

I have restricted this account to the society and its development, while recognizing that the records also constitute a rich lode of material on the conceptual development of our science, as revealed especially in the programs of the meetings, but also in the contents of the journals, as recently mined by Charles M. Super (1982). I found myself caught up in the affairs of the society in a way I would not have imagined possible. Although I did not become a member until late in the period I have covered, I knew of the people, knew the literature, and knew firsthand the problems of living through the depression years in which the society was formed and the war years in which it almost foundered. I was deeply moved by the many letters of members and officers that showed so much concern not only for the society but also for each other, for their demanding schedules, and, yes, for their comfort and peace of mind. Still, I cannot claim to have done my subject full justice. Fortunately, there are in the society those who can round out the account from personal knowledge.

APPENDIX: THE SOCIETY FOR RESEARCH IN CHILD DEVELOPMENT COMMITTEE ON PRESERVATION OF HISTORICAL MATERIALS IN CHILD DEVELOPMENT, 1977–1983

ROBERT R. SEARS

Stanford University

HAMILTON CRAVENS

Iowa State University

The establishment of the Committee on Preservation of Historical Materials was the first major effort by the Society for Research in Child Development (SRCD) to encourage historical research. In March 1977, Alice Smuts, the society's only historian member, reported to the governing council on the precarious state of the primary source materials for the history of the field of child development (Smuts, 1977). Some already had been lost or destroyed; most were in jeopardy. Pointing out the importance of these sources as a basis for the reconstruction of the history of the field, Smuts urged the council to appoint a committee to locate and preserve the papers of individuals and organizations that had been influential in the founding and early growth of the field. The council responded promptly, appointing a committee composed of Dale Harris, Philip Sapir, Alice Smuts, and Robert Sears (chair).

At the first meeting of the committee, in September 1977, Smuts proposed and other members agreed that the first step should be to hold a conference of historians and archivists for the purpose of securing advice. The William T. Grant Foundation provided financial support for the 2-day conference held in New York in January 1978. It proved to be most worthwhile. The 18 historians and archivists who attended thought that the preservation project proposed by the committee was both important and feasible. They helped the committee set priorities, educated it about procedures, recommended the employment of a part-time archivist, and suggested possible sources of funding. Three of the conference participants agreed to serve as a board of advisers to the committee: Robert Warner (University of Michigan), Joan Warnow (American Institute of Physics), and Manfred Waserman (National Library of Medicine). Herbert Finch (Cornell University) replaced Warner when he was appointed archivist of the United States. Lynn Bonfield was employed as part-time archivist early in 1979.

With additional support from the Grant Foundation, we conducted a pilot study during 1978–1979 to test the feasibility of the committee's plans to recover papers of early leaders, many of whom had died. The study quickly revealed the complexities of our task. Only a few developmentalists had deposited their papers in reputable repositories. Most collections of individuals were in boxes in university departments or in private homes or had disappeared. Many records of organizations had been lost, were in storage in warehouses or basements, or, at best, were unprocessed and unavailable to scholars. Indeed, SRCD's own records were stored in a Chicago warehouse.

Some foundations, child development research institutes, and child guidance clinics were cordial to the idea of preserving and processing their records; a few, such as the Judge Baker Foundation and the Commonwealth Fund, proceeded to do so with help and suggestions from members of the committee. Early leaders and family members of leaders who had died were friendly but slow to respond to requests for information. Our discovery that some families had disposed of significant papers because they did not recognize their value or did not know what to do with them convinced us of the importance and urgency of our task. We decided to seek funds for a full-scale, 3-year program to search for and preserve the papers of individuals who had been important to the establishment of the scientific study of children from around 1880, when developmental research began, until World War II.

With substantial help from the archivists on our advisory board, the committee drafted a proposal for submission to the National Historical Publications and Records Commission for financial support for a part-time archivist and modest secretarial help. The commission responded favorably. Lynn Bonfield agreed to continue as archivist, and Arthur Parmelee joined the committee in 1979 and Hoben Thomas and Hamilton Cravens in 1980. The committee won an additional grant from the History and Philosophy of Science Program of the National Science Foundation to cover the cost of travel to archives and libraries, particularly to those that already possessed important child development collections. Archivists and historians at the 1978 conference had stressed the importance of communicating to the directors and staff of these institutions the committee's purpose and securing their active participation in the search for important collections and in negotiations for their transferral to a reputable repository.

With the assistance of professional colleagues, the committee prepared a list of about 200 individuals and 50 organizations that had contributed significantly to the field of child development from 1880 through World War II. It determined that phase 1 of the committee's task should be the recovery of the papers of individuals and organizations. Phase 2 would emphasize education rather than the search for sources and would focus on arousing the interest of contemporary senior developmentalists in the preservation of their own papers and those of the organizations with which they are affiliated.

PHASE 1

Assuming that the records of organizations were less likely than those of individuals to be dispersed adventitiously, our initial efforts focused on the search for papers of individuals. The archivist was responsible for locating these papers. Committee members, with the aid of many colleagues, provided her with information about individuals' institutional and family connections to enable her to inquire about collections not already preserved and identified in standard listings. Locating these papers and negotiating for their eventual preservation was a task that was often protracted. The archivist also met with librarians and archivists to educate them about the field of child development, to discuss the committee's program, and to encourage them to locate and secure for their own organizations significant child development collections. During the first 2 years of the project these educational efforts proved to be the most successful and have had longlasting consequences. Thus the editors of the National Union Catalog of Manuscript Collections agreed to add the heading "child development" to their indexing system. Another coup, in large part engineered by the committee, was arranging the successful transfer of valuable historical materials in the Merrill-Palmer Library to Wayne State University at the time of Merrill-Palmer's dissolution.

We cannot emphasize too strongly that the program proceeded very slowly during the first 2 years. Many developmentalists or their descendants did not understand the historical importance of their papers; many did not even understand what we meant by papers. Some assumed that we meant publications rather than correspondence, memorandums, and other manuscript materials. The need for education was apparent, and our more recent experience with phase 2 of the program demonstrates that education is a continuing need. The first 2 years were extremely useful in laying the groundwork with potential donors and in opening up many lines of communication with living developmentalists, with families or colleagues of dead ones, and with the staff of repositories where collections might be deposited. The importance of this last task cannot be overemphasized because it was indispensable to wrapping up phase 1 in the project's third year.

In 1982 Sears asked to be replaced as chair, and Hamilton Cravens took over the responsibility. A new archivist, Linda Heath Curry, was employed to work under his supervision. Cravens and Curry drew up biographical charts for each pending target, contacted every institution where there was a significant connection, and continued the search for missing papers through relatives, colleagues, and friends. Not all these efforts were successful, but part of their purpose was to guarantee that these steps need never be retraced. The records of this search are in the committee's own archive.

The committee met in January 1983 at the Hoover Institution, Stanford University, as guests of the Hanna Collection and its curator, Gerald A. Dorfman. At this meeting, Curry and Cravens reported on the disposition of all pending cases. Of the 209 individual targets, most had been successfully followed to one degree of completeness or another. Only eight appeared to be complete dead ends. In September 1983 the score was (1) papers preserved independent of committee efforts—41; (2) papers secured by SRCD, arrangements completed—77; (3) negotiations pending between donors and archives—28; (4) papers located but negotiations incomplete—55; and (5) dead ends, papers missing—8. We hope and expect that the majority of papers in the fourth category will eventually be placed in reputable depositories.

The committee published its findings in a listing in a special section of *Child Development Abstracts and Bibliography* ("Archives," 1984). The listing, in the form customary for the National Union Catalog of Manuscript Collections, contains a description of the papers of early developmentalists and of their location, including both the collections the committee helped to secure and those placed in repositories prior to or independent of the committee's efforts. Collections deposited but not yet processed and available to scholars were not listed.

During our 6 years of work, we discovered that the situation with respect to institutions was similar to that for individuals. The Rockefeller Foundation has an excellent archive, but 38 other institutions belong, at this point, to our category 3 (pending), and eight appear to be dead ends (category 5). The committee hopes to publish additional lists in the future that will include the papers of institutions as well as of individuals.

PHASE 2

The committee's second purpose was to arouse interest among senior researchers and clinicians in the preservation of their own papers. To further this educational effort, a brochure was prepared by archivist Curry that provided advice on preservation and deposit, including descriptions of the kinds of materials that developmentalists should keep and instruction on how to care for these materials until ready for deposit. At the 1983 anniversary meeting of SRCD, as part of the historical program, Cravens chaired a special breakfast meeting attended by about 70 senior developmentalists at which the work of the committee was described and plans for future work discussed. In 1984, the History and Philosophy of Science Program of the National Science Foundation gave the committee an additional small grant for phase 2.

Full records of the committee's work to 1983 are on file in the first author's papers in the Department of Special Collections, Stanford University Library; the nearly 2 feet of documents provide the necessary minutiae for a more careful study of what we did and how we did it.

Members of the committee during the 6 years were Hamilton Cravens, professor of history, Iowa State University (1980–1983, chair, 1982–1983); Dale B. Harris, emeritus professor of psychology, Pennsylvania State University (1977–1985); Marjorie Honzik, research psychologist, University of California, Berkeley (1981–1985); Arthur H. Parmelee, professor of pediatrics, University of California, Los Angeles (1979–1982); Philip Sapir, president, William T. Grant Foundation (1977–1982); Robert R. Sears, emeritus professor of psychology, Stanford University (1977–1983, chair, 1978–1982); Alice Smuts, historian, Bush Program in Child Development and Social Policy, University of Michigan (1977–1983); and Hoben Thomas, professor of psychology, Pennsylvania State University (1980–). The professional archivists were Lynn Bonfield, San Francisco (1979–1982), and Linda Curry, Santa Rosa (1982–1984). Members of the advisory board were Herbert Finch, archivist, Cornell University; Robert Warner, director, Bentley Historical Library, University of Michigan; Joan Warnow, director of archives, American Institute of Physics; and Manfred Waserman, curator of modern manuscripts, History of Medicine Division, National Library of Medicine.

REFERENCES

I. PUBLISHED SOURCES

Abbott, G. (1923). Ten years' work for children. *North Amerian Review,* **218,** 189–200.

Ainsworth, M. D., Anders, T. F., Caldwell, B. M., Hetherington, E. M., & Kennell, J. H. (1979, Winter). Forum on interdisciplinary issues. *Society for Research in Child Development Newsletter,* pp. 1–4.

Ambidexterity: Its possibility and advisability [Review of Dextrality and sinistrality, by G. M. Gould]. (1904). *Westminster Review,* **162,** 649–664.

American Psychiatric Association. (1980). *Diagnostic and statistical manual of mental disorders* (3d ed.). Washington, DC: American Psychiatric Association.

Anderson, J. E. (1936). *The young child in the home* (1929–1930 White House Conference on Child Health and Protection, Sec. 3, Education and Training Committee on the Infant and Preschool Child). New York and London: Appleton-Century.

Anderson, J. E. (1956). Child development: An historical perspective. *Child Development,* **27,** 181–196.

Anderson, M. (1971). *Family structure in nineteenth-century Lancashire.* Cambridge: Cambridge University Press.

Anderson, V. E., & McDonnell, P. M. (1979, June). *The sinister infant: Unexpected laterality at three to eight weeks.* Paper presented at the meeting of the Canadian Psychological Association, Quebec.

Archives. (1984). *Child Development Abstracts and Bibliography,* **58**(1), 123–141.

Ariès, P. (1962). *Centuries of childhood: A social history of family life* (R. Baldick, Trans.). New York: Vintage.

Ashton, R. (Ed.). (1851). *The works of John Robinson* (Vol. 1).

Auwers, L. (1980). Reading the marks of Connecticut. *Historical Methods,* **4,** 204–214.

Axtell, J. (1974). *The school upon a hill: Education and society in colonial New England.* New Haven, CT: Yale University Press.

Baldwin, J. M. (1889–1891). *Handbook of psychology* (Vols. **1–2**). New York: Henry Holt.

Baldwin, J. M. (1890a). Origin of right or left handedness. *Science,* **16,** 247–248.

Baldwin, J. M. (1890b). Right-handedness and effort. *Science,* **16,** 302–303.

Baldwin, J. M. (1894). The origin of right-handedness. *Popular Science Monthly,* **44,** 606–615.

Baldwin, J. M. (1895). *Mental development in the child and the race* (1st ed.). New York: Macmillan. (2d ed., 1900; 3d ed., 1906)

Baldwin, J. M. (1896). A new factor in evolution. *American Naturalist,* **30,** 441–451; 536–553.

Baldwin, J. M. (1897). Color perception in children. *American Journal of Psychology,* **9,** 61–62.

Baldwin, J. M. (1926). *Between two wars, 1861–1921, being memories, opinions and letters received* (Vols. **1–2**). Boston: Stratford.

Baltes, P. (1979). *Life-span developmental psychology: Some converging observations on history and theory* (Vol. **2** of P. Baltes & O. Brim, Jr. [Eds.], *Life-span development and behavior*). New York: Academic Press.

Bardeleben, K. von. (1909). Ueber bilaterale Asymmetrie beim Menschen und bei hoheren Tieren. *Anatomischer Anzeiger Centralblatt für die Gesamte Wissenschaftliche Anatomie.* Jena: Gustav Fischer.

Bay Area Association of Black Psychologists. (1972). Position statement on use of IQ and ability tests. In R. L. Jones (Ed.), *Black psychology* (pp. 92–94). New York: Harper & Row.

Bayton, J. A. (1975). Francis Sumner, Max Meenes, and the training of the black psychologists. *American Psychologist, **30**,* 185–186.

Beck, C. H. M., & Barton, R. L. (1972). Deviation and laterality of hand preference in monkeys. *Cortex, **8**,* 339–363.

Beeley, A. L. (1919). Left-handedness. *American Journal of Physical Anthropology, **2**,* 389–400.

Bell, R. (1985). *Holy anorexia.* Chicago: University of Chicago Press.

Bellugi, U., Poizner, H., & Klima, E. S. (1983). Brain organization for language: Clues from sign aphasia. *Human Neurobiology, **2**,* 155–170.

Berkner, L. K. (1972). The stem family and the developmental cycle of the peasant household: An eighteenth-century Austrian example. *American Historical Review, **77**,* 398–418.

Better Times. (1920a). **1**(January).

Better Times. (1920b). **1**(December).

Bloom, B. S. (1964). *Stability and change in human characteristics.* New York: Wiley.

Blumin, S. (1977). Rip Van Winkle's grandchildren: Family and household in the Hudson Valley, 1800–1860. In T. K. Hareven (Ed.), *Family and kin in urban communities, 1700–1930* (pp. 100–121). New York: New Viewpoints.

Bolton, T. L. (1895). [Review of *Mental development in the child and the race* (1st ed., 1895), by J. M. Baldwin]. *American Journal of Psychology, **7**,* 142–145.

Bond, H. M. (1924). Intelligence tests and propaganda. *Crisis, **28**,* 61–64.

Boring, E. G. (1957). *A history of experimental psychology.* New York: Appleton-Century-Crofts.

Bradbury, D. E., & Stoddard, G. E. (1933). *Pioneering in child welfare: A history of the Iowa Child Welfare Research Station, 1917–1933.* Iowa City: State University of Iowa Press.

Bremner, R. H. (1960). *American philanthropy.* Chicago: University of Chicago Press.

Bremner, R. H. (1983). Other people's children. *Journal of Social History, **16**(3),* 83–103.

Bremner, R. H. (Ed.). Barnard, J., Hareven, T. K., & Mennel, R. M. (Assoc. Eds.). (1971). *Children and youth in America: A documentary history: Vol. **2**. 1866–1932.* Cambridge, MA: Harvard University Press.

Brennemann, J. (1932). Psychological aspects of nutrition in childhood. *Journal of Pediatrics, **1**,* 145–171.

Bresson, F., Maury, L., Pieraut–le Bonniec, G., & de Schonen, S. (1977). Organization and lateralization of reaching in infants: An instance of asymmetric functions in hands collaboration. *Neuropsychologia, **15**,* 311–320.

Brewster, E. T. (1913, June). The ways of the left hand. *McClure's Magazine,* pp. 168–183.

Brigham, A. (1833). *Remarks on the influence of mental cultivation and mental excitement upon health* (2d ed.). Boston: Marsh, Capen & Lyon.

Brim, O., Jr. (1959). *Education for child rearing.* New York: Free Press.

Brisbane, R. H. (1974). *Black activism: Racial revolution in the United States, 1954–1970.* Valley Forge, PA: Judson.

REFERENCES

Brizzolara, D., de Nobili, G. L., & Ferretti, G. (1982). Tactile discrimination of direction of lines in relation to hemispheric specialization. *Perceptual and Motor Skills*, **54,** 655–660.

Broca, P. (1861). Remarques sur le siège de la faculté du langage articulé, suivies d'une observation d'aphémie (perte de la parole). *Bulletins de la Société Anatomique*, **6,** 330–357.

Broca, P. (1865). Sur le siège de la faculté de langage articulé. *Bulletins de la Société d'Anthropologie de Paris*, **6,** 377–393.

Broca, P. (1877). Recherches sur la circulation cérébrale. *Bulletin de l'Académie de Médecine*, **6**(2d Ser.), 508–539.

Bronfenbrenner, U., Kessel, F., Kessen, W., & White, S. (in press). Towards a critical social history of developmental psychology. *American Psychologist.*

Brooks, S. (1984). Diabetes mellitus and anorexia nervosa. *British Journal of Psychiatry*, **144,** 640–642.

Broughton, J. M. (1981). The genetic psychology of James Mark Baldwin. *American Psychologist*, **36,** 396–407.

Broughton, J. M., & Freeman-Moir, D. J. (Eds.). (1982). *The cognitive-developmental psychology of James Mark Baldwin.* Norwood, NJ: Ablex.

Bruch, H. (1973). *Eating disorders, obesity, anorexia nervosa and the person within.* New York: Basic.

Bruch, H. (1982). Anorexia nervosa: Therapy and theory. *American Journal of Psychiatry*, **139,** 1531–1538.

Brumberg, J. J. (1982). Chlorotic girls, 1870–1910: An historical perspective on female adolescence. *Child Development*, **53,** 1468–1474.

Brumberg, J. J. (1985). *Fasting girls: The emergence of anorexia nervosa.* Unpublished manuscript.

Bruner, J. S. (1969). Eye, hand, and mind. In D. Elkind & J. H. Flavell (Eds.), *Studies in cognitive development: Essays in honor of Jean Piaget* (pp. 223–235). New York: Oxford University Press.

Buchanan, A. (1862). Mechanical theory of the predominance of the right hand over the left, or, more generally, of the limbs of the right side over those of the left side of the body. *Proceedings of the Philosophical Society of Glasgow*, **5,** 142–167.

Burnham, J. C. (1968). The new psychology: From narcissism to social control. In J. Braeman, R. H. Bremner, & D. Brody (Eds.), *Change and continuity in twentieth century America: The 1920's* (pp. 351–398). Columbus: Ohio State University Press.

Buss, A. R. (1975). The emerging field of the sociology of psychological knowledge. *American Psychologist*, **30,** 988–1002.

Bynum, C. (1982). *Jesus as mother: Studies in the spirituality of the High Middle Ages.* Berkeley and Los Angeles: University of California Press.

Bynum, C. (1984). Women mystics and eucharistic devotion in the thirteenth century. *Women's Studies*, **2,** 179–213.

Cairns, R. B., & Ornstein, P. A. (1979). Developmental psychology. In E. Hearst (Ed.), *The first century of experimental psychology* (pp. 459–512). Hillsdale, NJ: Erlbaum.

Caplan, N., & Nelson, S. D. (1973). On being useful: The nature and consequences of psychological research on social problems. *American Psychologist*, **28,** 199–211.

Carlson, D. F., & Harris, L. J. (1985). Development of the infant's hand preference for visually-directed reaching: Preliminary report of a longitudinal study. *Infant Mental Health Journal*, **6,** 158–172.

Carrington, H. (1908). Left-handedness. *Annals of Psychical Science*, **7,** 494–502.

Cattell, R. B. (1929). Psychology in America. *Science*, **70,** 335–347.

Chambers, C. C. (1963). *Seedtime of reform: American social services in social action, 1918–1933.* Minneapolis: University of Minnesota Press.

Child Development Abstracts and Bibliography. (1927–1933). (Vols. **1–9**). Washington, DC: National Research Council.

Child, I. L., & Van de Water, M. (Eds.). (1945). *Psychology for the returning serviceman* (Prepared by a committee of the National Research Council). Washington, DC: Infantry Journal; Penguin Books.

Chudacoff, H., & Hareven, T. K. (1978). Family transitions and household structure in the later years of life. In T. K. Hareven (Ed.), *Transitions: The family and the life course in historical perspective* (pp. 217–243). New York: Academic Press.

Chudacoff, H., & Hareven, T. K. (1979). From the empty nest to family dissolution. *Journal of Family History,* **4,** 59–63.

Clark, C. (1972). Black studies or the study of black people? In R. L. Jones (Ed.), *Black psychology* (pp. 3–17). New York: Harper & Row.

Coben, S. (1979). American foundations as patrons of science: The commitment to individual research. In N. Reingold (Ed.), *The sciences in the American context: New perspectives* (pp. 229–248). Washington, DC: Smithsonian Institute Press.

Coffman, H. C. (1936). *American foundations: A study of their role in the child welfare movement.* New York: Russell Sage.

Cohen, S. (1980). The mental hygiene movement, the Commonwealth Fund and public education. In G. Benjamin (Ed.), *Proceedings of the Rockefeller Archive Center Conference, June 8, 1979* (pp. 33–46). North Tarrytown, NY: Rockefeller Archive Center.

Cole, M., & Bruner, J. (1971). Cultural differences and inferences about psychological processes. *American Psychologist,* **26,** 867–876.

Comte, A. J. (1828). Recherches anatomico-physiologiques, relatives à la prédominance du bras droit sur le bras gauche. *Journal de Physiologie Expérimentale et Pathologie,* **8,** 41–80.

Corballis, M. C., & Morgan, M. J. (1978). On the biological basis of human laterality: 1. Evidence for a maturational left-right gradient. *Behavioral and Brain Sciences,* **2,** 261–269.

Cornwell, K. S., Harris, L. J., & Fitzgerald, H. E. (1985a). Developmental discontinuities in handedness: The role of age and task variables. *Journal of Clinical and Experimental Neuropsychology,* **7,** 625. (Abstract)

Cornwell, K. S., Harris, L. J., & Fitzgerald, H. E. (1985b). The development of the relationship between language, gestures, and handedness. *Journal of Clinical and Experimental Neuropsychology,* **7,** 625. (Abstract)

Cott, N. F. (1977). *The bonds of womanhood: Woman's sphere in New England, 1780–1835.* New Haven, CT: Yale University Press.

Cravens, H. (1979, December). *The Laura Spelman Rockefeller Memorial, the child welfare institutes, and the creation of the science of the child, 1917–1940.* Paper presented at the annual meeting of the American Historical Association, New York.

Cravens, H. (1985). Child saving in the age of professionalism, 1915–1930. In J. M. Hawes & N. R. Hiner (Eds.), *American childhood: A research guide and historical handbook* (pp. 415–488). Westport, CT: Greenwood.

Cressy, D. (1980). *Literacy and the social order: Reading and writing in Tudor and Stuart England.* Cambridge: Cambridge University Press.

Crichton-Browne, J. (1907). Dexterity and the bend sinister. *Proceedings of the Royal Institution of Great Britain,* **18,** 623–652.

Crisp, A. H. (1976). How common is anorexia nervosa? A prevalence study. *British Journal of Psychiatry,* **128,** 349–354.

Cunningham, D. J. (1902). Right-handedness and left-brainedness: The Huxley Lecture for 1902. *Journal of the Royal Anthropological Institute of Great Britain and Ireland,* **32,** 273–296.

Curti, M. (1958). American philanthropy and the national character. *American Quarterly,* **10**(Winter), 420–437.

Cushing, F. H. (1892). Manual concepts: A study of the influence of hand usage on culture-growth. *American Anthropologist, 5,* 289–317.

Daniels, B. C. (1979). *The Connecticut town: Growth and development, 1635–1790.* Middletown, CT: Wesleyan University Press.

Degler, C. N. (1980). *At odds: Women and the family in America from the Revolution to the present.* New York: Oxford University Press.

Demos, J. (1970). *A little commonwealth: Family life in Plymouth Colony.* New York: Oxford University Press.

Demos, J. (1971). Developmental perspectives on the history of childhood. In T. K. Rabb & R. Rotberg (Eds.), *The family in history* (pp. 127–139). New York: Harper Torchbooks.

Demos, J. (1974). The American family in past time. *American Scholar, 43,* 422–446.

Demos, J. (1982). *Entertaining Satan: Witchcraft and the culture of early New England.* New York: Oxford University Press.

Demos, J., & Boocock, S. S. (Eds.). (1978). *Turning points: Historical and sociological essays on the family.* Chicago: University of Chicago Press.

Demos, J., & Demos, V. (1969). Adolescence in historical perspective. *Journal of Marriage and the Family, 4,* 632–639.

Dennis, W. (1935). Laterality of function in early infancy under controlled developmental conditions. *Child Development, 6,* 242–252.

Devereux, G. (1979). *Basic problems of ethnopsychiatry.* Chicago: University of Chicago Press.

Dougherty, G., Rockwell, W., Sutton, G., & Ellingwood, E. (1983). Anorexia nervosa in gonadal dysgenesis: Case report and review. *Journal of Clinical Psychiatry, 44,* 219–221.

Dowse, T. S. (1881). Anorexia nervosa. *Lancet, 1,* 827.

Duddle, M. (1973). An increase in anorexia nervosa in the university population. *British Journal of Psychiatry, 123,* 711–712.

Dupree, A. H. (1957). *Science in the federal government: A history of policies and activities to 1940.* Cambridge, MA: Belknap Press.

Earle, A. M. (1899). *Child life in colonial days.* New York: Macmillan.

Elder, G. H., Jr. (1974). *Children of the Great Depression: Social change in life experience.* Chicago: University of Chicago Press.

Elder, G. H., Jr. (1978a). Approaches to social change and the family. In J. Demos & S. S. Boocock (Eds.), *Turning points: Historical and sociological essays on the family* (pp. S1–S38). Chicago: University of Chicago Press.

Elder, G. H., Jr. (1978b). Family history and the life course. In T. K. Hareven (Ed.), *Transitions: The family and the life course in historical perspective* (pp. 17–64). New York: Academic Press.

Elder, G. H., Jr. (1981). History and the family: The discovery of complexity. *Journal of Marriage and the Family, 43,* 489–519.

Ellis, J. H. (Ed.). (1867). *Works of Anne Bradstreet.* Charlestown, MA.

Englehardt, H. T. (1974). The disease of masturbation: Values and the concept of disease. *Bulletin of the History of Medicine, 48,* 234–248.

Evans, C. (1941). *American bibliography: A chronological dictionary of all books, pamphlets and periodical publications in the U.S.A., 1639–1820.* New York: P. Smith.

Feighner, J., Robins, E., Guze, S., Woodruff, R., Winokur, G., & Munoz, R. (1972). Diagnostic criteria for use in psychiatric research. *Archives of General Psychiatry, 26,* 57–63.

Féré, C. (1889). La gaucherie acquise. *Revue Scientifique, 44,* 605–606.

Ferris, D. (1855). *Memoirs of the life of David Ferris, an approved minister of the Society of Friends . . . written by himself.* Philadelphia.

Fiering, N. (1981). *Jonathan Edward's thought and its British context.* Chapel Hill: University of North Carolina Press.

Fischer, D. H. (1977). *Growing old in America.* New York: Oxford University Press.

Fischer, R. B., Meunier, G. F., & White, P. J. (1982). Evidence of laterality in the lowland gorilla. *Perceptual and Motor Skills,* **54,** 1093–1094.

Fleming, S. (1933). *Children and Puritanism: The place of children in the life and thought of the New England churches, 1620–1847.* New Haven, CT: Yale University Press.

Fosdick, R. B. (1952). *The story of the Rockefeller Foundation.* New York: Harper & Row.

Fosdick, R. B. (1962). *Adventures in giving: The story of the General Education Board.* New York: Harper & Row.

Frank, L. K. (1933). Childhood and youth. In President's Research Committee on Social Trends (W. C. Mitchell, Chair), *Recent social trends in the United States: Report of the President's Research Committee on Social Trends* (pp. 751–800). New York and London: McGraw-Hill.

Franz, S. I. (1912). New phrenology. *Science,* **35,** 321–328.

Friedman, H., & Davis, M. (1938). "Left-handedness" in parrots. *Auk,* **55,** 478–480.

Furstenberg, F., Jr. (1985). Sociological ventures in child development. *Child Development,* **56,** 281–288.

Gallimore, R., Boggs, J., & Jordan, C. (1974). *Culture, behavior and education: A study of Hawaiian-Americans.* Beverly Hills, CA: Sage Publications.

Games, P. A. (1967). *Elementary statistics.* New York: McGraw-Hill.

Gee, S. (1908). *Medical lectures and aphorisms.* London: Oxford University Press.

George Joseph Hecht. (1975). New York: Parents' Magazine Press.

Giesecke, M. (1936). The genesis of hand preference. *Monographs of the Society for Research in Child Development,* **1**(5, Serial No. 5).

Glick, P. C. (1947). The family cycle. *American Sociological Review,* **12,** 164–174.

Glick, P. C. (1955). The life cycle of the family. *Marriage and Family Living,* **17,** 3–9.

Glick, P. C. (1977). Updating the life cycle of the family. *Journal of Marriage and the Family,* **39,** 5–13.

Glick, P. C., & Parke, R., Jr. (1965). New approaches in studying the life cycle of the family. *Demography,* **2,** 187–212.

Glick, S. D. (Ed.). (1985). *Cerebral lateralization in nonhuman species.* Orlando, FL: Academic Press.

Goldstein, J. (1982). The hysteria diagnosis and the politics of anticlericalism in late nineteenth century France. *Journal of Modern History,* **54,** 209–239.

Goode, W. (1963). *World revolution and family patterns.* New York: Oxford University Press.

Gordon, M. (Ed.). (1983). *The American family in a socioeconomical perspective* (3d ed.). New York: St. Martin's Press.

Gottlieb, G. (1979). Comparative psychology and ethology. In E. Hearst (Ed.), *The first century of experimental psychology* (pp. 147–173). Hillsdale, NJ: Erlbaum.

Gould, G. M. (1904). Dextrality and sinistrality. *Popular Science Monthly,* **65,** 360–369.

Gowers, W. R. (1902). Right-handedness and left-brainedness. *Lancet,* **2,** 1719–1720.

Grant, C. T. (1968). Puritan catechizing. *Journal of Presbyterian History,* **46,** 107–127.

Greven, P. (1970). *Four generations: Population, land and family in colonial Andover, Massachusetts.* Ithaca, NY: Cornell University Press.

Greven, P. (1977). *Protestant temperament: Patterns of child-rearing, religious experience, and the self in early America.* New York: Knopf.

Groves, E. (1932). Parent education. *Annals of the American Academy of Political and Social Science,* **160,** 216–222.

Gull, W. W. (1873). Anorexia nervosa. *Transactions of the Clinical Society,* **1,** 22–28.

Guthrie, R. V. (1976). *Even the rat was white: A historical view of psychology.* New York: Harper & Row.

Gwirtsman, H., Roy-Byrne, P., Yager, J., & Gerner, R. (1983). Neuroendocrine abnormalities in bulimia. *American Journal of Psychiatry,* **140,** 559–567.

REFERENCES

Haeckel, E. (1905). *The evolution of man* (J. McCabe, Trans., Vols. 1–2). London: Watts. (From *Anthropogenie: Keimes-und Stammes-Geschichte des Menschen* [5th ed.]. Leipzig: W. Englemann, 1874)

Hall, D. D. (Ed.). (1968). *The Antinomian controversy, 1636–1638: A document history.* Middletown, CT: Wesleyan University Press.

Hall, G. S. (1904). *Adolescence: Its psychology and its relations to physiology, anthropology, sociology, sex, crime, religion, and education.* New York: Appleton.

Hall, G. S. (1923). *Life and confessions of a psychologist.* New York: Appleton.

Hall, G. S., & Hartwell, E. M. (1884). Research and discussion: Bilateral asymmetry of function. *Mind, 9,* 93–109.

Hall, W. S. (1974). Research in the black community: Child development. In J. Chunn (Ed.), *The survival of black children and youth* (pp. 79–104). Washington, DC: Nuclassics & Science Publishing.

Hammond, W. A. (1876). *Spiritualism and allied causes and conditions of nervosa derangement.* New York: Putnam's Sons.

Hammond, W. A. (1879). *Fasting girls: Their physiology and their pathology.* New York: Putnam's Sons.

Hareven, T. K. (1971). The history of the family as an interdisciplinary field. *Journal of Interdisciplinary History, 2,* 399–414.

Hareven, T. K. (1974). The family as process: The historical study of the family cycle. *Journal of Social History, 7*(Spring), 322–329.

Hareven, T. K. (1975). Family time and industrial time: Family and work in a planned corporation town, 1900–1924. *Journal of Urban History, 1,* 365–389.

Hareven, T. K. (1976). Modernization and family history: Perspectives on social change. *Signs, 2,* 190–207.

Hareven, T. K. (Ed.). (1977a). *Family and kin in urban communities, 1700–1930.* New York: New Viewpoints.

Hareven, T. K. (1977b). Family time and historical time. *Daedalus, 106*(Spring), 57–70.

Hareven, T. K. (1978a). Cycles, courses, and cohorts: Reflections on the theoretical and methodological approaches to the historical study of family development. *Journal of Social History, 12*(1), 97–109.

Hareven, T. K. (1978b). The dynamics of kin in an industrial community. In J. Demos & S. S. Boocock (Eds.), *Turning points: Historical and sociological essays on the family* (pp. S151–S182). Chicago: University of Chicago Press.

Hareven, T. K. (Ed.). (1978c). *Transitions: The family and the life course in historical perspective.* New York: Academic Press.

Hareven, T. K. (1982). *Family time and industrial time.* New York: Cambridge University Press.

Hareven, T. K., & Modell, J. (1980). Family patterns. In S. Thernstrom (Ed.), *Harvard encyclopedia of American ethnic groups* (pp. 345–354). Cambridge, MA: Harvard University Press.

Harnad, S. R., Steklis, H. D., & Lancaster, J. (Eds.). (1976). Origins and evolution of language and speech. *Annals of the New York Academy of Sciences, 280.*

Harris, D. B. (1953). Why an interdisciplinary Society for Research in Child Development. *Child Development, 24,* 249–255.

Harris, L. J. (1980a). Left-handedness: Early theories, facts, and fancies. In J. Herron (Ed.), *Neuropsychology of left-handedness* (pp. 3–78). New York: Academic Press.

Harris, L. J. (1980b). Which hand is the "eye" of the blind? A new look at an old question. In J. Herron (Ed.), *Neuropsychology of left-handedness* (pp. 303–329). New York: Academic Press.

Harris, L. J. (1983a, May). *John B. Watson's studies of laterality in infants: A re-examination.*

Paper presented at the annual meeting of the Midwestern Psychological Association, Chicago.

Harris, L. J. (1983b). *Laterality of function in the infant: Historical and contemporary trends in theory and research.* In G. Young, S. J. Segalowitz, C. Corter, & S. Trehub (Eds.), *Manual specialization and the developing brain* (pp. 177–247). New York: Academic Press.

Harris, L. J. (1984). Louis Pierre Gratiolet, Paul Broca, et al. on the question of a maturational left-right gradient: Some forerunners of current-day models. *Behavioral and Brain Sciences, 7,* 730–731.

Harris, L. J. (1985). Teaching the right brain: Historical perspective on a contemporary educational fad. In C. T. Best (Ed.), *Developmental neuropsychology and education* (pp. 231–273). Orlando, FL: Academic Press.

Harris, L. J., & Fitzgerald, H. E. (1983). Postural orientation in human infants: Changes from birth to three months. In G. Young, S. J. Segalowitz, C. Corter, & S. Trehub (Eds.), *Manual specialization and the developing brain* (pp. 285–305). New York: Academic Press.

Hecht, G. J. (1919). *The war in cartoons.* New York: Dutton.

Heinlein, J. H. (1930). Preferential manipulation in children. *Comparative Psychology Monographs, 7*(3, Serial No. 33).

Hendricks, J. (1968). *The child-study movement in American education, 1880–1910: A quest for educational reform through a scientific study of the child.* Unpublished doctoral dissertation, Indiana University.

Herman, C. P., & Polivy, J. (1975). Anxiety, restraint and eating behavior. *Journal of Abnormal Psychology, 84,* 666–672.

Herron, J. (Ed.). (1980). Neuropsychology of left-handedness. New York: Academic Press.

Hertz, R. (1909). La prééminence de la main droite: Etude sur la polarité religieuse. *Revue Philosophique de la France et de l'Etranger, 68,* 553–580.

Hicks, J. A. (Ed.). (1931). *National Research Council directory of research in child development* (Reprint and Circular Series of the National Research Council, No. 102). Washington, DC: National Research Council.

Hildreth, G. (1949). The development and training of hand dominance: 2. Developmental tendencies in handedness. *Journal of Genetic Psychology, 75,* 221–254.

Historical selections from the fiftieth anniversary meeting. (in press). *Society for Research in Child Development Newsletter* (Suppl.).

Hoffer, P., & Hull, N. E. H. (1981). *Murdering mothers: Infanticide in England and New England, 1558–1803.* New York: New York University Press.

Howard, A., & Scott, R. A. (1981). The study of minority groups in complex societies. In R. H. Munroe, R. L. Munroe, & B. Whiting (Eds.), *Handbook of cross-cultural human development* (pp. 113–152). New York: Garland.

Humphrey, H. (1840). *Domestic education.* Amherst, MA: J. S. & C. Adams.

Hunt, J. M. (1961). *Intelligence and experience.* New York: Ronald Press.

Illustrated London News. (1891, January 17).

Jackson, J. (1905). *Ambidexterity or two-handedness and two-brainedness.* London: Kegan Paul, Trench, Trubner.

James, W. (1890). Origin of right-handedness. *Science, 16,* 275.

Jastrow, J. (1901). *Dextrality.* In J. M. Baldwin (Ed.), *Dictionary of philosophy and psychology* (Vol. 1, pp. 277–278). New York: MacMillan.

Jedrey, C. M. (1979). *The world of John Cleaveland: Family and community in eighteenth-century New England.* New York: Norton.

Jobert, L. (1885). *Les gauchers comparés aux droitiers aux points de vue anthropologique et médico-légal.* Lyon. (Pamphlet no. 5076, National Library of Medicine, Medical History Department)

REFERENCES

Joncich, G. (1968). *The sane positivist.* Middletown, CT: Wesleyan University Press.

Jones, H. E. (1931). Dextrality as a function of age. *Journal of Experimental Psychology,* **14,** 125–143.

Jones, H. E. (1956). The replacement problem in child analysis. *Child Development,* **27,** 237–240.

Kaestle, C. F., & Vinovskis, M. A. (1978). From apron strings to ABC's: Parents, children, and schooling in nineteenth-century Massachusetts. In J. Demos & S. S. Boocock (Eds.), *Turning points: Historical and sociological essays on the family* (pp. S39–S80). Chicago: University of Chicago Press.

Kaestle, C. F., & Vinovskis, M. A. (1980). *Education and social change in nineteenth century Massachusetts.* Cambridge: Cambridge University Press.

Kahman, L., Richardson, H., & Kipley, H. S. (1939). Anorexia nervosa with psychiatric observations. *Psychosomatic Medicine,* **1,** 335–365.

Kail, R. V., & Herman, J. F. (1977). Structure in developmental psychology: An analysis of journal citations. *Human Development,* **20,** 309–316.

Keniston, K. (1971). Psychological development and historical change. *Journal of Interdisciplinary History,* **2,** 329–345.

Kessen, W. (1965). *The child.* New York: Wiley.

Kett, J. (1977). *Rites of passage: Adolescence in America, 1790 to the present.* New York: Basic.

Kett, J. F. (1978). Curing the disease of precocity. In J. Demos & S. S. Boocock (Eds.), *Turning points: Historical and sociological essays on the family* (pp. S183–S211). Chicago: University of Chicago Press.

Kimura, D. (1976). The neural basis of language qua gesture. In H. Whitaker & H. A. Whitaker (Eds.), *Studies in neurolinguistics* (Vol. **2,** pp. 145–156). New York: Academic Press.

Kimura, D. (1979). Neuromotor mechanisms in the evolution of human communication. In H. D. Steklis & M. J. Raleigh (Eds.), *Neurobiology of social communication in primates* (pp. 197–219). New York: Academic Press.

Kinsbourne, M., & Hiscock, M. (1977). Does cerebral dominance develop? In S. J. Segalowitz & F. Gruber (Eds.), *Language development and neurological theory* (pp. 172–191). New York: Academic Press.

Kleinman, A. (1980). *Patients and healers in the context of culture.* Berkeley and Los Angeles: University of California Press.

Komai, T., & Fukuoka, G. (1934). A study of the frequency of left-handedness and left-footedness among Japanese school children. *Human Biology,* **6,** 33–42.

Kowal, S. J. (1955). Emotions as a cause of cancer: Eighteenth and nineteenth century contributions. *Review of Psychoanalysis,* **42,** 3.

Kuhn, A. L. (1947). *The mother's role in childhood education.* New Haven, CT: Yale University Press.

Labov, W. (1970). The logic of non-standard English. In F. Williams (Ed.), *Language and poverty* (pp. 153–189). Chicago: Markham.

Ladd, G. T. (1894). *Psychology, descriptive and explanatory* (1st ed.). New York: Scribner's Sons.

Lasègue, C. (1873). On hysterical anorexia. *Medical Times and Gazette,* **2,** 265–266; 367–369.

Lashley, K. S. (1917). Modifiability of the preferential use of the hands in the Rhesus monkey. *Journal of Animal Behavior,* **7,** 178–186.

Lashley, K. S., & Watson, J. B. (1913). Notes on the development of a young monkey. *Journal of Animal Behavior,* **3,** 114–139.

Laslett, P., & Wall, R. (Eds.). (1972). *Households and family in past time.* Cambridge: Cambridge University Press.

Lederer, R. K. (1939). *An exploratory investigation of handed status in the first two years of life* (University of Iowa Studies in Child Welfare, Vol. **16**, No. 2). Iowa City: University of Iowa Press.

Lehmann-Nitschke, R. (1895). Untersuchungen über die langen Knochen der südbayerischen Reihengraberbevolkerung. *Beiträge zur Anthropologie und Urgeschichte Bayerns* (Vol. **2**, Bk. 3). Munich.

Lenneberg, E. H. (1967). *Biological foundations of language.* New York: Wiley.

Lesser, I. (1981). A review of the alexithymia concept. *Psychosomatic Medicine, 43,* 531–543.

Lester, J. (1971). The angry children of Malcolm X. In A. Meier, E. Rudwick, & F. L. Broderick (Eds.), *Black protest thought in the twentieth century* (pp. 469–484). Indianapolis: Bobbs-Merrill.

Leurat, F., & Gratiolet, P. (1857). *Anatomie comparée du système nerveux, considéré dans ses rapports avec l'intelligence* (Vol. **2,** written by P. Gratiolet). Paris: Baillière & Fils.

Levenkron, S. (1978). *The best little girl in the world.* Chicago: Contemporary Books.

Levenkron, S. (1982). *Treating and overcoming anorexia.* New York: Warner.

Levin, E. (1983, February). A sweet surface hid a troubled soul in the late Karen Carpenter: A victim of anorexia nervosa. *People,* p. 28.

Liederman, J. (1983). Is there a stage of left-sided precocity during early manual specialization? In G. Young, S. J. Segalowitz, C. M. Corter, & S. E. Trehub (Eds.), *Manual specialization and the developing brain* (pp. 321–330). New York: Academic Press.

Locke, J. (1964). *Some thoughts concerning education* (abridged ed., F. W. Garforth, Ed.). Woodbury, NY: Barron.

Lockridge, K. A. (1974). *Literacy in colonial New England: An inquiry into the social context of literacy in the early modern West.* New York: Norton.

Lomax, E., in collaboration with Kagan, J., & Rosenkrantz, B. (1978). *Science and patterns of child care.* San Francisco: Freeman.

Lucas, A. (1981). Toward the understanding of anorexia nervosa as a disease entity. *Mayo Clinic Proceedings, 56,* 254–264.

Lundie, R. A. (1896). Left-handedness. *Chambers Journal, 73,* 9–12.

Lynd, R. S., & Lynd, H. M. (1929). *Middletown.* New York: Harcourt Brace.

MacLeod, S. (1982). *The art of starvation: A story of anorexia nervosa and survival.* New York: Schocken.

Mallery, G. (1881). *Sign language among the North American Indians* (First Annual Report of the Bureau of Ethnology). Washington, DC: U.S. Government Printing Office.

Malmsheimer, L. M. (1973). *New England funeral sermons and changing attitudes towards women, 1672–1792.* Unpublished doctoral dissertation, University of Minnesota.

Marion, H. (1890). Les mouvements de l'enfant au premier age: Premiers progrès de la volonté. *Revue Scientifique, 65,* 769–777.

Marsden, R. E. (1903). A study of the early color sense. *Psychological Review, 10,* 37–47.

Marston, L. R. (Ed.). (1927). *Directory of research in child development* (Reprint and Circular Series of the National Research Council, No. 76). Washington, DC: National Research Council.

Mather, C. (1741). *Ornaments for the daughters of Zion* (3d ed.). Boston.

Mather, I. (1961). The autobiography of Increase Mather. *Proceedings of the American Antiquarian Society, 71,* 271–360.

Mathews, D. G. (1977). *Religion in the old south.* Chicago: University of Chicago Press.

May, D., & Vinovskis, M. A. (1977). A ray of millennial light: Early education and social reform in the infant school movement in Massachusetts, 1826–1840. In T. K. Hareven (Ed.), *Family and kin in American urban communities, 1800–1940* (pp. 62–99). New York: Watts.

May, H. F. (1954). Shifting perspectives on the 1920's. *Mississippi Valley Historical Review*, **18**, 405–427.

Mazel, F. (1891). Droiterie et gaucherie d'après Sir Daniel Wilson. *Revue Scientifique*, **48**, 492–495.

Mazel, F. (1892). Pourquoi l'on est droitier. *Revue Scientifique*, **49**, 112–114.

McDougall, W. (1908). An investigation of the colour sense of two infants. *British Journal of Psychology*, **2**, 338–352.

McLean, D. (1954). A generation of research. *Child Development*, **25**, 3–8.

McLoyd, V. C., & Randolph, S. M. (1984). The conduct and publication of research on Afro-American children: A content analysis. *Human Development*, **27**, 65–75.

Mead, M. (1928). *Coming of age in Samoa*. New York: Morrow.

Mead, M. (1930). *Growing up in New Guinea*. New York: Morrow.

Merton, R. K. (1957). *Social theory and social structure*. Glencoe, IL: Free Press.

Miles, S., & Wright, J. (1984). Psychoendocrine interaction in anorexia nervosa and the retreat from puberty: A study of attitudes to adolescent conflict, and luteinizing hormone response to luteinizing hormone releasing factor in refed anorexia nervosa subjects. *British Medical Psychology*, **57**(Pt. 1), 49–56.

Modell, J. (1978). Patterns of consumption, acculturation, and family income strategy in late nineteenth-century America. In T. K. Hareven & M. A. Vinovskis (Eds.), *Family and population in nineteenth century America* (pp. 206–244). Princeton, NJ: Princeton University Press.

Modell, J., Furstenburg, F., & Hershberg, T. (1976). Social change and transition to adulthood in historical perspective. *Journal of Family History*, **1**, 7–32.

Modell, J., & Hareven, T. K. (1973). Urbanization and the malleable household: An examination of boarding and lodging American families. *Journal of Marriage and the Family*, **35**, 467–479.

Modell, J., & Hareven, T. K. (1978). Transitions: Patterns of timing. In T. K. Hareven (Ed.), *Transitions: The family and the life course in historical perspective* (pp. 245–269). New York: Academic Press.

Moran, G. F. (1979). Religious renewal, Puritan tribalism, and the family in seventeenth-century Milford, Connecticut. *William and Mary Quarterly*, **36**(3d Ser.), 236–254.

Moran, G. F. (1980). Sisters in Christ: Women and the church in seventeenth-century New England. In J. W. James (Ed.), *Women in American religion* (pp. 47–64). Philadelphia: University of Pennsylvania Press.

Morgan, E. S. (1966). *The Puritan family: Religion and domestic relations in seventeenth-century New England*. New York: Harper & Row.

Morgan, H. G. (1977). Fasting girls and our attitudes to them. *British Medical Journal*, **2**, 1652–1655.

Mueller, R. H. (1974). The American era of James Mark Baldwin (1893–1903). Unpublished doctoral dissertation, University of New Hampshire.

Mueller, R. H. (1976). A chapter in the history of the relationship between psychology and sociology in America: James Mark Baldwin. *Journal of the History of the Behavioral Sciences*, **12**, 240–253.

Myers, C. S. (1908). Some observations on the development of the colour sense. *British Journal of Psychology*, **2**, 353–363.

Myers, H. F., Rana, P. G., & Harris, M. (1979). *Black child development in America, 1927–1977*. Westport, CT: Greenwood.

Nature. (1890). **1098**, 43.

Neugarten, B., & Hagestad, G. O. (1976). Age and the life course. In R. H. Binstock & E. Shavas (Eds.), *Handbook of aging and the social sciences* (pp. 35–65). New York: Van Nostrand.

Nice, M. M. (1918). Ambidexterity and delayed speech development. *Pedagogical Seminary*, **25**, 141–162.

O'Connor, J. T. (1890). Right-handedness. *Science*, **16**, 331–332.

Ogle, W. (1871). On dextral pre-eminence. *Medical-chirurgical Transactions* (Transactions of the Royal Medical and Chirurgical Society of London), **54**, 279–301.

O'Neill, C. B. (1982). *Starving for attention*. New York: Continuum.

Oyemade, U. J., & Rosser, P. L. (1980). Development in black children. In B. Camp (Ed.), *Advances in behavioral pediatrics* (Vol. **1**, pp. 153–179). Greenwich, CT: JAI.

Pardee, I. (1939). Cachexia nervosa: A psychoneurotic Simmond's syndrome. *Archives of Neurology and Psychiatry*, **411**, 840–844.

Peery, J. C., & Adams, G. R. (1981). Qualitative ratings of human development journals. *Human Development*, **24**, 312–319.

Powers, G. (1935). Infant feeding. *Journal of the American Medical Association*, **105**(10), 753–761.

Preyer, W. (1888). *The mind of the child: Pt. 1. The senses and the will* (2d ed., H. W. Brown, Trans.). New York: Appleton. (Originally published as *Die Seeles des Kindes* in 1881)

Provine, R. L., & Westerman, J. A. (1979). Crossing the midline: Limits of early eye-hand behavior. *Child Development*, **50**, 437–441.

Psychology for the fighting man. (1943?). (Prepared by a committee of the National Research Council with the collaboration of Science Service). Washington, DC: Infantry Journal.

Rabb, T. K., & Rotberg, R. I. (Eds.). (1971). *The family in history*. New York: Harper Torchbooks.

Ramsay, D. S. (1980). Onset of unimanual handedness in infants. *Infant Behavior and Development*, **3**, 377–386.

Reade, C. (1878, January 19, 26, February 2, March 2, 23, May 18). The coming man [Letters to the editor]. *Harper's Weekly*, pp. 50–51; 74; 94–95; 174–175; 234–235; 394–395.

Reese, H. (1984). Rational alternatives to Kuhn's analysis of scientific progress. In H. Reese (Ed.), *Advances in child development and behavior* (Vol. **18**, pp. 189–284). Orlando, FL: Academic Press.

Richards, T. W. (1949). Editorial comment. *Child Development*, **20**, 3–4.

Riegel, K. F. (1972). Influence of economic and political ideologies on the development of developmental psychology. *Psychological Bulletin*, **78**, 129–141.

Riley, M. W. (1978). Aging, social change and the power of ideas. *Daedalus*, **108**(Fall), 39–52.

Riley, M. W., Johnson, M. E., & Foner, A. (1972). *Aging and society: A sociology of age stratification* (Vols. **1–3**). New York: Russell Sage.

Rodin, J., Silberstein, L., & Streigel-Moore, R. (1983). *Women and weight: A normative discontent*. Unpublished manuscript.

Rogers, L. J. (1980). Lateralization in the avian brain. *Bird Behaviour*, **2**, 1–12.

Rosenberg, C. E. (1962). *The cholera years*. Chicago: University of Chicago Press.

Rosenberg, C. E. (Ed.). (1975). *The family in history*. Philadelphia: University of Pennsylvania Press.

Ross, D. (1972). *G. Stanley Hall: The psychologist as prophet*. Chicago: University of Chicago Press.

Ryan, M. P. (1981). *Cradle of the middle class: The family in Oneida County, New York, 1790–1865*. Cambridge: Cambridge University Press.

Saling, M., & Tyson, G. (1981). Lateral cradling preferences in nulliparous females. *Journal of Genetic Psychology*, **139**, 309–310.

Schallenberger, M. (1897a). Discussion: Professor Baldwin's method of studying color-perception of children. *American Journal of Psychology*, **8**, 560–576.

REFERENCES

Schallenberger, M. (1897b). [Reply to Baldwin]. *American Journal of Psychology,* **9,** 60.

Schlossman, S. (1976). Before home start: Notes toward a history of parent education in America, 1897–1929. *Harvard Educational Review,* **46,** 436–467.

Schlossman, S. (1979, January 30). [Interview with George J. Hecht].

Schlossman, S. (1981). Philanthropy and the gospel of child development. *History of Education Quarterly,* **21,** 275–299.

Schlossman, S. (1983, Spring). Science and the commercialization of parenthood: Notes toward a history of *Parents' Magazine. American Psychological Association, Division 7, Newsletter,* pp. 14–17.

Schwartz, D., & Thompson, M. (1981). Do anorectics get well? Current research and future needs. *American Journal of Psychiatry,* **138,** 319–323.

Scott, A., & Tilly, L. (1975). Women's work and family in nineteenth-century Europe. *Comparative Studies in Society and History,* **17,** 36–64.

Sears, R. R. (1975). Your ancients revisited: A history of child development. In E. M. Hetherington (Ed.), J. W. Hagen, R. Kron, & A. H. Stein (Assoc. Eds.), *Review of child development research* (Vol. **5,** pp. 1–73). Chicago: University of Chicago Press.

Seguin, E. (1976). *Report on education.* Delmar, NY: Scholars' Facsimiles & Reprints. (Photoreprint of the 2d ed., published 1880)

Senn, M. J. E. (1975). Insights on the child development movement in the United States. *Monographs of the Society for Research in Child Development,* **40**(3–4, Serial No. 161).

Sennett, R. (1971). *Families against the city: Middle-class homes of industrial Chicago, 1872–1890.* Cambridge, MA: Harvard University Press.

Sewny, V. D. (1945). *The social theory of James Mark Baldwin.* New York: Kings Crown.

Shea, C. (1980). *The ideology of mental health and the emergence of the therapeutic liberal state: The American mental hygiene movement, 1900–1930.* Unpublished doctoral dissertation, University of Illinois.

Shipman, P. (1985). The ancestor that wasn't. *Sciences,* **25**(2), 42–48.

Shorter, E. (1976). *The making of the modern family.* New York: Basic.

Siegel, A. W., & White, S. H. (1982). *The child study movement: Early growth and development of the symbolized child* (Advances in child development and behavior, Vol. **17**). New York: Academic Press.

Siegel, L. S. (1983). Child health and development in English Canada, 1790–1850. In C. G. Roland (Ed.), *Health, disease and medicine: Essays in Canadian history* (pp. 360–380). Agincourt: Clarke, Irwin.

Sifneos, P. (1973). The prevalence of alexithymic characteristics in psychosomatic patients. *Psychotherapy and Psychosomatics,* **22,** 255–262.

Sigourney, L. (1838). *Letters to mothers.* Hartford, CT: Hudson & Skinner.

Simmonds, M. (1914). Ueber embolische prozesse in der hypophysis. *Archives of Pathological Anatomy,* **217,** 226.

Simpson, G. G. (1953). The Baldwin effect. *Evolution,* **7,** 110–117.

Skrabanek, P. (1983). Notes towards the history of anorexia nervosa. *Janus,* **70,** 109–128.

Slater, P. G. (1977). *Children in the New England mind: In death and life.* Hamden, CT: Archon.

Slaughter, D. T., & McWorter, G. A. (1985). Social origins and early features of the scientific study of black American families. In M. Spencer, G. Brookins, & W. Allen (Eds.), *Beginnings: The social and affective development of black children* (pp. 5–18). Hillsdale, NJ: Erlbaum.

Smelser, N. J. (1959). *Social change and the Industrial Revolution.* Chicago: University of Chicago Press.

Smith, D. S. (1973). Parental power and marriage patterns: An analysis of historical trends in Hingham, Massachusetts. *Journal of Marriage and the Family,* **35,** 419–428.

Smith, L. G. (1917). A brief survey of right- and left-handedness. *Pedagogical Seminary*, **24**, 19–35.

Smith, W. (Ed.). (1973). *Theories of education in early America, 1655–1819*. Indianapolis: Bobbs-Merrill.

Smuts, A. (1977, Spring). Report to the governing council on preservation of primary sources. *Society for Research in Child Development Newsletter*, pp. 6–7.

Smuts, A. (1979, March). *The beginnings of child development research in America: Science in the service of reform*. Paper presented at the biennial meeting of the Society for Research in Child Development, San Francisco.

Soltow, L., & Stevens, E. (1981). *The rise of literacy and the common school in the United States: A socioeconomic analysis to 1870*. Chicago: University of Chicago Press.

Some suggestions relative to the study of the mental attitude of the Negro. (1916). *Pedagogical Seminary*, **23**, 199–203.

Sommerville, C. J. (1982). *The rise and fall of childhood*. Beverly Hills, CA: Sage Publications.

Sontag, S. (1977). *Illness as metaphor*. New York: Farrar, Straus & Giroux.

Spufford, M. (1979). First steps in literacy: The reading and writing experiences of the humblest seventeenth-century spiritual autobiographers. *Social History*, **4**, 407–435.

Stannard, D. E. (1975). Death and the Puritan child. In D. E. Stannard (Ed.), *Death in America* (pp. 9–29). Philadelphia: University of Pennsylvania Press.

Stannard, D. E. (1977). *The Puritan way of death: A study in religion, culture, and social change*. New Haven, CT: Yale University Press.

Steiner, G. Y. (1976). *The children's cause*. Washington, DC: Brookings Institution.

Stevens, H. C. (1908). Right-handedness and peripheral vision. *Science*, **27**, 272–273.

Stone, L. (1974, November 14). The massacre of the innocents. *New York Review of Books*, pp. 25–31.

Stone, L. (1977). *The family, sex, and marriage in England, 1500–1800*. New York: Harper & Row.

Stone, L. (1981). Family history in the 1980's. *Journal of Interdisciplinary History*, **12**, 51–57.

Streltzer, J., & Wade, T. C. (1981). The influence of cultural group on the undertreatment of postoperative pain. *Psychosomatic Medicine*, **43**, 397–403.

Striker, C. (1933). A case of Simmond's disease with recovery. *Journal of the American Medical Association*, **101**, 1994.

Sulley, J. (1896). *Studies of childhood*. London: Longmans, Green.

Super, C. M. (1982, Spring). Secular trends in child development and the institutionalization of professional disciplines. *Society for Research in Child Development Newsletter*, pp. 10–11.

Takanishi, R. (1979, March). *Notes on the historiography of child development research, 1920–1975*. Paper presented at the biennial meeting of the Society for Research in Child Development, San Francisco.

Teng, E. L., Yang, K. S., & Chang, P. C. (1976). Handedness in a Chinese population: Biological, social, and pathological factors. *Science*, **238**, 1148–1150.

Tilly, L., & Cohen, M. (1982). Does the family have a history? *Social Science History*, **6**, 181–199.

Todd, M. (1980). Humanists, Puritans and the spiritualized household. *Church History*, **49**, 18–34.

Tracy, F. (1893). *The psychology of childhood*. Boston: Heath.

Tseng, W. S., & McDermott, J. (1981). *Culture, mind, and therapy: An introduction to cultural psychiatry*. New York: Brunner/Mazel.

Tulkin, S. R. (1972). An analysis of the concept of cultural deprivation. *Developmental Psychology*, **6**, 326–339.

Turkewitz, G., & Creighton, S. (1974). Changes in lateral differentiation of head posture in the human neonate. *Development Psychobiology*, **8**, 8.

REFERENCES

Uhlenberg, P. (1974). Cohort variations in family life-cycle experiences of U.S. females. *Journal of Marriage and the Family*, **36**, 284–292.

Uhlenberg, P. (1978). Changing configurations of the life course. In T. K. Hareven (Ed.), *Transitions: The family and the life course in historical perspective* (pp. 65–97). New York: Academic Press.

Ulrich, L. T. (1976). Virtuous women found: New England ministerial literature, 1660–1735. *American Quarterly*, **28**, 20–40.

Ulrich, L. T. (1982). *Good wives: Image and reality in the lives of women in northern New England, 1650–1750*. New York: Knopf.

Vaid, J., Bellugi, U., & Poizner, H. (1984, March). *Hand dominance in a visual-gestural language*. Paper presented at the annual meeting of the Body for the Advancement of Brain, Behavior, and Language Enterprises (BABBLE), Niagara Falls, Ontario.

Valentine, C. W. (1914). The colour perception and colour preferences of an infant during its fourth and eighth months. *British Journal of Psychology*, **6**, 363–387.

Vandereycken, W., & Pierloot, R. (1981). Anorexia nervosa in twins. *Psychotherapy and Psychodynamics*, **35**, 55–63.

Van de Water, M. (1932). Why children tell lies. *Science News Letter*, **21**(May 28), 338–339.

Verdonik, F., & Sherrod, L. R. (1984). *Inventory of longitudinal research on childhood and adolescence*. New York: Social Science Research Council.

Vierordt, K. von. (1881). *Physiologie des Kindesalters*. Tübingen: Heinrich Laupp.

Vinovskis, M. A. (1977). From household size to the life course: Some observations on recent trends in family history. *American Behavioral Scientist*, **21**, 265–267.

Voelckel, E. (1913). Untersuchungen über die Rechtshändigkeit beim Saugling. *Zeitschrift für Kinderheilk*, **8**, 351–358.

Wadsworth, B. (1719). *The well-ordered family*. Boston.

Waller, J. V., Kaufman, R. M., & Deutsch, F. (1940). Anorexia nervosa: A psychosomatic entity. *Psychosomatic Medicine*, **2**, 3–16.

Warren, J. B. (1980). Handedness and laterality in humans and other animals. *Physiological Psychology*, **8**, 351–359.

Washburn, A. H. (1950). Presidential address. *Child Development*, **21**, 61–65.

Washington, E. D., & McLoyd, V. C. (1982). The external validity of research involving American minorities. *Human Development*, **25**, 324–339.

Watson, J. B. (1924). *Behaviorism*. New York: People's Institute.

Watson, J. B., & Rayner, R. (1920). Conditioned emotional reactions. *Journal of Experimental Psychology*, **3**, 1–4.

Watson, J. B., & Watson, R. R. (1921). Studies in infant psychology. *Scientific Monthly*, **13**, 493–515.

Weber, E. (1904). Eine Erklärung die Art der Verebung der Rechtshändigkeit. *Zentralblatt für Physiologie*, **18**, 426–432.

Weems, L. (1974). Black community research needs: Methods, models and modalities. In L. Gary (Ed.), *Social research and the black community: Selected issues and priorities* (pp. 25–38). Washington, DC: Howard University, Institute for Urban Affairs and Research.

Wells, R. V. (1982). *Revolution in Americans' lives: A demographic perspective on the history of Americans, their families, and their society*. Westport, CT: Greenwood.

Welter, B. (1966). The cult of true womanhood, 1820–1860. *American Quarterly*, **18**, 151–174.

White, W., & Moehlig, R. C. (1950). Differentiation of anorexia nervosa and pituitary cachexia. *Journal of the Michigan State Medical Society*, **49**, 665–667.

Willard, S. (1726). *A complete body of divinity on two hundred and fifty expository lectures on the assembly's shorter catechism*. Boston.

Williams, R. (1972). Abuses and misuses in testing black children. In R. L. Jones (Ed.), *Black psychology* (pp. 77–91). New York: Harper & Row.

Wilson, D. (1891). *The right hand: Left-handedness.* New York: Macmillan.

Wohlwill, J. (1985). Martha Muchow, 1892–1933: Her life, work and contribution to developmental and ecological psychology. *Human Development,* **28**(4), 198–200.

Wollons, R. (1983). *Educating mothers: Sidonie Gruenberg and the Child Study Association of America, 1881–1929.* Unpublished doctoral dissertation, University of Chicago.

Wood, A. (1981, July). Relating. *Seventeen,* p. 78.

Woodworth, R. S. (1958). *Dynamics of behavior.* New York: Holt.

Woolley, H. T. (1910). The development of right-handedness in a normal infant. *Psychological Review,* **17,** 37–41.

Wozniak, R. (1982). Metaphysics and science, reason, and reality: The intellectual origins of genetic epistemology. In J. M. Broughton & D. J. Freeman-Moir (Eds.), *The cognitive-developmental psychology of James Mark Baldwin* (pp. 13–45). Norwood, NJ: Ablex.

Yans-McLaughlin, V. (1977). *Family and community: Italian immigrants in Buffalo, 1880–1930.* Ithaca, NY: Cornell University Press.

Young, G., Segalowitz, S. J., Corter, C., & Trehub, S. (Eds.). (1983). *Manual specialization and the developing brain.* New York: Academic Press.

Young, G., Segalowitz, S. J., Misek, P., Alp, I. E., & Boulet, R. (1983). Is early reaching left-handed? Review of manual specialization research. In G. Young, S. J. Segalowitz, C. Corter, & S. Trehub (Eds.), *Manual specialization and the developing brain* (pp. 13–32). New York: Academic Press.

Zeitschrift für Psychologie und Physiologie der Sinnesorgane. (1891). Hamburg and Leipzig: Leopold Voss.

Zigler, E. F., & Anderson, K. (1979). An idea whose time had come: The intellectual and political climate. In E. F. Zigler & J. Valentine (Eds.), *Project Head Start: A legacy of the War on Poverty* (pp. 3–19). New York: Free Press.

Zuckerman, M. (1970). *Peaceable kingdoms: New England towns in the eighteenth century.* New York: Knopf.

II. UNPUBLISHED SOURCES

Unpublished sources from seven special collections in four major archives were used extensively by several contributors to this *Monograph.* Smuts and Rheingold provide sufficient information in the text of their chapters to permit an interested scholar to locate their unpublished sources from the National Academy of Sciences Archives (Smuts) and the Society for Research in Child Development Archive Collection in the National Library of Medicine (Rheingold). In order to save space, these sources are not included in the reference list of unpublished sources. Additional unpublished materials used by Schlossman and Smuts and in the introduction to Part 3 are shown in the reference list of unpublished sources. References to these additional sources in the text are identified by the letters "NP" (not published) following the date. A description of the four major archives and seven special collections used by the authors follows.

1. *National Academy of Sciences Archives, 2101 Constitution Ave., Washington, DC 20418.*—This is the repository for materials of the National Research Council. Particularly relevant to the field of child development are materials in the collections of (*a*) the National Research Council's Division of Anthropology and Psychology and (*b*) the division's Committee on Child Development (called the Committee on Child Welfare from its founding in 1920 until 1925). The collections include correspondence, memorandums, minutes of meetings, reports, and financial statements.

2. *Rockefeller Archive Center, Hillcrest, Pocantico Hills, North Tarrytown, NY 10591.*—
The Rockefeller Archive Center contains several large collections on child welfare, child study, and parent education related to organizations active in these areas founded or supported by various divisions of the Rockefeller Foundation. The two collections used by Schlossman and Smuts are (*a*) the Laura Spelman Rockefeller Memorial Collection, which covers the period 1918–1949 (materials on child study and parent education are primarily from the period 1923–1929), and (*b*) the General Education Board Collection, which contains papers and correspondence of all sorts, covering the entire history of the board (its child development sources are primarily from the 1930s and 1940s).

3. *National Library of Medicine, Bethesda, MD 20014.*—The National Library of Medicine possesses several collections in its History of Medicine Division that are relevant to the field of child development. Three of these collections were used by *Monograph* authors. (*a*) The Society for Research in Child Development Archive Collection contains correspondence, minutes of meetings, reports, financial statements, and conference proceedings from the society's founding in 1933. The society constantly adds material to this collection, which eventually will receive correspondence, reports, unpublished papers, and other materials relating to the 1983 historical program and to the preparation of this *Monograph*. Since Rheingold used the collection it has been processed, and an inventory of its materials and their location is available from the library. All Smuts's and Rheingold's unpublished sources dated after June 1933 are from this collection. (*b*) The Lawrence K. Frank Papers (1891–1968) contain 26 boxes of correspondence, memorandums, minutes of meetings, speeches, and other materials both published and unpublished. (*c*) The Milton J. E. Senn Oral History Collections in Child Development and in Child Guidance (only material on child development was used by *Monograph* authors) include almost 200 interviews. Transcripts of the interviews from both collections have been microfilmed and may be purchased from the library.

4. *Columbia University, Teachers College, 525 W. 120th St., New York, NY 10027.*—The Columbia University Teachers College possesses the Institute of Child Welfare Research Files. This institute was the first child development institute to be founded by the Laura Spelman Rockefeller Memorial.

The unpublished proceedings of the conferences held by the National Research Council Committee on Child Development in 1925, 1927, 1929 (2 vols.), and 1933 are available at the National Academy of Sciences Archives, the Rockefeller Archive Center, and the National Library of Medicine. Reproductions of the 1929 and 1933 conference proceedings from typed and mimeographed pages are available in some university libraries. Proceedings of the Society for Research in Child Development's biennial conferences in 1934, 1936, and 1938 were published and are also available in the Society for Research in Child Development Archive at the National Library of Medicine.

Caldwell, O. (1924a, November 1). [Letter to James Earl Russell]. Columbia University, Teachers College, Institute of Child Welfare Research Files, Folder 583.

Caldwell, O. (1924b, November 6). [Letter to James Earl Russell]. Columbia University, Teachers College, Institute of Child Welfare Research Files, Folder 583.

Committee on Child Development of the National Research Council. (1929a, September 24). [Minutes]. Rockefeller Archive Center, Laura Spelman Rockefeller Memorial Collection, Series III, Subseries 5, Box 30, Folder 322.

Committee on Child Development of the National Research Council. (1929b). Quadrennial Report. Rockefeller Archive Center, Laura Spelman Rockefeller Memorial Collection, Series III, Subseries 5, Box 30, Folder 322.

Frank, L. (1924a, November 6). [Memorandum of interview with George J. Hecht]. Rockefeller Archive Center, Laura Spelman Rockefeller Memorial Collection, Series III, Subseries 5, Folder 390.

Frank, L. (1924b, Spring). Training personnel and preparing teaching material [Memorandum]. Rockefeller Archive Center, Laura Spelman Rockefeller Memorial Collection, Series III, Subseries 5, Folder 315.

Frank, L. (1925a, December 5). [Letter to Beardsley Ruml]. Rockefeller Archive Center, Laura Spelman Rockefeller Memorial Collection, Series III, Subseries 5, Folder 446.

Frank, L. (1925b, December 22). [Memorandum]. Rockefeller Archive Center, Laura Spelman Rockefeller Memorial Collection, Series III, Subseries 5, Folder 446.

Frank, L. (1925c, November 16). [Memorandum of interview with Dean Russell]. Rockefeller Archive Center, Laura Spelman Rockefeller Memorial Collection, Series III, Subseries 5, Folder 446.

Frank, L. (1925d, December). Parents Publishing Association [Memorandum]. Rockefeller Archive Center, Laura Spelman Rockefeller Memorial Collection, Series III, Subseries 5, Folder 390.

Frank, L. (1926, December 23). Child study and parent education [Memorandum]. Rockefeller Archive Center, Laura Spelman Rockefeller Memorial Collection, Series III, Subseries 5, Folder 316.

Frank, L. K. (1932, July 30). [Letter to T. W. Todd]. Rockefeller Archive Center, General Education Board Collection, Series I, Subseries III, Box 373.

Frank, L. K. (1939). Forces leading to a child development viewpoint and study [Memorandum]. National Library of Medicine, History of Medicine Division, Lawrence K. Frank Papers, Box 12, Folder 4.

Marston, L. R. (1926, October 23). [Report]. Rockefeller Archive Center, Laura Spelman Rockefeller Memorial Collection, Series III, Subseries 5, Box 31, Folder 328.

Roberts, L. J. (1929). Review of recent literature on certain phases of nutrition research and its significance in child development. *Proceedings of the National Research Council third conference on research in child development.* Washington, DC: National Research Council.

Ruml, B. (1924, June 23). [Letter to Arthur Woods]. Rockefeller Archive Center, Laura Spelman Rockefeller Memorial Collection, Series III, Subseries 5, Folder 315.

Ruml, B. (1925, December 7). [Letter to L. K. Frank]. Rockefeller Archive Center, Laura Spelman Rockefeller Memorial Collection, Series III, Subseries 5, Folder 446.

Russell, J. E. (1925, November 19). [Letter to the Laura Spelman Rockefeller Memorial]. Rockefeller Archive Center, Laura Spelman Rockefeller Memorial Collection, Series III, Subseries 5, Folder 446.

Senn, M. J. E. (1963, December). [Recording of L. K. Frank on the history of child development centers in the United States]. National Library of Medicine, History of Medicine Division, Milton J. E. Senn Oral History Collection.

Senn, M. J. E. (1972a, July 27). [Interview with George Hecht]. National Library of Medicine, History of Medicine Division, Milton J. E. Senn Oral History Collection.

Senn, M. J. E. (1972b, May 9) [Interview with Myrtle McGraw]. National Library of Medicine, History of Medicine Division, Milton J. E. Senn Oral History Collection.

Society for Research in Child Development. (1934, November 3–4). [Proceedings of the first biennial meeting]. Society for Research in Child Development Archive, National Library of Medicine, Container 5.

Todd, T. W. (1932, August 26). [Letter to L. K. Frank]. Rockefeller Archive Center, General Education Board Collection, Series I, Subseries III, Box 373.

Todd, T. W. (1933, January 9). [Letter to L. K. Frank]. Rockefeller Archive Center, General Education Board Collection, Series I, Subseries III, Box 373.

Woodworth, R. S. (1925, April 21). [Report to the Committee on Child Welfare of results of questionnaire sent out from the office of the Division of Anthropology and Psychology.] Rockefeller Archive Center, Laura Spelman Rockefeller Memorial Collection, Series III, Subseries 5, Box 30, Folder 320.

MONOGRAPHS

OF THE SOCIETY FOR RESEARCH IN CHILD DEVELOPMENT

VOLUME 50, 1985

EDITOR
ROBERT N. EMDE
University of Colorado School of Medicine
ASSOCIATE EDITOR
MARSHALL M. HAITH
University of Denver
EDITORIAL ASSISTANT
DONNA BRADSHAW
University of Denver

EDITORIAL ADVISORY BOARD

ELIZABETH BATES
University of California, San Diego

HARRIETTE P. McADOO
Howard University

ROBERT B. McCALL
Boys Town Center

ARTHUR H. PARMELEE
University of California, Los Angeles

ANNE L. PETERSEN
Pennsylvania State University

SHELDON H. WHITE
Harvard University

PUBLISHED BY THE UNIVERSITY OF CHICAGO PRESS FOR THE

SOCIETY FOR RESEARCH IN CHILD DEVELOPMENT

VOLUME 50, NUMBERS 1–5

PUBLISHED BY THE UNIVERSITY OF CHICAGO PRESS
CHICAGO, ILLINOIS, U.S.A.

MONOGRAPHS OF THE SOCIETY FOR RESEARCH IN CHILD DEVELOPMENT

VOLUME 50, 1985